THOMPSONVILLE

PETER FLOYD SORENSON

THOMPSONVILLE

BOOK ONE

1763 - 1900

PETER FLOYD SORENSON

ISBN:979-8-9877739-2-5

DEDICATION

This book is dedicated to the many people and institutions that opened their doors and archives, allowing me to explore the documents they have carefully collected and memories they have preserved so that I might tell this tale.

AUTHOR'S NOTES

This story is about people as much as it is about a village.

Peter Sorenson
September 2025

Although the people, companies, and events in this book are real, they may be remembered and considered in a different light than they have been portrayed in this book by themselves and by others. No malice or evil intent is meant in how these individuals or companies have been represented within these pages.

TABLE OF CONTENTS

THOMPSONVILLE

0: THOMPSONVILLE

Even the town's name recalls scenes right out of a black-and-white film directed by Frank Capra.

A slice of Americana for hungry people.

Move aside, Bedford Falls, New York; you've been replaced by a snowy winter's day in sleepy Thompsonville, Connecticut, a small town steeped in history. A village built around the successes of businessman Orin Thompson, who drew skilled weavers from Scotland to work at his 'White Mill', and later attracted immigrant workers from France, Ireland, Italy, Scotland, Poland, England, and Canada, looking forward to the promise of a better life at the larger, more expansive mill downstream.

These immigrants not only brought their families and their friends, but their customs, beliefs, prejudices, desires, vices, culture, and cuisine.

Thompsonville was the Cuisinart of ethnicities, where people who shared common backgrounds worked at the same factory, shopped at the same markets, went to the same bars, sent their kids to neighborhood public or parochial schools, and attended the same churches.

These were good people, people built for a black-and-white world. People who cared for each other, celebrated and grieved together, watched each other's backs, and collectively raised each other's children.

The sound of laughter would ring between the closely packed homes which had been built by the mill owner and rented back to the employees. The happy reverberations reflected a contented people.

The town had an unmistakable personality created by the 'salt of the earth' residents who lived there. The emotional bond that connected these people and the neighborhoods was built on more than the trolleys and, later, the paved streets that ran through the village and exited to other, more populated locales.

There was a palpable caring emanating from the homes and businesses in the community.

The skills these people brought helped create the physical infrastructure and societal interweaving, not unlike the finely woven carpets from the company at the center of the village, which provided employment, social and sports outlets, and a sense of purpose to most of the people who lived there.

Festivals and holidays were celebrated as one people, regardless of an individual's country of origin or their practiced religion.

Catholic boys and girls would confess their sins and head back onto the streets to repeat those activities that they had just admitted in the sanctity of the confessional. But the sins were those that one would expect of energetic youths and were not the kind that would immorally stain a person or community.

Freshwater Pond, or the "Mill Pond" as the residents called it, in the center of the village, would freeze over during the winter months and become a haven of activity for the hundreds of children who could strap on a pair of skates and carve a line on the ice or fall ungainly to the frozen surface inciting laughter or applause from their friends. A walk across a gravel parking lot to the printing shop's basement for a cup of hot chocolate, to warm the hands, hearts, and bellies of the winter festivities participants.

Neighbors Francis Mario Joseph Nai and Roland Jaycox would test the Mill Pond ice and employ a truck to plow it clear. At times, they would break through the frozen surface, having misjudged its thickness, and require assistance from a tow truck to be pulled from the winter waters. At least once, an unlucky vehicle stayed beneath the surface waiting for a Springtime rescue.

There were no malls then, no bisecting interstate, and no big box stores. Family-owned restaurants, grocery stores, hotels, clothing stores, bicycle shops, bakeries, barber shops, banks, delis, package stores, bars, and even two Chinese laundries populated the streets, offering their services to the tight-knit community.

Despite recriminations from their parents, children would play in or walk through the Dingo/Dingle[1] to get to Lafayette Park and would likely later get a "talking to" from their mothers, who would be tasked with removing the red clay from clothing and shoes. Swimming holes, known only to the children of the community, which went by the names "Twenty Foot", "Deep Hole", and "Phil Doughney's Swimming Hole", would attract naked boys who would scream and shout and throw themselves from the shoreline into the cool waters with abandon.

After Prohibition ended, local watering holes were back in business, dotting the landscape around the carpet manufactory. With names like Hunter's Bar (Tiny's), Dukes, Eddie's Café, Ringside, The Silhouette Club, and the infamous Bucket of Blood, each had its committed clientele and reputation.

Sporting events were a big part of Thompsonville's life,

---

[1] Residents still pleasantly argue as to the correct spelling and pronunciation of this area

from the 3500-seat outdoor boxing arena on Belmont Avenue to the stock car races at the Cherry Park Speedway in Avon, Connecticut, which drew local talent from both Thompsonville and Hazardville.

Clubs and other local associations allowed residents to gather to socialize and further connect with their neighbors. Some had unique names, such as the *Enfield Society for the Detection of Thieves and Robbers*, the *Odd Fellows Club*, the *Greys Club*, the *Elks*, the *Mount Carmel Society*, the *DAR*, the *Road Gents*, the *Foresters of America*, the *Girls Friendly Society*, and the *Modern Woodmen*, among others.

But a town is more than a collection of buildings, services, social groups, and events.

Thompsonville was unique because of the camaraderie and caring of its residents. The emotional attachments formed in tight-knit neighborhoods where people cared for one another, helped each other when needed, grieved and laughed together, and took pride in themselves, their heritage, and their homes – whether they owned or rented them.

The village had its own local heroes, both those who served in the military and those who served the community. Colorful characters. The kind of people whose remembered antics bring a smile to wizened faces.

What happened? Where did it go?

Maybe the ember still burns there among the ruins left behind from the failed promise of urban renewal in the 1970s, waiting for the right moment or event to spark a rebirth to reclaim the promise from that earlier time.

1: THE WHITE MILL

The vibrancy and presence of a tree reflect the integrity of its root system, without which the tree cannot withstand the rigors of a changing, often harsh and unforgiving, environment.

Who among us hasn't stopped and stood in awe of a grand oak, a maple, a majestic elm, whose limbs, full of leaves, cast a great protective shadow over the land, providing respite from seasonal elements for all creatures?

The tree may stand among its peers, but it alone is the beacon that calls to those in need of comforting shelter.

How did it achieve this uniqueness?

Was it the caliber of the seedling?

Was it the quality of the tree from which it had sprung?

Was it natural selection or chance?

Similarly, the persona of a hamlet, village, or town reflects its founders and early residents as recalled in the following passage.

Both his parents possessed the best qualities of Scottish character, and transmitted them unimpaired to their son. A correspondent of the local paper, writing his personal recollections of this worthy Scotch couple, says that they and others like them so set their seal upon the character of the little village of Thompsonville, then a mere hamlet, that 'for fifty years it was a place in many ways unlike any other village of its size in New England. Strong, original, honest, intelligent men and women they were, whom it was both pleasant and profitable to know, whether one saw things just as they did or not. [2]

When villages are born of good stock, they are immediately recognizable and attract individuals of the same nature, as if the resonance of the land itself calls out to others with similar vibrations.

When did Thompsonville begin?

True beginnings are elusive. When attempting to locate the source of a stream or river, one can always find other potential progenitors. Similarly, each person and event is a reflection of those that precede them and, at the same time, the source for those that follow.

For the beginning of this story, we look to Matthew Thompson, Jr., who was born in Enfield on June 16, 1763, to parents Matthew Thompson, Sr, and his wife Mary, 14 years after the town was annexed to Connecticut. Little is known about Matthew Jr.'s childhood or his parents' qualities or skill sets. We do know that he joined the Revolutionary War at the age of 16,[3] on February 14th, 1778,[4] as a Private under the command of Colonel Samuel Blachley Webb in Charles Whiting's Company (9th

---

[2] Bulletin. (1898). United States: National Association of Wool Manufacturers. Page 198.

[3] American Genealogist. Page 233. Simple math tells us Thompson would only have been 14 years old.

[4] United States Revolutionary War Rolls 1775-1783. Other resources note the incorrect enlistment date of April 6, 1779

Connecticut Regiment).[5]

Adding a bit of confusion is a note attached to Matthew Thompson's Revolutionary War Record that he replaced William Leach on March 20th, 1779, after Leach was wounded in the Battle of Rhode Island in August 1778.

After completing his three-year enlistment, Thompson was discharged on January 10, 1781. He then turned to serve on an American war vessel, incorrectly referenced in some records as the USS Randolph[6]. Soon afterward, he was taken prisoner, carried to the British West Indies, and imprisoned there until the end of the war.

Upon his release, Thompson narrowly escaped being forcefully impressed into service as a crewman on a British naval ship, a common fate for released prisoners of war. By means unknown he secured passage back to the United States, albeit in a compromised state of health. The young man returned to Connecticut and settled in Suffield by the early 1780s. At some point, Thompson considered applying for a war pension, having certainly earned it, but his conscience seemed to get the better of him, and he did not, as he had returned to some form of work by that time and was better off than his fellow countrymen who had also completed their military service.

By the mid-1780s, Thompson had met and proposed to Elizabeth Betsy Collins of West Hartford. The two were wed on September 2, 1787. A son, Orrin, was born to the

---

[5] Of interest is that Matthew Thompson is identified as one of 414 men in Webb's regiment in 1777, which would have made the youth 14 years old at the time of his service.

[6] The USS Randolph was lost in battle against the British naval vessel the HMS Yarmouth on March 7, 1778, so Thompson could not have served on that warship. It could be that Thompson served as a privateer during that period, attacking British ships on behalf of the Revolutionary forces.

couple a mere seven months later on March 28, 1788, indicating the pair had consecrated their nuptials early in their relationship.

Several sources claim that Matthew Thompson made his living as a trader and a successful land speculator. While it is difficult to determine the 'trader' skillset source, the 'land speculator' skills are easier to determine. It is also clear that Thompson was well-connected to those in power in the young nation and must have spent a considerable amount of time in the nation's capital.

The 1783 Treaty of Paris, negotiated to end the American Revolution, set the western border of the United States at the Mississippi River.

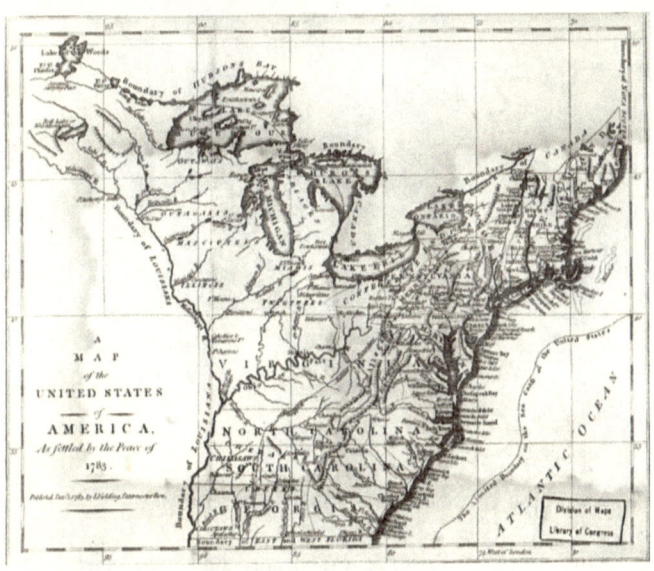

This 1783 map shows the boundaries of the United States as settled by the Treaty of Paris after the Revolutionary War (Library of Congress).

As the new Constitution was being written to replace the

Articles of Confederation, the states surrendered their sovereignty and could no longer coin money or raise armies independently. At the same time, states like Connecticut yielded back claims to any territories beyond their natural borders. Connecticut ceded land claims in Pennsylvania and Ohio, except for approximately 3,400,000 acres lying north and west of the Pennsylvania/Ohio border, which became known as the Connecticut Western Reserve.

General Moses Cleaveland circa 1885 (public domain)

The Western Reserve essentially had two parts. The western section was known as the 'Fire Lands', where Connecticut awarded plots to people who had lost property in the American Revolution. The eastern section was sold to a group of private investors who had formed the

Connecticut Land Company.

This group sent General Moses Cleaveland to survey the eastern lands (think of northern Ohio as it borders the Great Lakes) and carve out 'townships' of 25 square miles, which would attract land investors, speculators, and settlers.

The initiative was so successful that many Connecticut residents quickly moved to the northeastern section of Ohio, and the region became known as *New Connecticut*. One township, named Cleveland in the general's honor, was laid out with the help of Samuel Pease, a surname well known in Enfield.

To dispel any property challenges, in early 1800, President John Adams signed the Quieting Act, which legally recognized Connecticut's claim to these Western Lands.

Several original shareholders of the Connecticut Land Company were associated with Enfield, including Aaron Olmsted, Luther Loomis, Ebenezer King, and Jabez Stocking. A Suffield native, Gideon Granger Jr., a Yale graduate, was also an original shareholder. Granger, a lawyer in private practice, served in the Connecticut state legislature for ten years beginning in 1792.

The election of 1800 resulted in Vice President Thomas Jefferson ascending to the presidency, with Aaron Burr of New York assuming the vice presidency. Jefferson surprisingly tapped the nationally unknown Granger to become Postmaster General of the United States. Granger seemed to have both a personal and professional relationship with Matthew Thompson, which would serve the Enfield transplant well.

It was most likely Granger who introduced Thompson to the possibilities of land speculation through parcels offered by the Connecticut Land Company. Granger was a heavy buyer, and it appears that he influenced Thompson to make a purchase as well. So much so that Township 10 in range 6 of 'New Connecticut' was named 'Thompson Township' after Matthew Thompson of Enfield[7], Connecticut. Although the entire township was named after Thompson, he was one of three speculators in the venture, and he may never have even visited the lands he had purchased.

Thompson Township Town Hall, in Geauga County Ohio

Thompson certainly benefited from his speculation by subdividing the land and selling smaller parcels to the early settlers, the first of which was Dr. Isaac Palmer of Plainfield, Connecticut, in 1800.

---

[7] Thompson was a resident of Suffield at the time of the purchase, but would soon relocate to Enfield

Three years later, in 1803, Jefferson concluded negotiations with France and purchased the Louisiana Territory, effectively doubling the country's size overnight.

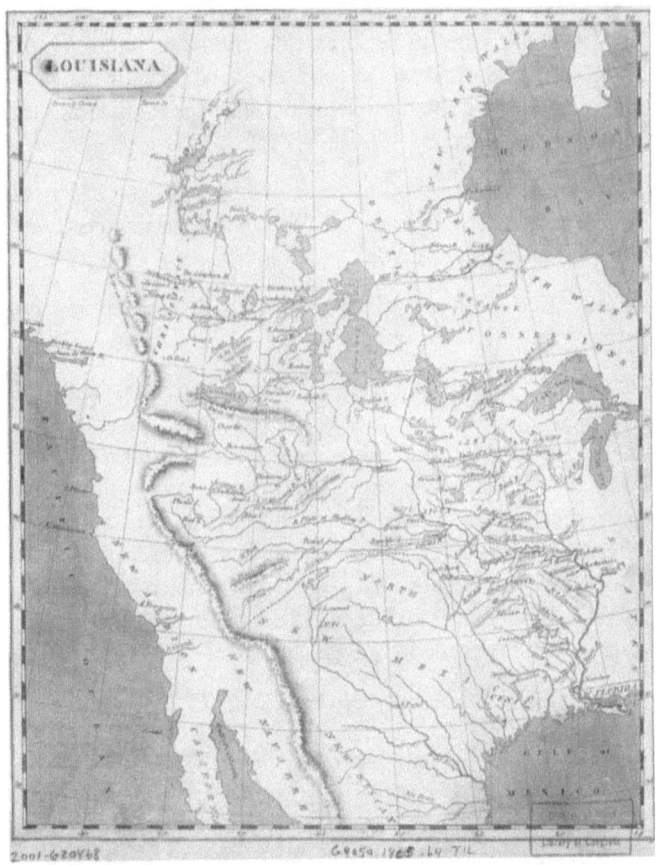

Lewis, Samuel and Aaron Arrowsmith, "Louisiana," 1805. Courtesy of Library of Congress

By 1804, rumors circulated within the government of a plan devised by Burr to separate the Western States and the newly acquired Louisiana Territory from the Union. Burr seemingly had the support of General James Wilkinson,

Commander-in-Chief of the U.S. Army. After acquiring the Louisiana lands, Burr convinced Jefferson to name Wilkinson as governor of Northern Louisiana.

In 1805, Burr traveled West to meet with Wilkinson to discuss the scheme to set up an independent nation in the Mississippi Valley. By all accounts, it seemed as if Burr had approached the British minister as well, seeking his financial and naval support.

In 1806, Burr and 60 others traveled to New Orleans to incite French settlers to revolt. Wilkinson, getting cold feet, betrayed Burr to Jefferson.

Burr fled but was quickly captured. He was returned to Virginia and tried for treason.

A participant in the trial of Aaron Burr was Enfield's own Matthew Thompson, who had been present for a meeting in Washington between Gideon Granger, the then Postmaster General of the United States, and William Ely, Representative from the Commonwealth of Massachusetts, where the two men discussed Vice President Aaron Burr's plan to divide the new nation. A solid citizen, Thompson put his recollections of the event in writing, and they were read into the trial record.

Springfield, Wednesday Morning, Oct. 15, 1806

I, Matthew Thompson, certify that I was present last evening in company with Wm Ely & Gideon Granger during a conversation between them of the subject of a plan to separate the Western States from the Union, and that the foregoing statement subscribed by G Granger is a correct and just narrative of the conversation.

Matthew Thompson[8]

---

[8] Quarterly Publication of the Historical and Philosophical Society of Ohio. Volume IX, 1914. Page 12.

In 1800, Thompson moved to Enfield, Connecticut, with his wife, Betsy, and their three sons, Orrin, Harvey, and Seth.

In addition to land speculation out West, Thompson had set up shop as a trader of goods in town. Why the family chose to move to Enfield to set up operations is unclear, as Suffield was a more populous town, but both locales were adjacent to the Connecticut River, so access to goods shipped into port at Warehouse Point made either location viable for business transactions.

Look to the right and dress.

SYLVESTER LUSK, HENRY KINGSBURY and MOSES ALLEN, Jun. have commenced business, under the Firm of

LUSK, KINGSBURY, & Co.

AND now offer for sale, at their Store in the North part of Enfield, an extensive assortment of European and India GOODS; together with a general assortment of Groceries, Crockery, Hardware, &c. Cash, approved Credit or most kinds of country Produce, received in payment.

SYLVESTER LUSK.
HENRY KINGSBURY.
MOSES ALLEN, Jun.

1st December. 35

1805 Advertisement for Lusk, Kingsbury, and Allen

In those days, trade shops opened and closed with regularity, with partners disassociating and reconnecting in various combinations. At various times, residents Sylvester Lusk, Henry Kingsbury, Moses Allen, and Matthew

Thompson had either opened shops together or managed ventures on their own. Lusk, Kingsbury, and Allen opened a store in December of 1805 and dissolved the partnership two years later, reopening at the same location without Lusk on the same day that the partnership dissolved.

NOTICE.

THE Copartnerſhip of LUSK, KINGS-BURY, & Co. is this day mutually diſ-ſolved. All thoſe who are indebted to the ſaid firm, are r queſted to call and ſettle their accounts without delay.

SYLVESTER LUSK,
HENRY KINGSBURY,
MOSES ALLEN, jr.

April 1.

BUSINESS will be continued at the old ſtand, under the firm of Allen, Kingſbury, & Co. where a more extenſive aſſortment of European and India goods are daily ex-pected, than has before been offered ; to-gether with a general aſſortment of Groce-ries, Crockery, Hardware, &c. all of which will be ſold on as liberal terms as at any country ſtore.

Enfield, April 1.

4

Lusk subsequently opened his own store, seemingly selling the same type of goods as his former partners. Some issues had obviously tainted the relationship among the proprietors, driving them to become competitors.

In 1805, Matthew's oldest son, Orrin, then 17 years of age, went to Hartford, Connecticut, where he was employed as an apprentice in the store of Nathaniel Patton [sic Patten].

Patten dabbled in a range of goods from books to clothing, and, because of this variety, his clientele spanned the less well-off to the very well-to-do. He may also have been involved in book printing, which would have exposed young Thompson to authors and publishers alike.

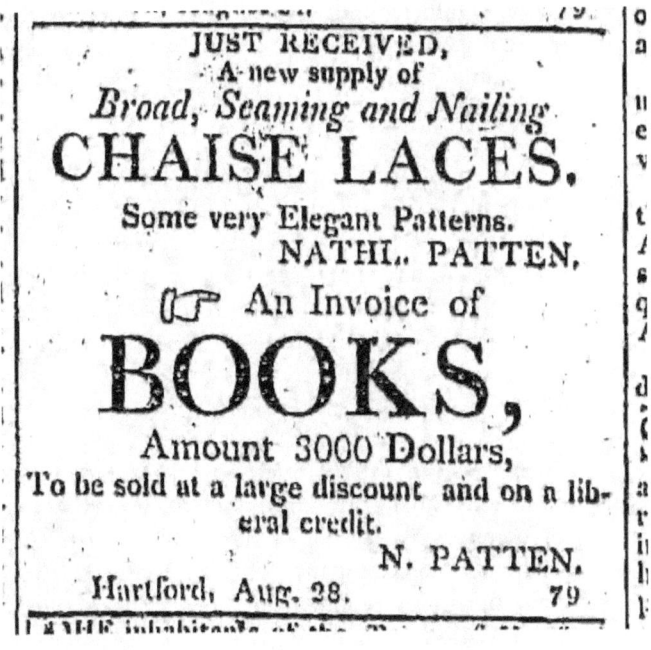

Hartford Courant advertisement for Nathan Patten's store located in the Capital City (1808)

Patten became a major stockholder and Director of the Hartford Fire Insurance Company when it was incorporated in 1810,[9] thereby introducing Thompson to the idea of diversifying one's finances.

---

[9] History of the Hartford Fire Insurance Company. Page 22.

Orrin remained in the employ of Nathaniel Patten for approximately five or six years, acquiring business acumen along the way while establishing his own contacts within the corporate community. Not unlike his father, Matthew, Orrin's employer owned a good amount of real estate in the Capital City, including a large house on Main Street with a barn and carriage house, a large vacant and buildable property along Mulberry and Wells (directly across from the Hartford and New Haven Railroad Depot), and a house and property on Little River.[10]

Beginning in 1806, on the eastern side of Connecticut, entrepreneur John W. Tibbets had been engaged in a series of unsuccessful water rights negotiations with multiple firms in an effort to establish a cotton mill manufactory. Finally, in 1809, he purchased the Nathan and Elisha Rose property, which included mill privileges and a dam along the Pachaug River where it met the Quinebaug.

The following year, in 1810, Tibbits, now with seven other partners, erected a small cotton mill along the waterway and formed a company under the name of The Jewett City Cotton Manufacturing Company[11]. Within months, the firm acquired additional water rights from Jebediah Barstow and John Wilson; Wilson's right having been initially established in 1781.

It was here that Orrin Thompson was employed as a clerk after leaving the employment of Nathaniel Patten in mid-1811. In less than one year, as the War of 1812 broke

---

[10] Hartford Courant, March 25, 1847. Page 2.

[11] In 1813 the name of the company was changed to Jewett City Manufacturing Company, dropping 'cotton' from the masthead. The company was formally incorporated in 1816.

out between the United States and Great Britain, Thompson was drafted into the Third Regiment of the Connecticut Militia and sent to Stonington, Connecticut, to help protect the port from British naval attack.

FACTORY NOTICE.

WHEREAS a Cotton manufacturing Company has lately been established who have been at great expence in purchasing water privileges, mills and other buildings in Jewet City, Preston, and have erected a Cotton Factory on an extensive scale, on one of the best mill seats in the State of Connecticut, which will contain and operate 2000 spindles; they have now a considerable number in operation, and 500 nearly completed, the whole being built of the best materials and executed by the first workmen—And to improve their privileges to the best advantage would wish to enlarge their capital to twenty or twenty-five thousand dollars more than it now is. Any gentlemen therefore wishing to become interested in a Cotton Factory and other water privileges are hereby invited to come and examine the situation, the privileges and works, and join them in the business.

JOHN WILSON, } Committee for said
JOHN DOUGLAS, } Company.
Preston, Jewett City, April 15, 1812.   67

Hartford Courant advertisement for the Wilson & Douglas cotton manufacturing company (1812)

Uncomfortable with the military, Thompson secured a substitute and returned to Enfield in 1814, where he partnered with his father, Matthew, and Henry Kingsbury to establish the trading firm of Orrin Thompson & Company.

The following year, he married Love Lusk, the sister of Sylvester Lusk, a resident of Enfield and a successful merchant. Three years after the wedding, in 1818, Orrin dissolved his partnership with Kingsbury and aligned himself with his brother-in-law, Sylvester, forming the firm of Thompson & Lusk. That partnership lasted until the middle of 1819, when the two went their separate ways, with Thompson retaining the business as a sole proprietor.

DISSOLUTION.

THE copartnership subsisting between the subscribers, under the firm of THOMPSON & LUSK, is by mutual consent, this day dissolved.   ORRIN THOMPSON,
                                 SYLVESTER LUSK.
August 25, 1819.   49

THE subscriber, who has taken an assignment of all the interest of SYLVESTER LUSK, in said copartnership, will continue business in his own name, at the store which was formerly occupied by Thompson & Lusk. And all persons indebted to said firm are requested to make payment to him.
                            ORRIN THOMPSON.

Hartford Courant advertisement announcing the dissolution of Thompson & Lusk (1819)

One hundred and thirty-five miles to the south, on November 5, 1817, the copartnership of Austin, Andrews & York was dissolved by mutual consent. Oliver York left the merchant company, and the business continued under the guidance of Daniel Austin and David Andrews as Austin & Andrews, working out of 180 Broadway Street in New York City.

Within three months, on February 2, 1818, the duo took on a new partner, Gad Taylor, renaming the company

Austin, Andrews & Company, with Taylor comprising the '& Company' part.

A little more than two years passed with relative harmony until, abruptly, on July 21, 1820, a post in regional newspapers announced that the copartnership of Austin, Andrews & Company was dissolving, with the firm closing under the directive of Daniel Austin and David Andrews. The firm had jettisoned Taylor and would continue under the former name, Austin & Andrews.

Taylor rebounded as he entered into a partnership with William Griffith on August 1, 1820, with the pair naming the firm Taylor & Griffith. Surprisingly, the company dissolved not two weeks later, on August 14, for reasons unknown. Perhaps some issue, business or personal, had tainted Gad Taylor, making him an unfit partner.

Undeterred, by March 26 of the following year, Taylor had aligned himself with William Swan, with the pair working out of 194 Pearl Street in lower Manhattan [corner of Fly Market] as Swan & Taylor transacting business in a line of "dry goods".

Partnerships in New York City seemed to be as fickle as those in Enfield.

Most resources indicate that Orrin Thompson relocated to New York City in 1821 and was subsequently employed by the importing firm of Austin & Andrews. This may be true, but there is no record of Thompson maintaining a residence in New York City before 1824, when he is first recorded in Longworth's American Almanac, New York Register, and City Directory as living at 9 Pine Street, at the southernmost tip of Manhattan. This apartment was a four-minute walk to the offices of Austin & Andrews. As some historical records are somewhat suspect, it may be that Thompson had lived at that location since his reported arrival in 1821.

Many sources also state that Thompson "bought out" Daniel Austin from the import partnership of Austin & Andrews, but that seems unlikely as Austin died on May 22, 1823, at the age of 54, and his probate record notes this:

> *To All Whom this may concern Know Ye that I Daniel Austin **of the house of Austin and Andrews**, merchants of the City and County of New York...*[12]

The caveat is that the organization had been rebranded as Andrews, Thompson & Company by early May 1823, weeks before Daniel Austin's death.[13] A safe assumption is that Thompson may have *bought Austin out*, as far as his partnership was concerned, shortly before his death. Still, Austin remained on the board as a member, thus continuing his association.

In any event, by 1824, Thompson was recorded as living in New York City and as a partner in a carpet-importing and wholesale company. He had achieved a sense of purpose, success, and stability.

It wasn't until the following year that a seismic shift would begin to adjust his plans.

In 1824, the United States Congress passed the appropriately named *Tariff Act of 1824*, which imposed an import duty of 30 percent on raw wool and $33^{1/3}$ percent on woolen goods, to protect domestic manufacturers from foreign competition. By then, stateside carpet manufacturers existed in Pennsylvania, Massachusetts, New

---

[12] New York Probate Record Volume 058, 1821-1825 page 96 for Daniel Austin

[13] Of interest is that Austin was born in Suffield, Connecticut, across the river from Enfield.

York, New Jersey, Rhode Island, and Maryland. However, with the new protections in place, a Connecticut firm also entered the market.

But not in Enfield.

In Simsbury, in the village of Tariffville.

In a strange twist, the *national carpet tariff* helped establish *the Tariff Manufacturing Company*, the first Connecticut carpet manufactory, incorporated in 1825 along the Farmington River. There locals and Scottish immigrants produced ingrain carpets from imported South American and Middle Eastern wool. Likely, the company sold its manufactured carpets through New York agents such as Andrews, Thompson & Company.

Thirty-five miles to the northeast of Tariffville, along the Connecticut River, lay the region referred to as *Head of the Falls* or *Lovejoy's Ferry*, which was, itself, nine miles north of Warehouse Point. This port had been established almost 200 years earlier by Colonel William Pynchon, the founder of Springfield, Massachusetts. There was a *distinctive quality* to the air along the real estate between the port and the falls in Enfield, as a mix of gin distilleries, grain mills, cow farms, and pig farms dotted the riverbank landscape, the stench of the effluence brought water to the eyes of the traveler (unless the wind was coming from the west). Other, less pungent businesses, such as sawmills and blacksmith shops that supported farming in the region, were clustered along the Freshwater Brook, an eastern tributary of the larger Connecticut River.

At that time, the primary inhibitor to commerce on the Connecticut River from Long Island Sound to Springfield, Massachusetts, was the 'falls' at Enfield, which presented as more of a treacherous, rock-strewn field of rapids rather than a single, or series of, true falls. The navigation challenge had been the reason Pynchon had established the southern Warehouse Point as a waypoint to offload goods and carry them north to a point where the water flowed freely once again, thereby effectively bypassing the *falls*.

It was at this same location where a ferry service to span the river had been granted to Joe Alline [sic John Allyn] of Suffield in 1691. Allyn subsequently sold his farm and ferry service to John Trumbull, and Trumbull's Ferry began. That service was supplanted by John Penguilly [sic Pengilley], who renamed his short-lived service as Gillies Ferry. That service, though, was soon repurchased by Trumbell and rebranded once again.

Captain Phineas Lovejoy, who was born in 1762 and commanded his own Company in Colonel Rogers Enos's regiment in the War of the Revolution, purchased land in Suffield bordering the Connecticut River as well as the rights to Trumbell's ferry service soon after returning from the war. At that time, crossing the waters by the *wired ferry* proved to be

> *...wholly impracticable, frequently difficult, and dangerous, and always attended with considerable delay*[14]

...although it was, at the same time, serviceable, carrying beasts of burden, wagons, and other implements and goods required by the farm communities of Suffield and Freshwater/Enfield.

Why the sparsely populated area of Enfield was referred to as Lovejoy's Ferry and not Gillies Ferry or Trumbell's

---

[14] As noted in the October 2, 1793, petition to the Connecticut State Legislature seeking the right to erect a Toll Bridge over the Connecticut River near a place called Mad Tom Bar, about 1.5 miles south of Lovejoy's Ferry [later Thompsonville]

Ferry is most likely based on Phineas Lovejoy's longevity of ferry ownership rather than anything more significant.

FARMS FOR SALE.

THE Farm whereon Gaius Pease lately lived in Enfield, of 100 acres, with good buildings thereon.

A small Farm of 25 acres by Lovejoy's Ferry in Suffield, with a good house and barn thereon, together with the right of ferry and a good ferry boat.

A Farm on the west side of the river, a little north of the above ferry, with a house and barn thereon, and containing sixty acres of excellent land.

Three Farms in Stafford—one of 60 acres one of 70, and one of 73 acres; and on each is a house and barn, in good repair.

If the above Farms are not sold by the first of March next, they will be to be rented. Apply to the subscriber in Enfield!

MATTHEW THOMPSON.

January 26. 67

1818 Hartford Courant advertisement noting Suffield property with ferry rights offered by Matthew Thompson

Whatever the actual reason, the name 'Lovejoy's Ferry' stuck and was generally used to refer to the region in the late 1700s through the early 1800s.

By 1818, real estate entrepreneur Matthew Thompson offered a 25-acre farm in Suffield, including the rights to the ferry service and a ferry boat. Whether this was a result of Lovejoy's passing or some other event is unknown, although most records indicate Phineas Lovejoy had passed in early 1800. The ferry's proprietor thereafter is difficult to determine.

Near the mouth of the Freshwater Brook, and slightly south of the ferry landing, lay the Globe Hotel, which was built in 1804 by Comfort Smith and sold to Jotham Wright. The hotel, known later as the 'lower tavern', was the gathering spot for the many river pilots who guided flatboats over the Enfield Rapids between Warehouse Point and Lovejoy's Ferry. A later document referred to these pilots as:

> ...*useful hard laboring class of men, [who] are drawn to the tavern, there to spend their time, waste hard earnings, and too often contract habits which destroy their future usefulness.*[15]

The tavern seemed to have its fans and detractors.

On average, it took 12 men to 'pole' a single flatboat through the rapids with a load capacity from 12 to 18 tons. The trip would take several days to complete, but it was the most elegant solution available at the time. The Hotel would rent rooms to the boatmen and quench their thirst as they overnighted between trips.

At that time, Enfield had a population of about 2,129 people[16], and most of those were congregated around Enfield Street. It was there that the Thompsons had moved in 1800 and had set up their businesses, and from where Orrin had set out to define himself as a businessman.

At the less populated Lovejoy's Ferry section of town,

---

[15] Connecticut Mirror, March 1, 1824. Page 3. Report on Improving the Navigation of [the] Connecticut River
[16] The History of Enfield. Page 54 states the population as 2661 in 1820, the corrected population as recorded by the Connecticut State Government for Enfield in 1820 is 2,129

to the east of the Globe Hotel, the village:

> *"...consisted of a large distillery and store owned by the Dwights...a small clothing and carding mill, and a diminutive linseed oil mill belonging to Seth Talcott and a flouring mill belonging to Henry Loomis. These buildings were located on the north side of the brook which [ran] through the village.*
>
> *The land south of the brook was in possession of Major Horace Metcalf and was used by him for agricultural purposes. There was a small sawmill on the south side of the brook."*[17]

It was a relatively undeveloped region with a powerful stream available to drive mill equipment and water access for shipping products.

With the protective carpet duty in place, and noting the success of the Tariff Manufacturing Company, Orrin Thompson and David Andrews of the New York Importing firm of Andrews, Thompson, & Company discussed the idea of setting up a carpet manufactory in New England in a copartnership with the Scottish firm of Gregory, Thompson & Company[18].

---

[17] Springfield Republican, October 24, 1909. Page 6.

[18] Often incorrectly referenced as *Gregory, Thompson, & Company, Gregory, Thompsons, & Company,* or *Gregory Thomson & Company.* Messrs. Gregory and Thomson were partners and owners of the company identified as a *Worsted Spinner and Carpet Manufacturer* located on Green Street in Kilmarnock, Scotland (as noted in the 21st volume of the 1872 Reports from Commissioners arranged for the House of Commons). The company was incorrectly referenced as Gregory, Thomsons, & Company in multiple European

The carpet manufacturing company was headquartered in the village of Kilmarnock, Scotland, a region more notable for the Johnnie Walker whisky brand, established there in 1820. It was nationally known on the Isle of Britain for Kilmarnock [Balmoral] bonnets and internationally recognized for high-quality woven carpets.

A series of unfortunate events had negatively impacted the weaving industry, beginning in 1825 with the collapse of the Bank of England. This financial crisis was only alleviated by the intervention of the Bank of France, a country with which Britain had been at war only a few years earlier.

The crisis lasted until the Autumn of 1827, with the national depression continuing for some years longer, severely impacting the cotton trade and the handweaving industry more than others.

During the 1825-27 economic depression, where perhaps somewhere in the region of 50% to 75% of the handloom weavers were under-employed or without any work at all, starving to death was a real and constant danger. Their predicament was so severe that if the handloom weavers and their families went for more than three weeks without paid work they would be literally starving. It should not be forgotten that unemployment, chronic low wages and under-employment lasted around 21 months from late 1825 right the way through to August 1827. With virtually no financial assistance from the state to speak of, the east Lancashire handloom weavers were looking at death directly in its face. It was desperate times and in April 1826 they came up with a desperate plan to send a symbolic message to government through the destruction of the powerlooms in the local mills and thus raise

sources

awareness of their precarious plight.[19]

Contrary to the desperate plight of their East Lancashire brothers 300 miles to the south, Kilmarnock employed some 1,300 weavers working 300 looms to manufacture Scotch carpeting, and 50 advanced Brussels Looms, which required a higher degree of dexterity and skill on the part of the operator, producing carpets of distinct quality and intricate design.[20] The relative success of the Kilmarnock workers halted a proposed appropriation before the English Parliament that would have subsidized the relocation of skilled manufacturers to America (from which two-thirds of the carpet orders originated).

Even without a government policy intervention, carpet weavers began to look to the United States for work, with some paying their own passage to a country that had only ripped itself away from England 50 years earlier. The Hartford Courant reprinted an article from the Glasgow Chronicle, which referenced the situation where skilled craftsmen were leaving for America:

Among them is a number of fine young men, carpet weavers from Kilmarnock, who were forced by the want of work, to accept an engagement to go to a large manufactory in the State of New York. This manufactory was erected about one year ago, and is conducted and managed by Scotsmen, principally from Kilmarnock. The principal part of these emigrants have little money, and are going to America, as some of them have expressed it, to save their little all from falling into the hands of Jews

---

[19] 'Alas Poor Weavers': The context of the April 1826 Weavers Uprising in east Lancashire
[20] Hartford Courant July 2, 1827. Page 2.

and jobbers, sinecurists and pensioners.[21]

The employment troubles in the United Kingdom were lining up perfectly with the plans of Orrin Thompson and David Andrews and their Scottish partners, Gregory, Thomsons & Company.

In 1828, most people and businesses were concentrated along Enfield Street, with others scattered along Freshwater Brook, Lovejoy's Ferry, and the open farmlands to the east. Based on his familiarity with the area, Orrin Thompson suggested that the American/Scottish carpet partnership look to Enfield to establish their manufactory.

Orrin engaged his brother Seth, who was, at the time, a business associate of Peter Raynolds, to look for suitable property in his hometown.

Raynolds was the grandson of Reverend Peter Raynolds, who was born in Bristol, Rhode Island, in 1700, graduated from Harvard University in 1720, was ordained in Enfield in 1725, and pastored at the First Congregational Church on Enfield Street. In his early years, grandson Raynolds made his money as a bookbinder, giving up his store on Enfield Street in 1814 to Hylas Stiles and Normand Loomis,[22] who opened a boot & shoe-making operation at the same location[23]. Raynolds went on to manage both the Lion and Central Hotels in Enfield after leaving private business[24]. Raynolds was also a land speculator, purchasing and selling

---

[21] Hartford Courant April 27, 1830. Page 2.

[22] Brother of Henry Loomis who owned a flouring mill in the Lovejoy's Ferry section of Enfield

[23] Connecticut Mirror June 20, 1814. Page 4.

[24] New York Genealogical and Biographical Record volume 81 page 317. The Lion Hotel was another name for the William Abbe Hotel on Bridge Street. Where the Central Hotel was located remains a mystery.

property with an eye on profit.

At some time before 1824, Peter Raynolds moved on from managing others' properties and came into possession of the two-story hotel and tavern 'up the street' [east] of the Globe Hotel. It had been built, like the Globe Hotel, by Comfort Smith[25] in 1796, and was locally referred to as the 'middle tavern'.

It was at this hotel that numerous business meetings were held, and most likely where Seth Thompson met with potential property owners to discuss sales terms and conditions during 1827 and 1828.

In the early 1800s, Enfield was a merchant-heavy town, despite being more often defined as an agricultural region. Merchant stores lined Enfield Street, selling both 'wet' and 'dry' foodstuffs. Clothiers and cooper shops populated the street as well, and all along Freshwater Brook, one could find mills of every kind, sawmills and gristmills, and supportive shops like blacksmiths and tanneries. Hotels and, of course, taverns were interspersed equally between Enfield proper and Lovejoy's Ferry.

In 1813, James Brewer, James Dwight, and Edmond Dwight, along with John Cooley, formed a partnership and opened a store on Enfield Street to market an assortment of English and West Indian goods. Noted in their first announcement was that they would pay cash for rye to be used in their distillery, as well as for oak and pine wood delivered to their location, which would indicate the presence of a sawmill.

Nine years later, the store seemed to have run its course, and management was taken over by John Cooley and Hiram

---

[25] Thompsonville Press August 1, 1936. People's Column. *RELATES EARLY HISTORY OF THE GLOBE TAVERN*. Page 4.

Belcher, also Enfield residents, who continued the business of distillation and merchandising.

COOLEY & BELCHER,

Have recently taken the stand of James Brewe, and Co. where they continue the business of Distillation and Merchandize. They have now on hand an assortment of

Dry Goods, Groceries, Crockery & Hardware.

Saw-Mill ✕ cut and Tenanting Saws.

English Draft Chains.

Iron and Steel.

Mackerel and Codfish.

4d. 6d. 8d. 10d. 20d. and 40d. wrought and cut Nails.

6 by 8, 7 by 9, and 8 by 10 English and American Window Glass.

T. I. Salt—20,000 Brick,

Which are offered at prices it is believed will be found satisfactory. ALSO,

Have just received, in addition to their former supply of Goods, a complete assortment of Plain, colour'd, blue edged and blue printed

Crockery Ware, Glass Ware, Plain & figur'd Bombazetts and Broadcloths,

which will be sold very low.

WANTED—A Man to tend a stall of Hogs and Cattle, who is of steady habits, and has a small family, to whom liberal wages will be given.— None need apply who cannot come well recommended. Enfield, Aug. 10. 4

The duo hosted farm animals on the property and advertised them in the Connecticut Courant on August 20, 1822.

Within two years, though, the operation had hit a rough patch, and the business, property, buildings, and contents were put up for sale. The stated reason for the action was the death of one of the principals, but both Belcher and Cooley were still alive; therefore, we must consider that this may have provided cover for a failing business.

Distillery, Mills, Stores, Dwelling Houses, &c. &c.

FOR SALE, on a liberal credit, and at a low price, 40 acres of excellent Land, situated within 50 rods of Connecticut River, in the town of Enfield, with a Distillery and building in good repair, capable of running 75 bushels of grain per day ; and now in operation, a first rate Grist Mill with three run Stones, and well accustomed. From the decease of one of the partners it is necessary to dispose of the above property to close the concern. For a further description, and the terms, application may be made to Mr. HENRY DWIGHT, Wall-street, *New York :* to DAY, BREWER & DWIGHT, *Springfield*, Mass. or COOLEY & BELCHER, on the premises.

Enfield, Conn. May 10, 1825.   12w48

Regional papers carried the announcement that the remaining stock of goods and products would be *auctioned off* on November 8th, 1825, after the sale of the business and contents had also failed. In addition, there would follow a private sale to dispose of some fifty 'well-fatted' hogs of between 250 and 400 pounds to qualified buyers.

By the following month, the partnership of Cooley & Belcher was dissolved on December 10, 1825.

Surprisingly, the members of the organization included Edmund Dwight, James Dwight, and James Brewer of the original James Brewer & Co concern, son Jonathan Dwight Jr., Benjamin Day, and, of course, Cooley and Belcher themselves.

NOTICE

IS hereby given that the Copartnership heretofore existing under the firm of COOLEY & BELCHER, was dissolved by mutual consent the 1st instant.

> JONATHAN DWIGHT, Jr.
> EDMUND DWIGHT.
> BENJAMIN DAY.
> JAMES BREWER.
> JAMES S. DWIGHT.
> JOHN COOLEY.
> JOHN COOLEY, Jr.
> HIRAM BELCHER.

Enfield, Dec. 10, 1825.   77

And so, the business, contents, and animals were gone, but the disposition of the 40 acres, dwellings, and other buildings remained in limbo until one year later, when, on November 20, 1826, Jonathan Dwight, James Dwight, and James Brewer completed the sale of that same property, and a few other acres, to Peter Raynolds, Sylvester Lusk, and Henry Thompson. As best as can be determined without the assistance of a map of the region for that period, the plots of land were all located in the Lovejoy's Ferry section of Enfield, based on the land sale records.[26]

Although the sale was two years before David Andrews and Orrin Thompson decided to move ahead with their carpet manufacturing plan, the fact that Orrin's brother-in-law Sylvester Lusk and brother Henry Thompson were part of the property purchase seems to indicate that acquiring the land was in some way connected to Andrews, Thompson & Company, possibly influenced by the perceived success of the Tariffville manufacturing operation. The purchase certainly secured valuable real estate and mills on Freshwater Brook and Pond, which would prove valuable years later when the operation expanded. Most historical references point to the purchase of the 'Dwight' properties as being connected to the future carpet manufactory.

Speculation aside, on January 16, 1828, James Brewer sold another piece of Enfield property, this time directly to David Andrews and Orrin Thompson of the New York City company.[27] The location of this parcel is easier to determine as the southerly boundary was defined by the Freshwater Brook, westerly and northerly by 'the road leading from Main Street [today's North Main Street] to the Connecticut River' [today's Main Street], and easterly by, once again, Freshwater Brook. This slice of property, sandwiched between the street and the brook and extending from the Connecticut River to the upper pond, included the linseed oil mill owned by Seth Talcott and Henry Loomis's flouring mill[28] and all associated water privileges.

These privileges allowed the New York pair to contract with Hiram Williston of South Hadley, Massachusetts, and

---

[26] See Appendix Record 1
[27] See Appendix Record 2
[28] Springfield Republican October 24, 1909. Page 6.

Benjamin E. White of Springfield, Massachusetts, to

> *erect a dam across Freshwater Brook (where the dam now stands), near the clothing works now occupied by Seth Talcott.*[29]

The dimensions of the new dam were set at 118 feet long, 14 feet high, 15 feet thick at the bottom, and 4 feet thick at the top, far surpassing the dimensions of the dam it would replace and creating a much larger pond than existed at that time. The contract focused on construction requirements to ensure durability, given the greater outward pressure from a larger body of water. The cost of the new dam was set at one thousand dollars [$32,289 in 2024], payable in two installments.

Resources identify the elusive Captain Harvey[30] as the contractor engaged by Andrews, Thompson & Company to begin construction on multiple initiatives for the organization, which included the first mill and housing for arriving emigres.

Before construction work on the mill could begin, though, buildings on the former Seth Talcott property, below the dam, such as a sawmill, carding mill, and fulling mill[31], needed to be removed or moved, and Harvey directed his men to do so.

Five months later, the Thompsonville Carpet

---

[29] Contract between Hiram Williston, Benjamen E. White, Andrews, Thompson & Co., Sylvester Lusk, Henry Thompson
[30] Multiple Thompsonville Press articles point to Captain Harvey as the 'contractor' for multiple buildings in Lovejoy's Ferry without ever identifying him further EXCEPT to point out he was from Poquonock, Connecticut
[31] Fulling is a process to work wet cloth to encourage the fibers to interlock and become more homogenous

Manufacturing Company was incorporated by a resolution of the Connecticut State Assembly. Specifically noted in the document were the directors Sylvester Lusk, Henry Thompson, David Andrews, and Orrin Thompson. This resolution was passed before the organization's final purchase of the land and water rights had been secured, and the document noted that the land purchased for the company's use should not exceed 100 acres unless some land were transferred to the corporation as payment in kind for goods or services.

An initial valuation of the company was set at 150,000 dollars, with a single share valued at 500 dollars, but the company was allowed to go into operation with a 30,000-dollar capitalization [approximately $1 million in 2024].[32] The stated amount would have to be paid to the Town Clerk of the Town of Enfield within 12 months of the passage of the declaration.

By November 28 of the same year, the company's directors sold parcels of property in the Lovejoy's section of Enfield, which they had personally acquired over the previous years, to the new carpet organization.[33] All four parcels of property were sold to the organization for a total of thirty-four thousand dollars [$1,097,827 in 2024], which was generally defined as follows: to the West by the Connecticut River, to the North by the Catholic Cemetery, to the East by Church Street/North Main/South Main, and to the South by High Street. The water rights were secured for Freshwater Pond, as well as for the brook leading to the Connecticut River.

The corporation had its land and its water rights.

But not yet a dam. The dam had been contracted and

---

[32] Resolves and Private Laws of the State of Connecticut. Page 923
[33] See Appendix Record 3

was projected to be completed by August 1828, yet it wasn't erected until the middle of December 1828.

The personality of a community reflects the collective makeup of its residents, and a property transfer on December 12, 1828, demonstrated the qualities of the Thompson children that were imbued into the very land of Lovejoy's Ferry. [34]

For the price of one dollar, and in *'consideration of the love and good will we bear to our Mother Betsy Thompson'*, the children, now adults, bequeathed four parcels of land and the buildings thereon to their mother for the rest of her life. Surprisingly there was a caveat inserted into the land transfer which might have negated the sale in the future. The contingency stated that the transfer was valid as *'long as she remains the widow of Matthew Thompson deceased.'*

The children didn't want another man benefitting from their act of love and loyalty, thus demonstrating both their affection and their business chops at the same time.

While work on the dam had been progressing, Captain Harvey had been busy elsewhere.

Directly below the dam, a crew of men was busy constructing a three-story wooden frame building, which would later be referred to as the 'White Mill' and would be the first factory building to be completed[35].

The Henry Loomis flouring mill, on the north side of Freshwater Brook, which had been part of the January land

---

[34] See Appendix Record 4
[35] In the Spring of 1829

purchase, was lifted and turned around and repurposed. [36]

By October of 1828, the first group of skilled Scottish weavers and mechanics, some with their families, arrived at Warehouse Point. The men had been recruited by Scottish business partners Gregory, Thomsons & Company. They had been shepherded northward from New York by Seth and Henry Thompson upon the emigres' arrival in the city.

The White Mill on Freshwater Brook in Thompsonville. Completed in 1829. The Newman S. Hungerford Museum Fund. Probably photographed by Nathan Page Palmer (American, 1843 - 1918)

The need for housing had somehow escaped the planners, so the group of newcomers was distributed among the available spaces at the 'lower tavern', or Globe Hotel managed by the Widow Wright, the 'middle tavern', or the soon-to-be-named Thompsonville Hotel managed by Peter Raynolds, and the 'upper tavern', or the Yellow Tavern

---

[36] As a dye house in 1829

managed by Hiram S. Belcher located on the southwest corner of Enfield and North Main Street.

With no mills prepared to ply their skills, the Scots worked on the dam and pitched in on the construction of the White Mill, which was perilously behind schedule.

It was around the same time, soon after the arrival of the first wave of Scotsmen, that the village known as Lovejoy's Ferry became rebranded as 'Thompsonville', in honor of Orrin Thompson and to acknowledge the influx of skilled foreigners populating the area.

For those not working on projects near or on the dam, Captain Harvey directed them to the western border of the village to hand-dig foundations along the Connecticut River to prepare for the construction of cottages to house immigrant families. Along the river ran a dirt road where construction materials were delivered to the men assembling the small homes. Due to the bloodline of the future inhabitants, the street was known as 'Scotch Row'.

The name itself was a misnomer of sorts as there would eventually be three sets, or rows, of homes constructed along the riverbank.[37] The first, nearest the river, was called 'River Row', the next 'Middle Row', and the third, closest to the street, 'Scotch Row'.

Besides the cold weather, the workers along the river had to deal with the challenges posed by the changing nature of the Connecticut River itself, which, in November of 1828,

---

[37] Thompsonville Press October 31, 1911. *Story of a Thompsonville Soldier* Robert Liddell

was at its highest level in forty years.[38] Thankfully, the cottages/tenements had no cellars, or the construction itself would have been doomed.

Possibly considering the nature of the river, work began constructing a set of four tenements on 'Mutton Hill' [39] to house additional immigrants, expected early the following year.

By the Spring of 1829, the White Mill, as well as numerous cottages and tenements, had been completed.

The second wave of Scottish workers, the majority from Kilmarnock, arrived soon after, and their influence would begin to extend far beyond the weaving of fabric.

---

[38] Upper Ashuelot: a History of Keene New Hampshire. Page 585

[39] As best as can be determined, Mutton Hill was the first iteration of Asnuntuck Street. It was likely named as either a slight, or in deference, to the Scottish immigrants who would live there.

2: LITTLE SCOTLAND

I Hereby Certify that the moneys paid in by the secured stockholders of the Thompsonville Carpet Manufacturing Company up to the 20th Day of April 1829 amount in the aggregate to the sum of thirty two thousand two hundred and twenty five dollars and eighty one cents.

Henry Thompson Treasurer and Agent for the Thompsonville Carpet Manufacturing Company

Received April 21, 1829, and recorded by William Dixon

What motivates someone to leave the country of their birth? Certainly war, social upheaval, and persecution are understandable reasons to pack up and move. However, leaving the land of one's ancestors to begin a new life in a foreign land must be a difficult decision.

The first wave of Scottish workers was hand-selected recruits by the Scottish partners of Gregory, Thomson & Company. They had been signed to a two-year contract and had their travel costs from Scotland to New York City prepaid. There, they were met by company officials, Seth and Henry Thompson, and were escorted to Enfield. Theirs had been a relatively easy financial and quality-of-life decision.

The second wave of recruits was mostly from Kilmarnock and had volunteered or self-advocated for the opportunity to seek employment with the fledgling Connecticut company because the Scottish work climate had deteriorated from 1828 onward.

Fore Street, Kilmarnock, Scotland (1830). Public Domain

Some of the searing distress that had characterized 1826 returned to the Scottish handloom weavers in 1829. On April 3, 1829, an estimated 20,000 from Glasgow and surrounding weaving areas met at Glasgow Green to discuss their 'present destitute and pitiable condition'. Three weeks later, one-third of the 1,200 to 1,300 harness, plain shawl, and muslin weavers of Kilmarnock were without work, in addition to another 300 idle carpet weavers representing about twenty percent of that workforce.[40]

---

[40] Glasgow Herald, 3 Apr. 1829; 20 Apr. 1829; 14 July 1829

The weavers were starving, subsisting on one month's provisions over three months, and, at times, "without a morsel to appease their hunger".[41]

Relief at the time was available only through the church, and even that was of little value, as parishes were in no better shape than the communities they served. In Paisley, Scotland, twenty miles due north of Kilmarnock, a soup kitchen was suggested to address the plight of the handloom weavers. The community reflected, saying -

...unless he was actually dying from want, and if he stooped to such degradation he would never be able to hold up his head among his fellows.[42]

Friendly Societies had been protected and encouraged by the Scottish parliament since 1793 and had existed and thrived among the weavers. These precursors to unions strengthened the brotherhood among skilled workers and even gave them the strength in numbers when negotiating with mill owners. In many cases, these friendly societies also resolved to form cooperative societies, seeking to provide additional social services to their members beyond wage negotiations. But these societies were no match for the challenging economic times, nor for the influx of Irish weavers seeking work, which further drove down pay rates.

In many cases, rather than providing soup or sustenance to the downtrodden, destitute weavers were employed as manual laborers, not in jobs that reflected their skill sets.[43]

As a rule, Scottish weavers were accustomed to living in small, crowded homes without access to running water. Baths were few and far between unless they dipped themselves in the River Irvine, Kilmarnock Water, Fenwick

---

[41] Glasgow Chronicle, 17 April 1829
[42] The Scottish hand loom weavers, 1790-1850. Page 136
[43] The Scottish hand loom weavers, 1790-1850. Page 140

Water, Craufurdland Water, or any of the tributaries on the outskirts of the town. The absence of piped running water led to infrequent baths, even in the most prosperous of households.[44]

> *It may be asked why self-respecting Scotsmen should have been content to live in such conditions. Some were quite satisfied; they did not understand — most medical men even did not understand — how closely connected dirt and overcrowding were with disease, and if you found fault with them, they would at once have quoted the proverb 'the clartier the cosier'.*[45]

Despite the economic hardships and their penchant for 'a wee bit of the drink', the Scottish weavers were a deeply religious people, adhering, for the majority, to the tenets of the Presbyterian Church of Scotland. Surprisingly, due to Irish immigration, 25% of the weaving community in Scotland embraced the Roman Catholic faith. This is not to say all were devout churchgoers, as church attendance was waning as 1830 drew near. This most likely reflected the devastating effect of a tumbling economy rather than a moral decline. Church pews were rented annually, and contributions to the poor were collected from congregation members based on their individual circumstances. Free seats were available to the poor in churches, but weavers would have been highly reluctant to use them, as doing so would have been an admission of poverty.

It must have been challenging to seek solace and comfort in the House of God without money to pay for it.

The economy also had a deleterious effect on the leisure activities of the weavers. The activities of the early 19th century, such as bowling, curling, gardening, and fishing,

---

[44] Ibid Page 155
[45] Mackie's Short History of Scotland. Page 279. The proverb means *'the dirtier the more comfortable'*

gave way to longer working hours and the simpler and less costly joys of reading scripture. Drinking establishments also began to capture the weavers' time and attention, to the dismay of their wives and families.

Kilmarnock Handloom Weaver (1830) Public Domain

All the above were motivators to the weavers of Kilmarnock to leave their homes to seek a better opportunity offered by the promise of Thompsonville. [46]

The first group of Scots had been living in Thompsonville for six months by the time the second wave

---

[46] Previously known as Lovejoy's Ferry. Renamed sometime after the incorporation of the Thompsonville Carpet Mfg Company and the arrival of the first wave of immigrants

of Scotch Presbyterians arrived in June 1829. With their arrival, the emigres officially outnumbered the native Yankees in the village.

The area along the riverbank, just north of the ferry, was dotted with housing, while the four larger tenements on Mutton Hill were well underway. The newcomers pitched in to complete the construction, and soon all families had roofs over their heads and a place to sleep at night.

By early summer, the new dam had created a greater, more expansive Freshwater Pond. This new body of water would provide the power needed to drive the machinery at the White Mill. This equipment had been supplied by Gregory, Thomson & Company of Kilmarnock, Scotland, along with the workers. The first and second floors of the factory building were filled with four sets of carding machines and four jack looms.[47] The third-floor housed rug looms and Venetian carpet looms.[48]

The Scots had the necessary skill sets to work the looms to produce carpets, but also hired from the surrounding countryside for other, less skilled positions, such as spinners. The first included William and George Olmsted, Becket Allen of Enfield, Hiram and Henry Sykes, and Jewell Wright of Suffield.

---

[47] A Carding Machine is designed for processing cotton fibers, preparing them for the spinning process, and ensuring that they are clean, aligned, and ready for further processing into yarn or fabric.
Jack Looms are a type of floor loom that are often small and folding and are good choice for weaving rugs because they can produce longer lengths of fabric and are stable enough for complex designs
[48] Venetian carpet is woven on simple looms in narrow strips that are 18–36 inches wide. They are inexpensive and are often used for stairs and passages

According to most accounts, the first carpet was produced in either June or July 1829.[49]

> *The Thompsonville Company commenced weaving in June 1829. At that time they had from eight to ten looms in operation. I am Clerk of the establishment. There was some debate about the price of weaving. At first the company paid 16 cents per yard and then 15½ cts [cents]. until the average price in the country could be ascertained. This was ascertained in September and it was agreed that 14½ cts. [cents] should be afterwards paid…*[50]

Along with the second group of immigrants[51] came Robert Thompson, a partner in Gregory, Thomson & Company, who became manager of the Thompsonville operation. It was Thompson's job to hire and fire.

Looms were assigned to individual weavers as they arrived, and they were theirs and theirs alone to work and produce carpets, as quality and competency were unique to each tradesman.

In 1828, the population of Kilmarnock was close to 16,000 people.

In contrast, there were approximately 40 people in Lovejoy's Ferry when the first Scots arrived, and the population increase in the village in the following year was due to the influx of additional immigrants. Clearly, the Scots had exchanged the crowded streets of their European city

---

[49] Thompsonville Press December 12, 1883. Page 1

[50] A Documentary History of American Industrial Society *Volume IV Supplement.* Page 52

[51] Included in the group were James Ronalds, John Gray, Ewen and Robert McChristie, Charles Stewart, David Galt, James Logan, John Bain, William Hamilton, William Weir, Robert Doo, Alexander Merkle, and Thomas Smith. James Reid, in the first group, wove the first carpet at the mill

for the quiet of a New England hamlet.

One would have expected the emigres to feel socially out of place in their new environment, but the reality was that they felt at home. Each already knew the other, having worked together for years in the same industry in their native land. Their interests, ancestry, culture, language, and cuisine were the same. Rather than being uncomfortable, it was as if a Scottish village had been grafted onto the Enfield shoreline.

One welcome difference experienced by the emigres was that the United States had a stable economy and a wealth of inexpensive provisions.

With weaving rates settled in at 14½ cents per yard, and an average production of eight yards per day, a weaver earned anywhere from five to seven dollars per week. Room and board (should the single man or family be renting a room at any of the three local taverns) was two dollars per week. If the weaver rented an apartment along the river or on Mutton Hill, they would purchase their provisions. Food was inexpensive, with potatoes costing 18 to 20 cents per bushel, beef 3½ to 5 cents per pound[52], butter 14 cents a pound, and sugar 6 to 7 cents per pound. In addition…

…rye gin [was] not to be despised, but treated as one of God's good creatures – [and it] was abundant, cheap, and respectfully, sometimes, affectionately regarded.[53]

Boats from the south would drop foodstuffs off at the wharf near the Globe Hotel. These provisions might be left there for days until the purchaser who worked in the mill had time to collect them, without a worry that someone would steal their purchases in the meantime.

---

[52] Thompsonville Press December 12, 1883. Page 1
[53] Thompsonville Press July 12, 1883. Page 1

It was a faithful, loving, and supportive community.

Everyone was ready to help [one] another without asking 'How much is there in it?'.

Neighbors were always ready to visit and help the sick or bury the dead. Borrowing and lending was frequent.

There was no necessity to lock doors in those days.[54]

The Scots were a lively group. The spaces they lived in were small but -

...the fun and the life and the generous enthusiasm that they sheltered can only be known by those who lived [there], or who knew [them] in all their rich originality, the growing [families] who bore these names...[55]

- like the Donalds, the Stewarts, the Anguses, the Jacks, the David Clarks, the Bottomlys, the Hoods, the M'Crones, and the Andersons.

Residents from Enfield Street or beyond would venture into the Scottish Presbyterian Village of Thompsonville from time to time to engage the 'blue blood' of Kilmarnock, only to return to their neighborhoods to speak in amazement that these 'foreigners were as white as can be' [56] and not unlike themselves in appearance (as if they were expecting something totally different).

Most Scottish immigrants could read and write English, and their work ethic was beyond reproach. Unlike other immigrant groups, Scots were not met with religious discrimination, and they did not expect special or

---

[54] Thompsonville Press October 31, 1911. Page 1
Remembrances of Robert Liddle of Enfield Civil War Soldier
[55] Thompsonville Press July 7, 1883. Page 1
[56] Thompsonville Press July 12, 1883. Page 1

preferential treatment.[57]

> ...*The Scots in America would also demonstrate that the endless possibilities of this inventive self-fashioning and the pursuit of individual success [did] not have to end in chaos. They spawn[ed] a new kind of civic community, which respect[ed] the right of all people to pursue their own ends as long as they respect[ed] that right for others. It [was] an enlightened community...reinforced, like concrete with steel rods, by a traditional moral discipline, the legacy of Presbyterianism.[58]*

Nevertheless, the Scots remained a distinctive group apart from the locals, and the differences in culture, as well as their assertive approach to leveraging their skill set advantage with the mill owners, created a management challenge.

The weavers brought with them the idea of Friendly Societies when 'collectively bargaining' wages for the whole. It was a relatively new concept in the region, but quite effective because immigrants' unique skill sets strengthened their bargaining power.

> *To bolster their monopoly position, the Thompsonville weavers immediately established a joint bargaining agency. This was accepted by management without complaint. Through it, agreements were reached on the original wage rates, and negotiations relating to working rules, living conditions, and rates for new goods were carried on periodically.[59]*

On September 7, 1829, Major Horace Metcalf passed

---

[57] *How the Scots Invented the Modern World*

[58] IBID Page 329

[59] Labor in the Early New England Carpet Industry. Page 24

away at the age of 38, having experienced only the infancy of the carpet mill. It was Major Metcalf's property, sold years earlier, that had provided much of the land on which the early mill buildings had been erected.[60]

The Scots weren't alone in 1829 as Irish and British weavers began to emigrate to the United States, and to Thompsonville in particular. Those who showed promise were given housing and a loom to ply their trade. To bring balance to their lives, these immigrants were accustomed to attending the "Kirk"[61] in their native land.

The issue for these Presbyterians was that the only church within a reasonable distance was the Congregational Church, which was over two miles from the village—a challenging walk in inclement weather—and was not in direct alignment with their religious beliefs.

One of the Irishmen who sought work in Thompsonville was James Lynn, a linen weaver from Northern Ireland, who arrived in the village in mid-1829, presenting papers from a mill in New York that attested to his skills. Like others before him, he was assigned a loom and housing on Scotch Row.

As no photographs exist as to the nature of the dwellings

---

[60] Horace Metcalf's father was Reverend Thomas Metcalf of Worcester, Massachusetts who had answered the call in 1776 to fight as a private in Captain Lemuel Kollock's company during the War of the Revolution. Years later he married Sybil Chapin, a resident of Enfield, Connecticut, whose family roots could be traced back to her grandfather Nathaniel Chapin who had been born in Enfield in 1711.

[61] A Scottish word meaning 'Church' – informally referring to the Church of Scotland

along the Connecticut River, we have to look to the words used to describe them at the time, the most frequent being *tenements*. To think that individual houses or cottages were erected for one family is to misunderstand the goal of the construction effort, which was to most efficiently house as many individuals and families as possible with the smallest possible footprint. The Scots were accustomed to tenement living, as these buildings were constructed quickly and cheaply to accommodate the growing population of industrial workers in most cities.

Tenements in Glasgow, Scotland. Bert Hardy The Forgotten Gorbals.

Constructed with density in mind rather than comfort, they were cramped, poorly lit, under-ventilated, and lacked indoor plumbing. Although they were built with mill labor, they were nonetheless owned by the mill and leased to the employees. Like Thompsonville, other mill towns, such as Middletown, Connecticut, the largest city in Connecticut in 1790, constructed the same type of tenements to house their immigrant workers laboring in the salmon fisheries, livestock farms, textile mills, and brownstone quarries.

Three six-family tenements were built for the Ponemah Mills workers in Taftville, Connecticut (1866)

Unlike that in Scottish cities, Thompsonville tenement housing was most likely constructed of wood, given the availability of sawmills and robust woodlands. Wood also equated to speed, which was of primary concern.

The aforementioned James Lynn was an amicable man, welcomed among the Scotch, English, and Irish alike. A pious man, he would gather people together for weekly prayer meetings, which were only limited by available space.

In those early days, if the houses in Scotch Row had been larger, or the families inhabiting them smaller, there would have been a good many similar meetings, but small rooms and large families prevented.

Mr. Lynn made many calls on families where he found that his presence was agreeable, and as there were a good many North of Ireland people here about that time, he was made welcome by all, no matter what their religious proclivities were. Catholic as well as Presbyterian were pleased to see the genial Mr. Lynn.

He was a man of very commanding presence, well versed in Scripture history, and remarkably modest in advocating any views of his own, but resolute in maintaining them.[62]

James Lynn was by no means a preacher, and his prayer meetings were not sanctioned by any religious body. He was inducted into a Methodist class formed toward the latter part of 1829 that Alvah Symonds led[63] and assisted by Arnold Olmsted.[64] This class dissolved at some point soon after formation, with preachers from East Windsor filling the void, while Lynn continued his supplemental preachings.

In addition to attending services led by the Reverend Francis Le Baron Robbins at the Congregational Church, one newspaper source stated that:

…a Scotsman by the name of Mitchell preached the first sermon in the village in the old baleing [sic baling] room of the factory. Soon afterward the basement of the store was prepared for meetings and in this basement the first baptisms of the village were performed. The record says that Barbara Law, Flora Angus, and James Houston were the first children [christened] here in the Presbyterian faith.[65]

---

[62] Thompsonville Press August 16, 1883.

[63] Also recorded in other sources as Simonds and Simons

[64] Thompsonville Press October 10, 1884.

[65] The Thompsonville Press November 15, 1914. Page 1. As of this date, additional information on the "preacher" Mitchell remains

It seems as if Reverend Mitchell's tenure was only for a short time, as, after a few weeks, he left the village[66] and the weavers and their families continued to attend the Congregational Church.

From 1830 to mid-1831, the carpet manufactory slowly expanded, adding looms and weavers to increase production as orders continued to be placed through the sales arm of Andrews, Thompson & Company of New York. Orrin Thompson still resided in New York City, and his brother Henry lived in Enfield, serving as treasurer and agent for the carpet company. James Elnathan Smith, a longtime employee of the New York import firm, continued to split his time between Manhattan and England, keeping his finger on the pulse of new carpet designs coming from European manufacturers.

During this same period, a long-weave shop, blacksmith shop, machine shop, drying shed, dyehouse, and baling room were constructed on the Metcalf property, completing the original layout of the fledgling carpet company.

The carpet company seemed to have settled in as nicely as had their Scottish, Irish, and English employees.

At times, though, looks can be deceiving.

. The store referenced in the quote was one located at the corner of Prospect and Asnuntuck Streets
[66] The Thompsonville Press July 7, 1889. Page 1.

3: DISHARMONY

Thompsonville was a tight-knit Scottish community. Though independent of mind and culture, they shared some of the same hardheadedness of their Yankee cohorts, which, at least in the beginning, gave the immigrants greater bargaining power over their managers and employers.

Contract orders for products came directly from the New York parent firm of Andrews, Thompson & Company, which meant periodic shutdowns for some of the weavers as rugs were woven "on demand". So skilled were the workers employed in Thompsonville that their output consistently surpassed that of the competition in terms of both quality and style.

While working overseas, James Elnathan Smith promptly forwarded three-foot copies of the latest European carpet styles to New York, where they were quickly sent to Thompsonville and converted into saleable products. The company was so efficient in this practice that it often beat not only its stateside rivals but also its European competitors to market.

Smith not only forwarded patterns but also convinced skilled rug and carpet weavers to emigrate to Thompsonville whenever he encountered them. As had been precedent, new contract employees would be assigned appropriate equipment and mill-owned housing.

All was harmonious until March 1, 1831, when James E. Smith withdrew from the partnership of Andrews, Thompson & Company.[67] By April 12th of that same year, Smith had partnered with Thomas L. Chester to form a new co-partnership transacting business as Thomas L. Chester & Company in New York City and as J. Elnathan Smith & Company in London.[68]

COPARTNERSHIP —*Thomas L. Chester*, late of the house of **W. W. & T. L. Chester**, and *James Elnathan Smith*, late of the house of Andrews, Thompson & Co. have entered into copartnership, and will transact business in this city under the firm of THOMAS L. CHESTER & Co. and in London under the firm of J. ELNATHAN SMITH & Co. New York, 12th April, 1831. THOMAS L CHESTER, J. ELNATHAN SMITH.

T. L. Chester, who has recently sailed for England, intends returning to this city in the month of August next, with an extensive assortment of every description of Carpeting, carefully selected from the most celebrated manufactories. a12 1w*

The status of the relationship between Smith and Andrews, Thompson & Company after the split is unknown, but it appears that the original working arrangement remained in place, albeit without partnership responsibilities.

There was an agreement between the Thompsonville Carpet Company and the proprietors of the three village taverns insofar as setting weekly rental rates to be charged to the weavers.

If the workers represented a monopoly of skills, then,

---

[67] The Law Advertiser March 1, 1831. Page 278
[68] The Evening Post April 13, 1831. Page 3

based on availability, the taverns, Scotch Row, and Mutton Hill tenements represented a housing monopoly. Which group would prove the stronger was settled when an attempt was made to raise housing rates. This prompted a work action that ultimately led to a return to earlier rental rates.

The Scots were not to be trifled with.

Expansion hadn't come without its costs. Despite brisk sales and unmatched quality, the company's stockholders' meeting in July of 1831 at the company offices (then on Church Street) in Thompsonville did not sit well with local shareholders.

Robert Thomson had emigrated to the United States to represent the interests of the Scottish partners, Gregory, Thomsons & Company, in the first wave of emigration in 1828. He had acted as supervisor of the Thompsonville manufactory site since his arrival. For two difficult years, he had attempted to herd the cats—the Scottish, Irish, and English weavers —and by 1831, he had had enough. Thomson disengaged from the operation either by having his stock shares bought out or by simply resigning from the Scottish board. He withdrew to Paterson, New Jersey[69], nicknamed 'Silk City', most likely to the Great Falls District. That area was rife with mills of all types, including carpet, and even had 260 hand looms in operation in 1825, exclusive of industrial operations.[70]

One of the challenges Thomson faced was controlling weavers' behavior to manage production better. A three-headed approach of prohibition, time management, and incentivization was employed to corral and focus

---

[69] The Thompsonville Press September 9, 1882. Page 1
[70] An Incorporation of the Adventurers. Page 147

production efforts.

On the prohibition front, management had instituted bans on smoking, reading newspapers, and on breaks lasting longer than 15 minutes.

For time management, weavers were required to declare the status of their piece[71] before leaving for the day, or if they intended to leave for other opportunities. Additionally, failure to complete two pieces within the allotted time may result in termination.

To encourage weavers to increase production, the company took the *stick-and-carrot* approach.

Failure to weave a piece – 90 yards – of fine carpeting in 12 days or superfine in 15 days cost the worker a shilling[72] for each extra day. For completing a fine piece in 10 days or superfine in 12, the weaver received a bonus of 50 cents.[73]

The challenge of enforcing these rules weighed more heavily on Thomson than on the Scots or Irish and likely contributed to his exit.

With the principals of Gregory, Thomsons & Company, Andrews, Thompson & Company, and Enfield stockholders assembled in the tiny Connecticut village, a review of the operation left the Enfield shareholders unsettled. Startup and expansion costs had impacted on the profitability of the manufactory, and, while that was not unexpected by the larger firms, the individual investors went so far as to question the viability of the operation.

To address the concerns of the small investor, Andrews,

---

[71] Commonly referred to as a *webb's notice*
[72] Approximately 12 cents
[73] Labor in the Early New England Carpet Industry. Page 48

Thompson & Company offered to purchase their shares outright. With this action, Sylvester Lusk and other minor Enfield investors were relieved of their association with the enterprise.

Their business concluded; the partners withdrew to their respective locales. Within two weeks, on July 29th, the unexpected happened as David Andrews, at 59 years of age, drew his last breath at his home at 75 Anthony Street, Brooklyn, New York. Surprisingly, for a man of his status, Andrews left no will to address how and to whom his assets should be distributed. This required his son, Robert Walsh Andrews, to petition the court to appoint him, James Magee, and Joseph Ripley as administrators of his father's estate, which was granted on October 3, 1831. Andrews shares in Andrews, Thompson & Company were then purchased from the estate by the surviving partner, Orrin Thompson. This purchase was added to the shares previously acquired from the Enfield investors.

The New York mercantile partnership was rebranded as Thompson & Company, with Orrin assuming all business and financial responsibilities. Into the business, Thompson welcomed Thaddeus Phelps, Vice President of the New York Democratic-Republican General Committee and a wealthy shipping merchant, and two salesmen who had been working at the New York store, William Douglas and Thomas McCrindle. Phelps injected capital and business *know-how,* while Douglas and McCrindle contributed youthful energy.

Thaddeus Phelps was a shipping magnate whose business, Thaddeus Phelps & Company, was located at 47 South Street in New York City. In addition to running a fleet of packing ships ferrying products along the Eastern Seaboard as well as across the Atlantic, he had founded the *Swallow-Tail Line* with another ship-building firm, Fish, Grinnell, & Company. The line was called the Swallow-Tail due to its forked pennant. The fleet of ships, which weighed from 600 to 1,500 tons each, departed on the 8th of every month from New York Harbor to Liverpool in 23 days, returning in 40.

FOR LIVERPOOL—To sail 8th proximo. The line ship SILAS RICHARDS, H. Holdredge, master, to sail 8th proximo for Liverpool, can take the bulk of 300 bales cotton.— For freight of which, or passage in cabin, having elegant furnished accommodations, or steerage, apply on board, at Pine-street wharf, to THADDEUS PHELPS & CO. 47 South-street, or

nov 27   FISH, GRINNELL & CO 136 Front-st.

William Douglas was born in 1795 in Dunfermline, Fife, Scotland. He had emigrated to the United States sometime in the early 1820s, where he secured a position as a salesman for the firm Andrews, Thompson & Company.

Thomas McCrindell was born in Aberdeen, Scotland, and emigrated to the United States in 1817. By the early 1820s, he was a partner in the firm of Barker and McCrindell, importing and selling carpets from their store at 196 Broadway, New York. Closing that operation in 1825, he partnered with his brother as *George and Thomas McCrindell,* marketing a similar line of carpets. By 1829, the siblings had closed their store, and Thomas joined the firm of Andrews, Thompson & Company as a salesman, leveraging his knowledge of the product. He became fast friends with Douglas, and the pair were brought into the rebranded firm of Thompson & Company as partners in 1831, after the death of David Andrews.

With the new hierarchy in place, the company was ready to move forward as a stable entity.

In 1832, a new covered bridge was completed connecting Enfield to Suffield. Begun in 1826, the 70-foot-wide, 1000-foot-long toll bridge was constructed under the guidance of William Dixon. It had been built with funds provided through a lottery, but was owned by Dixon, an Enfield resident who had served as Town Clerk for 12 years, represented the town in the General Assembly for 9 years, and had recently been elected Judge of Probate for the district.

The new bridge had replaced an earlier version that had been poorly constructed and had fallen into ruin of its own accord. With the bridge completed, the road leading to it was appropriately renamed Bridge Lane.

Thompsonville, though, was still isolated from the greater community, the only roadway in and out of the hamlet being the Main Street/Enfield Street connection—that, and, of course, traffic on the Connecticut River.

The first significant addition to the original manufactory layout was completed sometime around 1832[74]. The Black Mill, or Lower Mill, was a four-story brick and stone building constructed on the lower water privileges. It was dedicated to the production of three-ply carpeting, and the space and additional looms beckoned even more Scottish and Irish weavers to emigrate to the village.

The Dye House and the Black Mill (with cupola) are in the foreground of this photo. (~1892). Photographer: likely Nathan Page Palmer. The Newman S. Hungerford Museum Fund. View is looking west on Main Street toward the Connecticut River

In June 1832, the company once again held its annual shareholders' meeting in Thompsonville, with only the principals from New York attending, as the Enfield

---

[74] Sources vary as to the construction year – the earliest cited as 1830 in the publication *Fibre and Fabric A Record of American Textile Industries in the Cotton and Woolen Trade · Volume 36* [1902] to as late as 1833 in numerous others.

shareholders had been dismissed the previous year.

CHOLERA
AND
WATER.

BOARD OF WORKS
FOR THE LIMEHOUSE DISTRICT,
Comprising Limehouse, Ratcliff, Shadwell, and Wapping.

The INHABITANTS of the District within which **CHOLERA IS PREVAILING**, are earnestly advised

NOT TO DRINK ANY WATER
WHICH HAS NOT
PREVIOUSLY BEEN BOILED.

Fresh Water ought to be Boiled every Morning for the day's use, and what remains of it ought to be thrown away at night. The Water ought not to stand where any kind of dirt can get into it, and great care ought to be given to see that Water Butts and Cisterns are free from dirt.

BY ORDER,

THOS. W. RATCLIFF,
CLERK OF THE BOARD.

For the New York members, the trip was a welcome opportunity to escape the city, which was in the grip of a cholera epidemic that had originated in Asia, spread across Europe, and made its way to Canada, eventually reaching

Lower Manhattan via the Hudson River. The impact of the disease on Europe prevented the Scottish partners from making the trip.

At the time, most medical professionals believed that poisonous vapors from rotting matter caused cholera and that it was not contagious. Doctors attempted to treat patients using traditional methods such as bleeding or dosing with calomel (mercury chloride) or with laudanum (an opiate).[75]

With most infected people dying within one or two days of admittance to hospitals, those with other options fled Manhattan for more isolated environments.

Many theories abounded as to how to address and prevent succumbing to the disease.

An early explanation was that it affected only the shiftless, the ignorant, and the drunkards. If a person avoided alcohol and closed their windows tight at night to keep out the *dangerous night air*, all would be well.

The most widely accepted theory was that cholera was spread through some form of airborne vapor. Some canal towns in upstate New York hung meat on poles in the hope that it would absorb the cholera vapor. Other towns burned barrels of tar around the clock in the belief that the heavy black smoke would rid the air of cholera.

Beyond tar barrels, lime was believed to have the same power, and vats of lime bubbled on street corners to fumigate the air in canal and river towns. Some locations refused to let boats dock, fearing the dreaded disease would somehow waft ashore.

During the height of the cholera outbreak, New York steamboats, which generally ran up to Springfield, stopped

---

[75] Years later the same treatment would be used on Augustus Hazard as he lay dying in a New York Hotel in 1868

making their runs and were replaced by ships from *the Hartford Steamboat Company* and the *Steam Navigation Company*.

> *In the midst of the greatest excitement of the time, burning tar barrels in different sections of the city [New York], closing of business stores and offices, and a general stampede of citizens, a violent thunderstorm burst over the city in the night, the lightning striking several buildings and steamboats lying at the wharves, and among the rest, Thompson & Company's store, demolishing the windows on the east side of the store and unroofing the salesroom, and doing other material damage.*[76]

The violent weather seemed to have a palliative effect on the cholera outbreak as it gradually began to diminish over the summer months, with a feeling of normalcy returning to Manhattan. The financial impact of the disease carried on into the Fall and Winter months as banks began to curtail the relaxed credit policies that had been their general policy before the epidemic.

Churches also leveraged cholera to incite and motivate greater church attendance. The passage of Biela's Comet through the solar system during that same period was used by the clergy as a sign from above to associate the outbreak with a need to draw closer to God.

The direct impact of the disease in Enfield is challenging to determine, as regional papers focused on the dire situations in U.S. metropolitan and European cities.

The Bank War of 1832 had a significant impact on the financial well-being of most businesses from that Fall into the following year.

---

[76] Thompsonville Press September 28, 1882. Page 1

The Second Bank of the United States (B.U.S.) was established in 1816 as a private organization with a 20-year charter, having the exclusive right to conduct banking on a national scale. The original goal was to stabilize the American economy by establishing a uniform currency and strengthening the federal government. Generally, the goal was achieved, as the business community performed well with generous and flexible lending policies (easy credit).

However, as it did, politics complicated the issue, and the Republican Party encouraged the B.U.S. to submit its renewal application four years before it was due, in an attempt to draw a distinction between Democratic candidate Andrew Jackson and Republican Henry Clay in the 1832 presidential race. The Republican-controlled Congress reauthorized the bank's charter, but Jackson vetoed it.

With Jackson winning an overwhelming victory in 1832, he directed that all federal funds be removed from the B.U.S. and redistributed to dozens of state banks. The B.U.S. retaliated by constricting credit, which triggered a mild national economic downturn as loans became harder to obtain. In short order, the B.U.S. reversed its policy, but it was doomed as a national power, as state banks recaptured the attention of businesses.

As a result, businesses with sound fiscal policies were safe, especially those that were cash-rich, while others floundered and closed.

For companies like Thompson's, which generally sold products on six- and eight-month credit, tight banking policies trickled down, forcing them to renegotiate with their buyers and their employees. This new reality struck at a time when the Scotch and Irish weavers thought it best to flex their muscles in response to a tightening wage policy.

Even as monetary policy tightened in 1832, Thompson built his brick mansion on 32 acres bordering Enfield Street.

On the property, the carpet magnate erected a large stock barn as well as several outbuildings.

Thompson's Greek Revival house was set well back from the road on the southeast corner of Enfield Street and South Road overlooking the Revolutionary parade ground. The house had a central square block with a hip roof and cupola flanked by rectangular wings. Each wing had a two-story Doric portico with four columns. Long brownstone porches led to two main doors to the house located on the central block. The architect of the mansion was a talented man, but his identity remains unknown.

Orrin Thompson's home on Enfield Street. (Author photo)

The fact that Thompson elected to construct his house on Enfield Street rather than near his carpet mill did more to raise the prominence of Enfield Street than to diminish the importance of the Thompsonville mill. At the same time, the palatial estate was removed from the daily view of the Thompsonville weavers and, therefore, was not a constant reminder of the economic disparity between the immigrant workers and the owner.

To squeeze greater production from the Scotch, Irish, and English workers, management increased penalties and fines for activities the company deemed non-productive. The immigrants collectively shrugged off the attempt to force enhanced performance and stricter compliance, given the tight labor market and the skill sets of the Thompsonville weavers.

In 1833, the tariffs on imported carpets were reduced, specifically the less costly two-ply carpets, and the organization rescinded worker incentives in an attempt to better compete with imports. European carpets were once again attractive to the importer, especially given worker discontent.

Early in the year, the company introduced three-ply ingrains in Thompsonville to differentiate itself from lesser competitors. In response, the weavers demanded an increase in pay in the three-ply rate from 29 to 30 cents a yard, from $14^{1/2}$ cents to 15 cents per yard for superfine two-ply, and from $10^{1/2}$ cents to 11 cents per yard for fine two-ply ingrain.

Management reacted by shutting down the plant in July of 1833, effectively halting local production and shifting the fulfillment of orders to carpets imported from Europe.

The immigrants had prepared for this type of action, as they were largely unionized and had resources to sustain them during a lengthy work stoppage. They were connected to the other regional carpet mills and communicated with each location, requesting that weavers from those brother sites not migrate to Thompsonville to replace them during the work stoppage. Additionally, the other sites contributed to the fund that the Thompsonville weavers had established in 1828, which was drawn upon to pay each worker between two and three dollars per week while the mill was idle.

For three weeks, the company attempted to break the worker's will to no avail. Minor victories by the carpet company were achieved through bribery, such as when the president of the weavers' union was appointed to a supervisory position, softening the resistance's governance. Other leaders were arrested, and strikebreakers from the company's New York City warehouse were brought in to further weaken the workers' resolve. Linen weavers, friends of the Manhattan crewmen, less skilled at carpet weaving, were brought to Enfield as replacements on the company-owned looms.

Unable to dissuade the newcomers, the Thompsonville weavers returned to work at lower rates than they had left.

But the episode wasn't forgotten by either side.

4: ODDS AND ENDS

Across the river, west of Thompsonville, Simeon Viets introduced cigar manufacturing in the town of Suffield as early as 1810. At that time, the smokes were principally *principes*[77] forged by the hands of local farmhouse wives.

An established industry by 1830, cigars were plentiful and often used as 'legal tender' in the villages of Thompsonville and Warehouse Point when purchasing or bartering for items. David Woodruff, the acknowledged tinsmith of Thompsonville, gifted boxes of cigars to the peddlers who helped move and deliver his wares throughout the region.

Although records are limited, an unnamed cigar box manufacturer in the village reportedly supplied boxes to regional cigar manufacturers, facilitating the delivery of the product to both individuals and stores. This cigar-box factory sourced the finely cut lumber for the boxes from a buzzsaw mill located along Freshwater Brook, south of the gristmill, just below the White Mill.

As with many beliefs of that time, this report was based on a published recollection in a newspaper article and not

---

[77] Narrow hand-rolled cigars with twisted ends

from 'official' records.[78]

In the sister village of Suffield, a small cigar box manufacturing company owned and operated by George Gamble existed around the same time as the reported Thompsonville facility. Years later, a large cigar box factory owned by Henry Cowles was established in the Boston Neck area of Suffield. Cowles was highly successful and even innovated in production, using advanced equipment that increased output by 1200 percent.

Historical records and personal recollections often mention the antics of the young boys known as tread boys. The regionally unique name *tread boy* seems to be the equivalent of the European name for a weaver's assistant - the *draw boy*. Floor looms of the day were mostly *treadle looms*, and one can see it wasn't a reach to understand where the moniker *tread boy* came from.

A tread boy was taken out of school at an early age — somewhere between eight and ten years old — and assigned to a weaver as his assistant. The intricate patterns of the woven carpets required that a tread boy work with a weaver to help him create the desired patterns, as the weaver could not work the shuttle and the warp at the same time. Together, even the most skilled duo couldn't weave more than a couple of complex rows per minute. Workdays for the tread boy were long, often from five in the morning until eight (or later) in the evening, with unpaid breaks interspersed for meals.

The tread boy would manage the harnesses of colored longitudinal threads (the warp) per the designer's instructions to create the pattern as they were woven to the horizontal threads (the weft) as the weaver managed the

---

[78] Thompsonville Press January 11, 1894. Page 2

loom and the shuttle, which flew back and forth through the shed (the space between the raised and unraised warp yarns). One mistake could ruin a carpet, so communication and collaboration between the master weaver and the tread boy were necessary, as well as attention to detail.

Legend has it that the Thompsonville tread boy was an intelligent rascal, capable of both weaving and causing innocuous trouble. Notable tread boys in the village were John Ronald, Jr., James Gorman, Andrew Mair, Alexander Law, and James Alexander, Jr., among many others.

Tread boys were known to pelt visiting Shaker farmers with the farmers' own fruits and vegetables as they delivered their goods to stores in the village. It's safe to assume a certain gleefulness accompanied assaulting the oddly garbed Shakers, a sect the Scottish youths would not have encountered in their native land, making the activity all the more enjoyable.

The taunting of the tread boys was undoubtedly worth the patience demonstrated by both the religious farming sect and local farmers, as outlets for their crops had been somewhat limited up to that time. Rye, of course, was grown and sold to local distilleries, but most Enfield farms grew produce for their own use rather than for marketing. When the Morrison Store opened in Thompsonville on Main Street, both dry and wet goods flowed from provider to consumer, and a relationship was established that benefited all parties.

One story about these young hoodlums concerned a stockpile of empty boxes piled up opposite the brick mill on Main Street one winter. The tread boys cut and manipulated the cartons into containers and cages for a veritable Barnum Brothers menagerie of lions, tigers, hyenas, and monkeys – each of which was played by a howling youth, which, taken together, produced a cacophony of circus sounds.

In the Springtime, when those boxes were required to

pack and ship rugs, not a one could be found that hadn't been bastardized, and of course, when questioned, no tread boy would admit to any knowledge of how that could have happened. Henry Thompson, it was reported, was less than amused, and the three-ply weavers were required to make good on replacement boxes, and they, in turn, settled with the youths.

One specific Shaker, John Slate, a deacon in the religious community, seemed to draw inordinate attention from the tread boys. Legend has it that the tread boys used to extort a *toll* from the farmer whenever he crossed into their *territory*, which was purported to be the entirety of Main Street. A payment would be promised — usually a bag of apples — but never made; the negotiations were more important than the payment itself.

At rare times, the Shaker would bring home-brewed metheglin[79] into town, and it would call to the youths like a siren to seafarers, the boys circling the farmer in his one-horse wagon, looking for an opportunity to make off with the honey-based drink. Slate would hold the jug close to his chest with one hand and draw out his horsewhip with the other to fend off the tread boys until help arrived.

It was all fun and games until one evening, during a driving rain, the Shaker deacon sought shelter under a grist mill as he drove into the village. Slate misjudged the clearance, the top of his head slamming into a supporting beam, opening the farmer's head up and knocking him to the ground. The *Friends* were called and arrived soon after, the wounded Shaker was loaded into another wagon and taken back to the religious compound, where he passed within a few days. He was sure to have been missed by his

---

[79] Metheglin has its roots in folk medicine in Wales, as a cure for numerous ailments, but, at its core, it's a simple fermented drink (alcohol).

mischievous combatants, as the rivalry had always been good-natured and the village's residents were, at heart, caring people.

At the end of Main Street, on the left side past the Black Mill, as one traveled west, a two-story schoolhouse was erected[80] to accommodate the children of the village, whose numbers were steadily increasing. The schoolhouse was built by a village tax, assessed equally on each family, regardless of whether they had children. In a show of community, no resident resisted paying their share. Whether the company contributed to the construction fund is unknown.

Almost every child of suitable age attended class there, regardless of creed, as religion did not play a significant role in children's general education. For that purpose, Sabbath schools were established, although Reverend Thompson would open each secular school day with a prayer and a brief address to the pupils.

James Anderson, of Kilmarnock, Ayrshire, Scotland, was appointed librarian for the school and so went about acquiring the necessary texts for the subjects covered. In truth, James and his wife, Janet (Marshall), could have started a school of their own, as children Helen (13), Matthew (12), James (9), Adam (7), and Janet (5) were of age to attend. Their other children, William (2) and Agness (1), would have been too young at the time but were slated to attend in the years following.

James Wallace, born in Ireland around 1805, was assigned as the first superintendent of schools in Enfield. Unlike Anderson, he and his wife, Mary, had only one child, James Jr, who would be born years later and would not

---

[80] Thompsonville Press November 22, 1883. Page 1

attend the Thompsonville school.

As mentioned, the tread boys were an intelligent lot, but due to their long work hours, they were unable to attend school. So, the parents of these boys petitioned the town and the school committee, of which both James Anderson and Francis Le Baron Robbins were members, to establish a night school for the youths, affording them the educational opportunities for which the parents were already being taxed but not provided. The town agreed, and Robert Galbraith was selected as an evening educator.

It wasn't only the tread boys who attended the evening exercises, although that was the committee's intent; other boys attended as well. At least the first review of the educational initiative by the committee demonstrated that the children were focused and intent on their studies.

Weeks later, the evening school was revisited at an agreed-upon time to assess the students' progress. As all the school committee members entered the room, they were astonished to find only the teacher and an empty classroom.

Crickets.

Then one or two heads bobbed above the windowsill, and the game was on, with members scrambling out the door, each chasing down and corralling a wayward child.

Brought back before the relieved and chagrined instructor, the committee members were assured that there had indeed been significant progress by the youths, which the parents of the boys present supported. The evening concluded to the satisfaction of all.

Even the Reverend had a good laugh.

As wool was washed in tubs below the Mill Pond dam,

the outflow water was deemed not clean enough to use in the Dye House. Workers installed a lead pipe down the middle of Main Street to funnel fresh water to the carpet building. Every so often, there would be a stoppage in the water flow, and workers would venture out into the street to dig up the pipe at varying intervals starting from the upstream source. When the pipe was uncovered, someone would prick a hole in it to check for water. If it flowed cleanly, the hole would be plugged, and the same process would be repeated farther south.

When the punctured pipe spurted blood instead of water, the lead conduit would be opened, the offending eels removed, and the section repaired with cotton cloth and white lead. This process would continue for years until the lead pipe was replaced with an iron pipe of larger dimensions.

Water was of no help on June 30, 1834, when a fire broke out in that same Dye House at 11 p.m. The continuous ringing of the bell atop the White Mill roused the neighboring farmers, who responded to the alarm, bringing pails with them to help form a bucket brigade from the brook to the burning building.

Brave men worked the bucket brigade vigorously, saving the adjoining brick warehouse, but the Dye House was a total loss.

...the desolation would without doubt, have been very extensive, were it not for the prompt and efficient exertions of the people in that village and neighborhood, and perilous exposure of individuals, together with the providential circumstance, noticeable in the unusual stillness of the night; by which the fire was extinguished, and a wooden building at the distance of a few feet

containing $15,000 worth of property was saved.[81]

Orrin Thompson and the board of the carpet manufactory were more than appreciative of the efforts of the villagers and farmers. Within a few days, a feast was held for those same people in an open field in Thompsonville. Over 300 people were accommodated at tables under shade trees, with appropriate food and beverages. It highlighted the underlying connection and mutual respect between employees, villagers, and management.

Being present, I was happy to observe the sobriety and decorum which pervaded throughout the company. I could not but contrast the orderly and respectful appearance on this occasion, with the profanity, contention, and boisterous merriment which have often attended convivial entertainments, especially previous to the temperance reformation.

I know not how far others may think it advisable to adopt such a course in similar circumstances, as a means of securing ready assistance in such a time of need, and promoting mutual satisfaction and harmony; but it is ardently hoped that the people of this village may ever support the character of peaceable, orderly, industrious citizens. And that those who have come across the waters in quest of useful employment, a majority of whom are from Scotland, will ever by their sound principles and correct moral habits, honor the places of their birth.[82]

With the Dye House building in ruins, a contract was drawn up with local builder Omri Gates Carrier to construct a modern brick building in its place.

At the annual meeting of the Carpet Board members in

---

[81] Connecticut Courant August 4, 1834. Page 3
[82] ibid

July, the topic of the fire was broached, with all in favor of forming an official fire company to respond to future fire emergencies. At the next legislative session of elected state representatives, a charter was granted to Thompsonville authorizing Thomas Moore, John Burbank Jr., John Brough, and James Wallace to raise a company of forty men as a formal response team to combat future fire emergencies. At their first meeting, the assembly elected James Wallace as the first captain, John Burbank Jr. as assistant captain, and John Brough as engineer.[83]

A single unnamed individual was assigned to travel to New York City to purchase the necessary equipment such as caps, belts, boots, and coats to dress the firemen.

A hand-pumping fire engine named the *Invincible* had been constructed on Elm Street in New York City and, upon completion, had been loaded onto the steamboat *Victory* and ferried to Hartford, Connecticut, and then on to Thompsonville.

Here again, records conflict as to the date of delivery and service of the fire engine. Some documents state that the engine was in use in fighting the 1834 Dye House fire, and had failed miserably – the record stating that as soon as water was forced into the hose [from pumping] it had burst, rendering it useless.[84] A separate article noted that it wasn't a failure of the apparatus, but rather the residents' unfamiliarity with the equipment, that proved the real

---

[83] See Addendum. There is some conflict as to the actual date of incorporation of the Fire Company. The official state record of the **Resolves and Private Laws of the State of Connecticut Volume Three** records the granting of the charter as 1839 but the Thompsonville Press article of 1882 notes the original request as 1834. The 1834 date seems most likely as the decision to form a department would have been a likely response to the Dye house fire of that same year.

[84] Thompsonville Press Oct 19, 1882. Page 2.

failure.[85] Other articles seem to indicate that the fire engine was delivered after the Dye House fire.[86]

Despite conflicting records, by 1835, Thompsonville had a functioning fire department, staffed by both Scots and locals. The new firemen took the engine out regularly on Saturdays to train and hone their skills.

The intent of the Temperance Movement, as mentioned, insofar as it positively influenced the villagers' social behavior at the picnic following the Dye House fire, was to limit or ban alcohol consumption. It was inspired by the religious revival of the early 1800s and was often associated with other reform movements because alcohol was linked to social issues like poverty and insanity.

Surprisingly, the movement found a home in Thompsonville among the Scots, who weren't known as teetotalers.

In the Fall of 1835, the village was visited by a society representative from outside the area who waxed poetic on the good deeds of his fellow abstainers to a group of villagers gathered in the schoolhouse. So enamored were the participants that they agreed to form their own society, electing Henry Thompson as president.

The group did not agree to total abstinence but did agree

---

[85] Thompsonville Press Nov 22, 1883.Page 1.
[86] A personal recollection from a reader/contributor of the Thompsonville Press in the Nov. 16, 1882, edition stated that the first fire engine was christened with a bottle of alcohol in front of the Middle Tavern (Thompsonville Hotel) by John Brough. This memory was corrected by the editor as Doctor James Reid had christened the vehicle with a bottle of water in front of the firehouse, which meant the firehouse had been constructed before the christening.

to:

> *...abstain from the use of malt or spirituous liquors in Thompsonville and vicinity.*[87]

Although the leading men of the village signed the pledge, no record exists of the strictness with which they adhered to it.

Overseas and at about the same time, the *Scottish Temperance Society* was founded as the *Glasgow and West of Scotland Temperance Society* by John Dunlop and William Collins. The group was renamed the Scottish Temperance Society to reflect the expanding breadth of its operations. Its influence did not extend to the United States, but the timing of each spiritless initiative, separated by the Atlantic, is interesting, nonetheless.

Thompsonville was not alone in considering the abandonment of alcohol, as the *Hartford County Temperance Society* was meeting weekly at the time, and its membership included representatives from thirteen regional societies, with a good possibility that Thompsonville was one of them.[88]

The Connecticut Temperance Society, a subgroup of the American Temperance Society, had been formed earlier and was actively soliciting members for the cause as early as 1833.[89] Perhaps it had been a member from that organization who had originally approached the good men of Thompsonville in 1835.

It is no secret that the temperance movement was rooted in religion, as the Bible defines temperance as *emotional*

---

[87] Thompsonville Press Nov. 16, 1882. Pg 2

[88] Hartford Courant July 11, 1836. Pg 3

[89] Litchfield Enquirer Jan 17, 1833. Pg 1

restraint or self-control. Beyond temperance, the Presbyterians were concerned with the challenging walk to the Congregational church in the center of town. The village residents decided to appropriate the second floor of the school on Main Street for weekly services.

Lacking a preacher, the village reached out to the East Windsor Theological Seminary to see if they might provide a pastor to lead Presbyterian services. The seminary agreed and provided Reverends Tyler, Cogswell, Thompson, and Nettleton on a rotating basis, establishing a continuous religious service in the growing hamlet.

The townspeople were rich in spirit but poor in wealth, and they reached out to the Connecticut Missionary Society for financial aid, but the request was refused. Nevertheless, the townspeople were resilient and somehow managed to cobble together the funds to pay their preachers each week without fail.

Linen whitening at the bleaching greens in Ireland, which consisted of large tracts of land on which to spread the linen.

Wool washing was an art form, and some hands had been dedicated to the task for years, such as John Boyd, head of the Thompsonville department and manager of Tub Number One. The management of the second tub had turned over several times, but one of the most notable washers was 'Old' John Moore, who had previously been employed in the same position in Ireland in a *bleach green*.

Moore wasn't just an efficient worker but a man who possessed an additional skill—predicting changes in the weather by *feeling the cloth*. An old weather lore says –

When the dew is on the grass
Rain will never come to pass.
When grass is dry at morning light,
Look for rain before the night.

Moore would frequently feel the drying cloth as it lay out on Wool Hollow to see if it was accumulating moisture. If the change seemed drastic, he would call out to his coworkers to warn them of an approaching storm.

On one occasion, in early June of 1837, Moore felt the wool and called to the men to alert them to a coming change in the weather. Casting their eyes about, the workers could see not a cloud in the sky in any direction, but there to the south, two riverboats were approaching, traveling up the Connecticut River at an alarming speed.

As they reached the point where the men toiled, a great wind arrived, scattering the wool about the hill, the hollow, the bushes lining the river, and into the river itself in the blink of an eye. A dead calm followed the violent wind, and the workers quickly recovered what wool they could from the land, and, looking west to the river, they noted only one boat remained upright, and that one had the sails torn clear from the masts.

The missing boat and cargo had been commanded by Captain John Harmon, who had managed to float to shore on a cask of flour. The other cargo had sunk beneath the waves, as had young boatman Giles Prior.[90] The contents of the boat, owned and operated by Parker, Douglas & Company, had been uninsured and had been transported at the risk of the owner. The human toll, though, was unrecoverable. Prior took ten days to locate and return to his mother, who owned a house on the riverbank, just above the falls.[91]

Prior wasn't the only fatality that summer, as scarlet fever had descended upon the town.

The cunker and rash, otherwise denominated as the scarlet fever, of a malignant type, now prevalent in many towns, has invaded a large portion of the families in Thompsonville, during four or five of the last few months, and while there has been several cases of recovery after a very distressing illness, twenty children, and it is believed more than that, under the age of nine years, have fallen victims, and have been conveyed unto the grave.

The mourning parents while sympathizing with each other in view of the early loss of these buds of promise, and with those in other places who are similarly affected, are loudly admonished to hold their offspring at the disposal of heaven.

While times enormous scythe
Strikes empires from the root; each moment plays.
His little weapon in the narrow sphere
Of sweet domestic comfort, and cuts down
The fairest bloom of sublunary bliss.[92]

---

[90] Connecticut Courant June 9, 1838. Page 1

[91] Hartford Courant June 23, 1838. Page 3

[92] Hartford Courant June 20, 1838. Page 3.

Once the wool had dried, it was carted to the picker rooms by a single man and a horse each morning. That same pair would take the yarn from the Mills to the Dye House (or storerooms), the freshly washed wool to the men waiting on the hill[93] to be spread out and dried, transport the dyed wool to storage, and take the bales of wool to be washed to the Wash Tubs in a continuous production cycle.

The *fly in the ointment* was the temperament of the horse, which was known to upset a cartful of product should he not get along with the driver. There were two men the horse did not like. One was a black man, commonly referred to as *Pug*, and the other was Patrick Hennesey, better known as *Red Patrick*, to distinguish him from the other Patrick working at the site.[94]

One story goes that Red Patrick had been tasked with disconnecting the horse from the wagon to lead him back to the stable after a day's labor. The grey mare took offense at something Red did at the time; there is no record of the offending activity, and took a bite out of the worker's backside, coming away with a mouthful of pants, but thankfully, no flesh.

From that moment forward, Red swore off any further interactions with the horse, ceding the job to others.

Red Patrick, Ewen McChristie, Edward Chipman, William Steel, and Doctor James Reid comprised the group of bailers, men who prepared the rugs for shipment each Monday while the river remained open. In the winter months, rugs would be piled in the storeroom until the

---

[93] Where Cottage Green is now located
[94] With so many Scots and Irish it's hard to believe only two Patricks were working at the mill simultaneously.

Spring when the river became navigable.

Red was what was, at the time, referred to as an *outdoor man*. He could neither spin nor weave and wasn't mechanically inclined. Still, he was invaluable at other tasks around the compound, having previously worked as a porter at Orrin Thompson's New York carpet store.

A sound worker, he had a penchant for imbibing, the only governor on that activity being finances. General labor wages were about $4 per week, and with board set at $2.25 per week at each hotel, Red often found himself at a loss for liquid refreshment funds. George Martin took a particular interest in Red as he was a good employee and could easily be taken advantage of by his wealthier co-workers. Reliable employees were coveted, so Martin worked out a deal with Patrick to manage his pay, with Red turning his paycheck over to Martin every four weeks (workers were paid the fourth Saturday of each month). Martin would pay the man's rent and set aside a little money for savings.

Usually, though, after the third or fourth day had passed after payday, Red would approach Martin looking for some money to go drinking with the boys. This was usually because the men would tease Patrick about having someone handle his money as if he were a little boy, and after they had plied him with a bit of drink to rile him up about the situation.

To try to address the issue once and for all, Martin went to the local tavern, located the rabble-rousers, and regaled them with a tale of Patrick's love for a local widow for whom he was pining, and had asked Martin to hold money back each week until the couple's wedding day. Martin asked the men to keep the knowledge to themselves, which they did, until the day, years later, when Patrick left the mill for employment once again in New York, and the men realized they had been fooled.

As had the unnamed widow, I suppose.

Henry Barter is enjoying a pint of Guinness in Dublin, Ireland. (Photo by Bert Hardy used with permission for representative purposes).

Pranks were not exclusive to the tread boys as the adults often took advantage of their colleagues' naivety.

When an individual only known today as 'W'[95] first arrived in Thompsonville, on a Sunday afternoon, he was met by Orrin Thompson, Deacon Smith, and Doctor James Reid, the good doctor seemingly taking the young accountant under his wing.

After an evening's rest W was rousted and directed to the bailing room where he found James Ronold, Ewen McChristie, Edward Chipman, William Steele, James Reid, and Red Patrick waiting, as Monday was bailing day and the carpets were being prepared for shipment.

---

[95] This individual was a writer penning his recollections for the Thompsonville Press and signed his articles as 'W'. A typewritten letter uncovered at the Connecticut Library identifies the mystery author as James Wallace

As W was about to begin to enter each piece into his logbook, Mr. Ronold selected it, and Doctor Reid halted him.

"Wait awe; ye hae not paid your *fittin* yet." [96]

W, not knowing much about factory policies, inquired about the amount of the fee required, to which Dr. Reaid responded – fifty cents (~$5.50 in 2020).

W paid the charge to Reid and the bailing and recording activities were completed and the group went to breakfast together.

Once the meal was completed, Dr. Reid informed W that a load of wool had arrived at the dock and needed to be logged in and compared to the invoice.

As W began to count the bales and record their weight Dr. Reid stopped him once again.

"Avast lad, ye hae na paid y'er fittin yet."

Responding that he had indeed paid the fee earlier that morning Reid responded.

"This was na the bail'n room and ye must pay anew."

W asked how much the fee was and, to no one's surprise, the answer was fifty cents once again.

Soon the new bales had been secured in the storeroom.

In the afternoon of that same day the good doctor approached W once more as yarn was about to be transferred from one storehouse to another and an accounting of the same needed to be done for the upcoming July board meeting.

Once again, the topic of paying the activity fee was

---

[96] As best as can be determined – *fittin* represented some fee that must be paid to engage in an activity.

broached, as this job and location were different from the previous two. After complying, W asked his host how many more of these fees might be required.

Sensing W had finally caught on, Reid told W that his factory training had been completed and that no more *fittins* would be required of him. He added that if any employees brought up the topic again then the doctor could be called upon to set them straight.

All in all, a relatively inexpensive education.

When Ewen McChristie first arrived in the village, he was put up in the attic of George W. Martin's house, which bordered the brook. At that time bullfrogs made the stream their home and made their presence known from dusk to dawn during the late Spring into early Summer.[97]

Unaccustomed to the sound, McChristie found no rest during a uniquely loud and boisterous evening, and he rose to roust the homeowner to complain of a herd of cows mooing outside the property. Understanding the issue Mr. Martin told the Scotsman to go back to bed and he would address the problem, which was, of course, impossible.

Having gotten no sleep the rest of the evening, McChristie arose the following morning to survey the damage that must have been done to the yard by the braying bovines.

Surprised that the grounds were as they had been the day before, it took hours to convince the recent émigré that he had simply been treated to a bullfrog concert, and that he had best become used to their noise as mating season was upon them.

---

[97] American male bullfrogs croak to attract interested females, the louder the croak the better.

By 1838, the number of Thompsonville residents who had met the voting requirements had increased substantially, and the effects were felt at the polls. For the first time, Gilbert Allen of the Whig Party had been elected Sheriff for the county, and William Harrison Taylor and the Honorable James Dixon were elected to serve as the state representatives for Enfield.

To celebrate their victory the men of the little Scottish village needed something momentous to mark the event; and what better device than a cannon?

Responsible parties were sent both to Springfield to procure the cannon and to Hazard Powder to purchase the needed gunpowder. Both arrived safely; the gun was stored in Seth Alden's barn, and the powder was in an undisclosed location. It had been agreed to fire off a single charge the day before the celebration to announce the arrival of the cannon and to alert the villagers of the coming parade.

The Grand Marshall for the affair was to be Gilbert Allen, and his aids Colonel David Abbe and James Wallace, each on horseback. To lead the brigade, the people selected Peter Mann, who was to be decked out in a Highlander costume.

With everything in preparation for the following day, the assembled waited for the firing of the cannon.

But no resounding boom came forth.

The cannon had been spiked.[98]

By nine o'clock, the offensive plug had been extracted, and the gun was moved to a spot in front of the Thompsonville Hotel and guarded to prevent another

---

[98] Spiking a gun was a method of temporarily disabling a cannon by hammering a barbed steel spike into the touch hole; this could be removed only with great difficulty.

attempt at thwarting the celebration.

An example of a Scot adorned in Highlander gear.

Early the next morning, the village was awakened by the thunderous roar of the cannon blasting from the center of the village, the cacophony echoing down Main Street to the River.

Slowly, villagers and townspeople exited their homes in holiday attire, lining the streets from Thompsonville to the Enfield Street cemetery. There, the procession turned, heading north past the Lion Tavern[99] where refreshments of food and drink were laid out on long tables.

Heading north on Springfield Road, the procession paused at Deacon Pierce's, where jugs of cider were liberally passed around.

At every opportunity, the cannon was loaded and fired to the delight of the assembled crowds.

As the parade passed the Yellow Tavern, the assembled were greeted with more libations from the then proprietor, Harris Meachem.

A stage had been erected in front of the Thompsonville Hotel, where the carriage ferrying the officials stopped to unload the newly elected politicians. Speeches were made to an ever-increasing multitude, as the cannon shots had drawn participants from other towns, curious as to the reason for the festivities.

Orations completed, the crowds slowly dispersed, glowing emotions enhanced by the plentiful drink.

Later in the evening, villagers gathered once again at the Thompsonville Hotel to share stories, drink heartily, and sing Scottish songs.

Without realizing it, the village had become integrated with the greater Enfield Street community, and the day of celebration spoke more about brotherhood and acceptance

---

[99] The Lion Hotel was another name for the William Abbe Hotel on Bridge Street.

than mere politics.

On January 8, 1839, near the Mersey River, a deadly hurricane blew off the coast of England as Henry Thompson and William Douglas traveled aboard the packet ship the Victoria. The vessel sank, a total loss, and two other ships were caught in the storm but were not badly wrecked, their contents recoverable.

Thompson and Douglas were the only two to make it to shore after the incident, with Henry the only survivor of the disaster. William, shortly after reaching dry land, succumbed to his injuries.

William Douglas and George W. Martin had met as clerks in the New York store of Andrews, Thompson & Company in 1826. Both had emigrated from Scotland: Douglas from Dunfermline and Martin from Aberdeen. However, they had never set eyes on each other until they were employed together in Manhattan.

When the carpet manufactory opened in Enfield in 1828, Martin was transferred to the village to manage the operation. Douglas was brought into the organization as a partner after the death of David Andrews in 1836. He had traveled in that capacity in 1839 to Europe on behalf of the firm, to both select goods and acquaint the younger Henry with their agents in Liverpool and connect with overseas manufacturers. It was on the return trip home that the duo met with tragedy, with Douglas's being fatal.

The newspaper The New York Enquirer of February 26, 1839, said it best:

> *We are prompted by the sacred ties of friendship to pay a brief tribute to the memory of one who was lost by the wreck of the packet ship Pennsylvania; we allude to William Douglas, Esq., of this city.*

Mr. Douglas was a native of Scotland; he came to this country early in life, soon became a partner in one of the finest mercantile houses in New York. Faultless as a companion – a friend, and a husband – generous and manly in all his transactions with others, it may with truth be said, he never made an enemy.

Cut down in the prime of existence, the news of his untimely death brought with it no ordinary pangs to the bosoms of a large circle of friends; and in the heart of one, united to him by the nearest and dearest connection of life, the melancholy tidings opened a wound, which time itself, with its soothing influence, can never entirely heal.

He has gone through death's sleep unto God – the best of friends, and an honest man.

One more death before the end of the decade, and it was a strange one.[100]

On Friday, July 12, 1839, Thompsonville experienced a severe thunderstorm, shaking the heavens and lighting up the sky.

At the James Wallace home, Mrs. George Martin sat looking out the window toward the river and exclaimed:

I see a great ball of fire falling down into the brook.

We all started to look out but it was all over – nothing to be seen.

The weekend passed without incident, as they often do in a sleepy village, but on the afternoon of the 15th, John

---

[100] The following story is taken from the historical writings of James Wallace recorded in longhand in archives held at Harvard University. Direct transcription in italics.

Adams failed to appear at his station in the factory.

Concerned, Esther Frank McGraw, Andrew Marr, and Lauren Gray went to call on him at his house and reported back that he was dead. The men had opened the back door and had found the man prone on the floor, cold and lifeless. They did not enter the building past the entryway but returned to Wallace's home as quickly as possible.

Wallace rose from his chair and accompanied the workers to the home the Adams had been renting from the company, although only Wallace would enter the house.

Wallace went in alone and had to step over the separated body of Adams.

His head and shoulders [were] out in the kitchen [and] his body and limbs in the pantry. As I looked around the first thing I noticed was the broken window and I called out to the boys to come in as I thought some one had broken in through the window and he had been murdered, but they both refused to come in.

I took a careful look at the body [and] I saw he had a cup in one hand and a piece of bread in the other and a piece of bread in his mouth and his whiskers on the right side of his face [were] a little singed.

I then called out to the boys again to come in as he was [likely] killed by lightning but they still refused to enter the house.

I then requested that one of them inform Squire Kingsbury and the other to inform Henry Thompson.

Henry Thompson soon arrived on the scene, as did Henry Kingsbury, and a jury of inquest was set up to officially determine the cause of death, which was death by lightning – clearly ruling out homicide. Aiding in the determination was a large tree that stood near the rear of the house that had been blackened and splintered, and the back window of the home, which had been shattered. Even for the untrained eye, as a bolt of lightning had connected with Adams as if he were a human lightning rod, the body cleaved and the wooden floor charred.

Adams had been a family man, well respected with obliging manners. Like so many others, he had emigrated from Kilmarnock with his wife and children to seek out a better life and had seemingly found it until his untimely passing.

In order to settle the affairs of the late John Adams Squire [William] Dixon was [appointed] as Judge of Probate to select an administrator to take charge of the property and James Wallace was identified

Mrs. Adams returned for a short time to address those items that were to be moved with her family to relatives in New Jersey. Once that was completed village residents, who were also employees of the carpet mill, were free to apply to be considered new lessees of the vacant house. Private homes were still scarce in the village as company-owned housing was about the only option available to employees besides local hotel boarding rooms, and management was eager to accommodate those with families.

The family of William Morrison was selected to take over occupancy of the house, and they moved into the space in the middle of that summer. The group of eleven settled quietly into the abode.

As Fall arrived, however, the family began to be awakened during the night by unusual noises, sounds that could not be identified. Soon, word spread around the village that the ghost of John Adams was visiting the house.

The Morrisons sought relief from the administrator.

As the town was swept up in the possibility of a real

haunting in the village, numerous young men offered their services to watch the house night after night.

Every morning [the volunteers] reported that there were terrible noises all over the house upstairs and down and nothing to be seen. Sometimes they felt as if the roof was coming down and then again it would sometimes [the noises would be] in the front and [then] in the rear.

The Morrisons' oldest daughter was about worn out by anxiety, as were the other members of the family, all younger.

The house was examined in the daytime — inside and out. At one point it was suggested that some person had gotten up in the branches of the stricken tree. At another, a search was made for some muskrat or water animal coming from the brook in [a] quest [for] food.

Still, the noises continued.

Notwithstanding this, applications continued to be made for taking up residence in the haunted house should the Morrisons decide to vacate.

On Monday morning Mrs. Roxy Steny[?] who then lived in the nearest house came and informed the writer [Wallace] that she and two or three other neighbors had been in on Sunday afternoon and were walking through the rooms and feeling the walls when all at once there came such a crash against the wall that they had their hands on that all were completely frightened and made sense that there was something supernatural about it.

As [the] administrator, it was necessary to view the wall and by reason to find out all about it to protect the family, and for that purpose called Mr. Henry Thompson who stated his intention of going to keep watch.

Mr. Thompson was, by his admission, not handy with firearms, so would instead bring his shillelagh as a weapon – ready to strike the ghost should he appear.

The watchmen took their positions and requested the family retire early as they would be protected from harm by the village volunteers. Mr. Thompson held steady in a lot across the brook from the home, Mr. Wallace near a home whose land was filled with trees and low brush, and others scattered in areas with a clear view of the Alden home. The sky was clear, and a fresh coat of snow lent a crispness and brilliance to the landscape.

The men were at the ready.

Nothing had occurred up to the first bell of the morning, and Mr. Thompson declared that no ghost who had any respect for himself would appear after that hour.

The group of men who had watched that entire evening checked in on the house and found that all had rested quietly and comfortably. Each man returned to their respective home to recover and recuperate.

Not a half hour had passed when Mr. Wallace was rousted at his home and told that the ghost had struck again after the men had retreated, carrying some of the young children down the stairs of the home, their cries waking the Morrisons and driving the entire family to the side of the road outside the house. It was there that Mr. Wallace found them, terrified and sobbing.

The family could not be consoled, and going back into the home was out of the question, as was staying in the village. The family moved away shortly thereafter.

With the house vacant, a single man who had earlier applied for tenancy reapplied, and...

was accepted by the administrator with the understanding that he must [handle] his risks and fight the ghost or make friends with him without any aid [from the administrator – Wallace] and to this, he agreed – and there was no more ghost.

Had it been the family that had been the problem? What would have stirred the spirit if indeed there had been one? Were the noises manmade or something from the beyond?

Whatever the source, all were able to agree that it certainly wasn't bullfrogs.

Years later, while in New York on business, Wallace ran into the same tenant who had been unfazed by the ghost and brought up the subject of the haunted house to which the man offered up the following:

An individual known to all villagers at that time had spearheaded the unearthly visitations. He was the person who had carried the children down the stairs in the early morning hours of that fateful last day and placed them on the road, making such a hideous noise about the home that it ultimately drove the family not only from the house but from the town as well.

When the former tenant revealed the name of the villager, who had long since passed away, to Wallace, he immediately realized how the individual had accomplished the ruse. The former housing administrator knew the person had been well-qualified and would have enjoyed, in a macabre sort of way, captivating the attention of everyone in the perceived haunting of Thompsonville.

Wallace never revealed the name of the perpetrator, a

villager himself, whose actions, in retrospect, cannot be viewed as benign. There were real consequences from the falsehood he created, certainly to his neighbors, who were kept on edge, but more so to the family living in the home he haunted, who, for a short while, had lived a nightmare.

Perhaps Wallace reflected the genuine kindness of the village by not revealing the individual's identity, even after the man's passing.

At least the culprit was able to rest in peace, even if he hadn't afforded the same allowance to others.

5: NEC TAMEN CONSUMEBATUR[101]

Below the dam, along the Freshwater Brook, toilets were attached to the rear of the company buildings that were to be used by workers to relieve themselves. These toilets were essentially outhouses nailed to the structures, with each *facility* extending beyond the one on the floor beneath, so that both could be occupied at the same time; this way, the person below wouldn't receive an unpleasant surprise.

The excrement would drop down to the water's edge, or possibly directly into it, creating a pleasing aroma for those downstream.

Those who think of 'the good old days' usually don't remember these less-than-ideal realities.

Long before sewers and waste treatment plants were conceptualized and implemented, excreta piled up wherever it landed. If one was lucky enough to have their land bounded by a stream, then that waste was carried downstream past the neighbors. If not, then it most likely ended up in a hole under an outhouse.

---

[101] The Church of Scotland's motto is "Nec tamen consumebatur", which means "Yet it was not consumed". The phrase refers to the Book of Exodus in the Bible, where Moses encounters a burning bush not consumed by flames.

And those holes had a finite capacity.

Enter the *night soil men.*

Night soil was the name assigned to human waste because it was removed from latrines under the cloak of darkness. Removing the waste at night meant people would be spared confronting their feces as they were carted away, leaving a horrific, festering stench as the only evidence of the activity.

Human excrement was a valuable fertilizer used by farmers for their crops when mixed with other waste materials, such as charcoal dust, limestone, or dried peat, to mask the smell and stabilize the acidity. Although regional resources are limited, it would only seem natural that Enfield farmers would have availed themselves of this nutrient enrichment.

A regional farm publication addressed the value of night soil in an article:

> *We speak of this first, because it is not only the most generally wasted, but one of, if not the most valuable of fertilizers. It is certainly the most valuable of the animal manures. Its value is greater in comparison with other animal manures in proportion as the food of man is better and richer than the food of inferior animals. The food of man is usually rich in nitrogen, phosphates and other inorganic matters; hence this manure is valuable as containing these matters.*[102]

> *Something over a year since I had 120 barrels of night soil put upon three-fourths of an acre (of which the above piece was a part) which, after being mixed with ashes, lime, and stable manure, was thoroughly incorporated with the soil; and this, I believe, was the immediate cause*

---

[102] Moore's *Rural New-Yorker* September 10, 1864. Page One

*of the extraordinary crops which I gathered. But there
were plain indications in the fall that the manure had only
begun its work, and hence I am expecting a more
remarkable yield from that land the ensuing year.[103]*

Whether any enterprising young men in Enfield or
Thompsonville took up the challenge of becoming night
soil men as a career is left to the unrecovered ledgers of
history. However, an incident reported in a medical journal
lends credence to the fact that excavating human waste and
selling it was not an uncommon practice in the Enfield
village.

On August 24, 1894, Mrs. Annie 'H' of Thompsonville
was diagnosed as suffering from typhoid fever. Her
symptoms were addressed by her physician, John F.
Dowling, MD, Thompsonville, and she ultimately
recovered. There were two other cases in the same
household at the time.

*The source of the poison was traced by Dr. Parsons and
myself [Dr. Dowling] to contamination of the well water
on this farm by night-soil carried on the footwear of the
farm help to the vicinity of the well when going for water
and then washed from the surface by rain into the well.
This water was used by all in the house for drinking
purposes.*

*The night-soil was gathered from different vaults in the
town and deposited on the land of this farm. The water
was analyzed and found to be impure. Its use was
discontinued.[104]*

Acquiring and selling night-soil was a practice already

---

[103] The Cultivator February 4, 1846.
[104] Proceedings of the Connecticut Medical Society. Cases of
Typhoid Fever. Page 155

known by the Scots, and humanure was highly valued as a fertilizer in their home country, as was urine.

> *The next manure to be noticed is night-soil which is exceedingly valuable, but it is much neglected on account of its unpleasant smell; this however can be removed in great measure by various ingredients, the most powerful of which is powdered charcoal, or peat in a half-burnt state.*[105]

Night Soil collectors emptying their carts onto allotment land – Hull Public Health Department, Scotland (used with permission)

It's not a great leap to believe that the practice of gathering this socially distasteful yet highly profitable product was not beyond the grasp of the Thompsonville immigrants, especially for those who were not weavers.

Given that most of Enfield was still farmland, there was a steady demand for manure, regardless of its source.

---

[105] Kelso Chronicle July 12, 1844. Page 12. Published by Tweeddale Press Group in Kelso, Roxburghshire, Scotland.

Joseph Harvey was born on March 1, 1787, to Deacon Ithamar Harvey and Electa Harvey of East Haddam, Connecticut. He was raised in a pious household and was prepared for university by his pastor, Reverend Joseph Vaill, a Dartmouth graduate who was also his uncle.

After graduating from Yale in 1809, he moved on to study theology under the Reverend Dr. Ebenezer Porter, pastor in Washington, Connecticut. Twelve months later, he accepted the duties of the pulpit at the Congregational Church of Goshen, in Litchfield County, on June 12, 1810, where he remained pastor for 15 years. It was there that he married Catherine Desire Selden.

Harvey resigned his position in 1825 to work as General Agent of the American Education Society, whose office was in Boston. While there, his health suffered greatly, and he retired from that position ten months later, returning to his hometown of Goshen.

Recovering quickly, he accepted a call from the Congregational Church in Colchester, Connecticut, where he was installed as pastor on January 17, 1827. While there, he founded The Evangelical Magazine, serving as editor from 1834 to 1835. For his efforts, he was awarded the honorary degree of Doctor of Divinity by Amherst College.

On December 13, 1835, he was dismissed from his pastoral charge and moved to South Windsor, where he founded and edited a weekly religious paper called The Watchman.[106]

While there, he served as an acting pastor in the South Windsor Congregational Church and participated in leading religious services in Thompsonville, as part of a rotating

---

[106] This periodical replaced the earlier publication The Evangelical Magazine.

troupe of evangelicals. In the latter part of 1838, he was engaged to preach exclusively in Thompsonville.

Reverend Joseph Harvey D.D. First Pastor of the First Presbyterian Church of Thompsonville, Connecticut

With that action, the village had a preacher but no formal church, and, as the majority of the residents were of the Presbyterian faith, Harvey associated himself with the Presbytery of New York. On his trip to conclude this alignment, the following was recorded in the minutes of that body;

At a meeting of the Presbytery of New York in the chapel of the Brick Church, [on] June 25th, 1839, a communication was received from sundry individuals, resident[s] in the village of Thompsonville, State of Connecticut, containing a request that this presbytery will constitute and organize a Presbyterian church in said village.

Whereupon:

Resolved, that this request be granted; and that the Reverend Messrs. Mines, Goldsmith, Dewing, Proudfit, and Dr. Harvey be a community to organize said church on Friday the 5th day of July, 1839, at seven o'clock.

Resolved, that the Moderator be requested to call a special meeting of [the] Presbytery, on Tuesday the 9th of July at seven o'clock for the purpose of receiving said church into our connection and installing the pastor, if the way be clear.

John Goldsmith, Clerk.[107]

Not only was this the formal instituting of the 1st Presbyterian Church of Thompsonville, but it was also the first to be organized in the entire state of Connecticut.

On July 5, 1839, one of the first entries into the new church's records stated:

Letters of dismission and recommendations from other churches having been exhibited to the committee by 73 persons and nine having been duly examined as to the evidence of their faith, the 82 were constituted a Visible Church of Christ.[108]

By the following day, the church administration had

---

[107] Presbytery of New York, Archives. 1839
[108] Anniversary Sermon – Reverend William Voorhies. Thompsonville Press November 5, 1914. Page 1

been completed, with Robert Galbraith, James Ronald, James Alexander, and William Liddle elected as Ruling Elders.

Four days later, on July 10th, the carpet mill was closed for a celebratory event for which a great staging had been erected on the western lawn between G. W. Martin's home and the house of James Wallace.

People came from Springfield, Warehouse Point, Longmeadow, and Suffield to bear witness to the installation of Reverend Dr. Joseph Harvey as pastor of the Presbyterian Church of Thompsonville.[109] Reverend Krebs of the New York Presbytery delivered the opening sermon to the delight of those gathered.

It was a wonderful and uplifting ceremony, and the joy and brotherhood of that day spread throughout the village.

The first meeting of the church was held eight days later, moderated by the new minister, on the second floor of the schoolhouse, as a formal house of worship had yet to be constructed, and the villagers' finances were insufficient to consider the task.

But the wholesome impact of the new church on the town had not escaped Orrin Thompson, and the company voted, in their annual meeting in 1840, to apportion three thousand dollars [about $108K in 2020] targeted to the construction of a Presbyterian Church in the village. The company agents, Henry Thompson and George Martin, were tasked with ensuring the building was erected by the following year.

Life was good for Orrin Thompson. The business was booming, and orders were piling up in the New York office.

---

[109] Harvey would hold this post for 18 years, resigning at the age of 70 on April 29, 1857.

The only challenge he faced was that his Thompsonville manufactories didn't have the capacity to meet the orders.

The answer lay 18 miles to the southwest, along the Farmington River, in the village of Tariffville. The area had been named after the Tariff Manufacturing Company, incorporated in 1825[110]. Before that, the same site and buildings had originally housed a peppermint distillery.[111] It was subsequently home to a wire mill, founded by Job Allyn and Guy Phelps, where iron rods, sourced from Simsbury ore, were drawn down to the fineness of wire, which was sold for use in making cards for combing wool.

The Tariffville site had been a minor competitor to Thompsonville and had fallen on hard times, as it lacked the capital to upgrade to the power looms required for profitable carpet manufacturing.

Sensing an opportunity, Orrin Thompson partnered with George Beach, the then president of the Phoenix Bank of Hartford, to purchase the Tariff Manufacturing Company in 1840 at a cost of half a million dollars [$18 million in 2020], not a trifling amount.

With this acquisition, yet another challenge faced the entrepreneur: ready access to worsted wool.

Like Thompsonville, Tariffville employed Scottish weavers to make ingrain carpets with coarse-grain wool obtained from abroad and manufactured on water-powered carding and spinning machines. Thompsonville had recently been expanded as well, by 41 looms, to produce brussels

---

[110] So named after Congress passed the Tariff Act of 1824 which imposed a rate of 30 percent on raw wool and 33 1/3 percent on woolen goods to protect domestic textile firms from British competitors
[111] The distillery was founded and run by Reverend Whitfield Cowles of Spoonville (East Granby)

carpeting.[112] To lower costs and facilitate production, Thompson and his new partner, Beach, engaged Henry G. Ellsworth of Hazardville, formerly from Painesville, Ohio, to erect buildings and to install steam-driven machinery to produce worsted[113] yarn in sufficient quantities for both carpet manufactories – Thompsonville and Tariffville. Ellsworth owned patents[114] on much of the machinery required to produce worsted yarn, and so was a credible choice to spearhead the effort.

H. G. Ellsworth is a historically elusive figure, with only snippets of information available to offer insight into him.

According to burial records, he was born on April 9, 1811, in Johnstown [or Jamestown], NY, to parents Henry Ellsworth and Miriam Brown [Ellsworth].

He seemed to have a deep familiarity with wool and wool mills, and it is quite possible that he had lived in, worked in, or had family in Painesville, Concord, or Lake County, Ohio.[115] H. G. Ellsworth, or his father, Henry, had likely been associated with the Lake County Woolen Mills, as along the river in that town, there had been a small woolen mill, a card and fulling mill, a small cotton factory, and a

---

[112] Brussels carpet is a type of machine-made floor covering with uncut pile loops. The loops are coiled extra tight, which leads to a durable finish that lasts for ages.

[113] See Appendix Worsted

[114] Ellsworth patents are difficult to determine before 1848. Broadlooms and Businessmen mentions the precedent worsted equipment patent/s without references

[115] The Painesville Telegraph of December 8, 1881, noted that letters from the family of Colonel H. G. Ellsworth, formerly of the Lake County Woolen Mills, stated that H. G. was putting up machinery for a silk factory of 300 looms, about 18 miles from Hazardville.

larger wool mill all owned by the Lake Company.[116]

The Painesville (Ohio) Telegraph of February 1, 1883, reported that H. G. Ellsworth, of Hazardville, Connecticut, was visiting the area for a few days, suggesting he had friends and/or family there.

There is a good possibility that H. G. Ellsworth was a descendant or a blood relative of Yale scholar Henry Leavitt Ellsworth (1791-1858), who was born in Windsor, Connecticut, and was the son of Chief Justice Oliver Ellsworth. A passage in the book *Ohio and Its People* noted that H. L. Ellsworth had, at the very least, traveled in the vicinity of Painesville in the early 1800s:

> *Henry Ellsworth, a young Yale graduate, and his companion found themselves in a predicament near Mantua in 1811.[117] They were forced to take shelter in a house that was barely large enough to accommodate the owner's family. Dinner was abysmal and served in such a 'sluttish manner' that the guests lost their appetite. "In all my life" said this well-bred easterner, "I have never seen so much dirt and filth in any human habitation."[118]*

As proof of his experience with wool, Ellsworth was awarded, in 1848 and 1878, patents tied explicitly to the industry. The 1848 patent was filed by H. G. Ellsworth of Enfield, Hartford County, Connecticut, while H. G. Ellsworth of Painesville, Ohio, filed the 1878 patent. Both were more than likely the same man despite the different locales cited in the applications. Ellsworth was buried in the New Hazardville Cemetery upon his death in 1890.

According to his obituary, he began as an apprentice at the Tariffville carpet manufactory in 1827 and relocated to

---

[116] Ancient Homes of Lakeport. Page 54
[117] Painesville is about 45 miles due north of Mantua, Ohio.
[118] Ohio and Its People. Page 141

the Lowell, Massachusetts, carpet mills in 1832, where he assisted in setting up the worsted wool works. The following year, in 1833, Ellsworth married Elizabeth Downey, and the two settled down in the area.

To muddy the waters further, Ellsworth seemed to have been the superintendent of the Ipswich (MA) Woolen Mills in 1867, as he was advertising in the Boston Journal for three or four good families to work in the mills there. The 1870 federal census listed Henry G. Ellsworth as the overseer of the Ipswich plant, with 26 employees under his control, and his wife, Elizabeth, noted as 'keeping house'. By 1872, the mill had closed, with Ellsworth seemingly finding employment elsewhere, possibly back in Ohio.

No matter the challenge of research, it was clear that Henry G. Ellsworth was embedded in Enfield (in either Thompsonville or Hazardville) and had been contracted by the Thompsonville Carpet Company, in the summer of 1840, to lead the initiative to manufacture worsted yarn, on a contract basis, in the village along Freshwater Brook. Ellsworth would be responsible for designing the new facilities, overseeing their construction, purchasing the necessary machinery, staffing the facilities, and paying employees' wages.

New brick buildings were constructed on the north side of Main Street to house the required equipment and provide space to store the finished product.

At about the same time, Erastus Bigelow had been busy building on the success of his coach-lace power loom, for which he had been granted a patent in 1837, and his knotted counterpane loom, for which he was granted a patent in 1838. In 1840, Bigelow turned his attention to the manufacture of ingrain carpeting using power looms and, believing that he could design and construct looms for this purpose, proposed the idea to both the Lowell Manufacturing Company in Lowell, Massachusetts, and the Thompsonville Carpet Company.

Without a working model to support Bigelow's ideas, a skeptical Thompsonville board of directors decided not to pursue a business relationship with the entrepreneur, despite his earlier successes.

It would be a decision they would later regret.

... Lowell Manufacturing Company decided to engage in the enterprise, and agreed to pay the expense of building trial looms and obtaining patents, and pay him [Bigelow] a royalty on their manufacture; he retained the exclusive use of his inventions for all other purposes than that of weaving ingrain carpets.

Mr. Bigelow went to Lowell, and in less than a year had built two automatic looms—one to make two-ply, and the other three-ply carpets. Each of these looms was successful, meeting the required conditions, surpassing in the perfection of the fabric the best work of hand-looms, and exceeding it in product by at least fifty percent.

Bigelow [then] commenced the construction of a second two-ply loom, with various modifications, suggested by the working of the first. This loom, when completed, made eighteen, instead of twelve yards.

He next began a third loom, with essential changes, which, when finished, made thirty yards a day, the ordinary work of an expert hand-weaver being eight yards per day. Similar improvements were made in the three-ply loom in the summer of 1841.

Patents for the two and three-ply ingrain carpet looms

were granted on May 16 and May 26, 1842.[119]

The Thompsonville board had severely miscalculated.

1842 agreement between Frances A. Calvert, Henry Thompson, George Martin, and Henry Ellsworth for the exclusive use of his technology.

Most likely, there had been too much on their plates at the time, with the acquisition of the Tariffville operation and the construction of the worsted mill works.

---

[119] Representatives of New England — Manufacturers. Pages 97-98

Based on his specifications, Ellsworth contracted with the Ames Manufacturing Company[120] of Chicopee, Massachusetts, incorporated in 1834, to create the castings and produce the equipment required to manufacture worsted yarn. Some equipment required Ellsworth to agree to a 'letters patent'[121] to ward off competition in design and production, making it more costly. Two of those patents were licensed from Frances A. Calvert of Chelmsford, Massachusetts, both for the process of picking and separating burrs and other foreign materials from wool, each for a period of exclusive use of 14 years. One license was acquired from Calvert for $1,400, and the other for $750.

In a moment of brilliance, due to ingenuity as much as necessity,[122] Ellsworth opted to purchase a steam engine built by Clark, Fairbanks, & Company of Providence, Rhode Island, and have it installed in the new mill to provide power for the works.[123]

Ellsworth's ingenuity was demonstrated by diverting the exhaust steam from the worsted mill to the dye house to power the machinery and facilitate production, thereby negating the need for the massive quantities of wood required to fuel the boilers and the personnel to man them.

Ames was also contracted to build four wool 'combers',

---

[120] Ames's foundry cast cannons, swords, and even manufactured the bell for the City Hall of New York in 1838.
[121] A letters patent is a type of legal instrument giving a person/company an **exclusive** right to use something
[122] Freshwater Brook had reached the limit as to its ability to power machinery by 1841
[123] John Barstow had founded the company in 1838 having foreseen the need for steam power to drive industry forward. Misreported as Clark, Fairbrother, & Company in the Holyoke Transcript-Telegram obituary April 8, 1899. Page 8

based on Calvert's designs, which were cast, assembled, and installed in the new Thompsonville factory in 1841. Workers skilled in the field were brought over from England, and soon the mill was turning out 500 pounds of worsted wool daily, which brought the need to import the product to a close.

The English workers joined the locals, Scots, and Irish in the village, the numbers of which were recorded yearly in the minutes of the Carpet Mill. In August of 1840, the population of the hamlet was registered as:

Children under 4	116
4 years to under 16	205
16 years to under 30	141
30 years to under 40	146
40 years to under 50	57
50 years to under 60	18
60 years to under 70	11
70 years to under 80	2
Total Residents	696

Each new émigré was put up in company-owned housing, as the business had been reluctant to sell or lease land to individuals for private homes. The organization would be motivated to do so shortly, though, as orders were piling up and the availability of worsted wool was no longer a governor on production, which meant more employees who needed roofs over their heads.

In the Fall of 1841, the dye house caught fire once again, this time on the fourth Sunday of the month. The bell atop the White Mill called out to all to aid in the effort of fighting the flames.

As payday was the fourth Saturday of every month, it just so happened that Ellsworth had an excess of cash after paying his employees.

As was his custom, he stored the funds and the account journal in the cabinet in his office, which was near the dye house. When the bell rang that morning, he rushed to his building, secured the money and cash book, and ran to the orchard to the north, away from the flames and activity, placing the items in a memorable location.

Returning, he joined his fellow residents in containing the fire, which took up much of the rest of the day. Once again, the dye house was in ruins except for the brick walls. The building was a smoldering shell and would have to be rebuilt. As dusk fell, Ellsworth returned to the orchard but could not locate the financial journal or the funds he had hidden. Had he forgotten the location? Each tree looked similar.

Crestfallen, he returned home.

As he entered the abode, Elizabeth asked her forlorn husband if anything was the matter.

Had he suffered any loss?

Was anything important missing?

Her questioning piqued his interest, and he asked her why she seemed so concerned.

She responded that Mrs. Gibson had stopped by with a substantial amount of cash and a logbook with Mr. Ellsworth's name on the cover and that if it weren't his, then perhaps she would consider keeping it herself.

Overcome with relief, the businessman admitted all, and the book and proceeds were returned to him.

Mrs. Gibson's action was not unique to the village.

It was an honesty shared by all who lived there. If something wasn't yours, then you found out who it belonged to and returned it to them.

Integrity. Morality. Ethics. Principles. Honesty.

It was the credo of the hard-working blue-collar men and women of the village.

Perhaps it came from their religious roots.

Perhaps it was simply 'who they were.'

Do unto others.

6: STOCKINET

The Hofwyl School was a progressive agricultural[124] boarding school in the village of Hofwil, Switzerland. Philipp Emanuel von Fellenberg founded it at the start of the 19th century.

The school was taken over by von Fellenberg's son, Emanuel, in 1799, who transformed it into several institutions, including one for the poor, a secondary school for local students, and an institute for the sons of wealthy European families. The students would live at the boarding school and work in the fields to sustain the school, keeping the institution financially stable and limiting the need for tuition.

The combination of academic and agricultural training enabled the development of innovative farming techniques, including the use of sowing and reaping machines, the

---

[124] Agricultural education is the systematic and organized teaching, instruction and training (theoretical as well as hands-on, real-world fieldwork-based) available to students, farmers or individuals interested in the science, business and technology of agriculture (animal and plant production) as well as the management of land, environment and natural resources.

introduction of new seeds and plants, and the improvement of existing species.

It was at this school where young Jonas Steiger, of Howfil, Switzerland, gained his primary agriculture experience before he became acquainted with the art of stockinet and with the machinery developed and patented in Europe for producing the same material.

On March 16, 1838, Jonas Steiger arrived at the Port of New York, Ellis Island, aboard the Ship Sully, which had sailed from Le Havre, France. His occupation was listed as 'merchant', not farmer, and his home country was registered as Switzerland. Surprisingly, the country he intended to become a citizen of was also Switzerland, indicating that his stay in the United States was not meant to be a long one. Indeed, Steiger was aboard the steamship the Great Western, headed back to Bristol, England, in mid-August, only five months after his arrival.[125]

As best as can be determined, the back and forth across the Atlantic voyages of Steiger were equated with his attempt to generate interest among New York merchants in the circular knitting machine, patented in Belgium, that had been developed to manufacture stockinet, or knit, goods. Finding these overtures of limited appeal, the House of Thompson in New York suggested that Steiger bring his technology and skills north to Thompsonville to ply his trade there.

Upon arriving in the small New England village, Steiger was introduced to the carpet manufactory and the new worsted works, which included steam generation capabilities. As an incentive, Orrin Thompson offered Steiger mill space and steam power at a reduced price for his manufacturing purposes, as well as 60 acres of farmland on Enfield Street, located about midway between the village

---

[125] The Evening post, August 17, 1838. Page 3

and the meeting house. All of this was dependent on Steiger agreeing to set up operations in Thompsonville.

The farm especially spoke to Steiger because of his personal agricultural history, as it included a large home, barns, stables, a washhouse, and an icehouse. The property was populated with an orchard, gardens, and enough hay to support a small herd of livestock.[126]

Steiger agreed and, by 1842, had settled on the farmland with his wife Barbara, sons Victor and Edmond, and daughters Edith, Emma, and Corina. Steiger installed the circular knitting machines in the space leased from Thompson, driven by the steam supplied by the worsted mill engines. The production materials were, for the most part, provided by Ellsworth and Thompson, although the cotton and silk were sourced elsewhere.

The quality of the goods was superior to that of conventionally woven materials in terms of durability and beauty, and the cost was lower than that of others due to the patented equipment employed.[127]   In addition, the machinery enabled one piece of equipment to produce 30 to 60 yards of finished material per day.

The ungoverned production did not translate into sales, as the Swiss émigré found marketing and distributing his goods challenging. In contrast, milk, eggs, fruit, and meat from his farm found a steady market in the stores in Enfield and Thompsonville.

A reporter from the Cultivator[128] waxed enthusiastically about the quality of manure management at the Steiger farm, going into specifics about how manure, straw, hay,

---

[126] Hartford Courant October 2, 1849. Page 3
[127] The Cultivator February 4, 1846. Page 46
[128] The Cultivator was a monthly magazine published by the New York State Agricultural Society sporadically throughout the mid-1800s.

and turf would be intermixed with urine to produce high-quality compost used on the farm to help grow abundant crops.

City of New-York, ss.

BE IT REMEMBERED,

THAT *Jonas Steiger —*

late of *Switzerland*

appeared in the Marine Court of the City of New-York, held in the City Hall of the said City on the *Twenty sixth* day of *September* in the year of our Lord one thousand eight hundred and forty-four, (the said Court being a Court of Record, having Common Law Jurisdiction, and a Clerk and Seal,) and declared **ON OATH**, in open Court, that it was bona fide his intention to become a CITIZEN OF THE UNITED STATES, and to renounce, forever, all allegiance and fidelity to any foreign Prince, Potentate, State or Sovereignty, whatsoever; and particularly to *The Authorities of the Canton of St. gall in Switzerland*

In Testimony Whereof, the SEAL of the said MARINE COURT of the City of New-York is hereunto affixed, this *26 th* day of *September* in the year of our Lord one thousand eight hundred and forty-four, and of our Independence the *69 th.*

Alex. Cotter CLERK.

133

By 1844, Steiger petitioned the courts of New York with a declaration to seek citizenship in the United States. That action provided Steiger with a path to seek stateside patent protection for the circular knitting equipment patented in Belgium a few years earlier.

The 1803 amendment to the U. S. patent laws gave 'aliens' who had resided in this country for two years the same rights as citizens, provided they submitted an affidavit declaring their intention to become citizens, which Steiger had done. Based on the granting of the overseas patent and the fact that Steiger had working equipment in Thompsonville, awarding patent protection to Steiger was a simple matter.

Unfortunately, neither Steiger's agricultural knowledge nor his patent ownership led to the success of his stockinette manufacturing initiative.

In 1845, Steiger agreed to sell out his equipment, patent ownership, and stock to W.G. Thompson, John Worthington, H. Schoonmaker, H. Allen Grant, F.S. & D. Lathrop, Samuel Parsons, James E. Smith, Condit & Scott, Joseph Steele, Steiger Enz[129], and Henry G. Thompson of The Enfield Manufacturing Company, which petitioned for incorporation in Connecticut that year.

It was at about that same time that the records of the Thompsonville Carpet Company indicated that August of 1845 was the last time worsted wool production was attributed to H. G. Ellsworth, as he had moved on to Warehouse Point, where he had constructed a worsted mill of his own to make cashmere and blankets[130]. Worsted

---

[129] Steiger Enz & Co. was not related to Jonas Steiger but was an East Windsor company engaged in the wool and silk industry.

[130] The mill was owned by the firm of Phelps, Sexton, &

production in Thompsonville continued under the direction of John Seekill and William Whitworth as 'Seekill and Whitworth' and later as 'John Seekill Worsted' in 1849.

Seekill's services were dismissed in 1850 due to poor yarn quality, as noted in the organization's minutes.

WE the subscribers pursuant to the provisions of an act entitled "An Act relating to Joint Stock Corporations" and a resolve of the Legislature of this State, do hereby associate and form ourselves into a Corporation under the name of the Enfield Manufacturing Company, for the purpose of manufacturing Wool, Cotton, Silk and other materials capable of being spun or wove. The capital stock of said Company is Three Hundred Thousand Dollars—one hundred thousand dollars of which only is subscribed.

H. G. THOMPSON,
H. SCHOONMAKER,
H. ALLEN GRANT,
JOHN WORTHINGTON,
F. S. & D. LATHROP,
SAMUEL PARSONS,
JAMES E. SMITH,
CONDIT & SCOTT,
JOSEPH STEEL.
STEIGER ENZ.

Hartford, July, 21st, 1845.   dtf

THE subscribers being three of the persons who have associated and formed a Corporation under the name of the Enfield Manufacturing Company, persuant to their charter and the provisions of the Statute Law of this State, hereby give notice that the first meeting of the stockholders of said Company will be holden on the 7th day of August, at the City Hotel, in Hartford, at 4 o'clock P. M. for the choice of officers and for the transaction of such other business as may come before the meeting.   H. G. THOMPSON,
H. SCHOONMAKER,
H. ALLEN GRANT.

Hartford, July 22d, 1845.   14d

The actual incorporation of the 'Enfield Manufacturing

Ellsworth. Ellsworth later left to become associated with the Auburn Woolen Company in upstate New York.

Company' listed several additional individuals as participants in the organization, compared with the original petition. Listed in the state document were [original members in bold, original NOT mentioned in incorporation document in bold italics]: **Henry G. Thompson**, *W.G. Thompson*, **John Worthington**, **Henry Schoonmaker**, **H. Allen Grant**, *F.S. & D. Lathrop*, **Samuel Parsons**, *James E. Smith*, **Condit & Scott**, **Joseph Steele**, *Steiger Enz*[131], George Burgess, George W. Betts, Joseph Blackwood, H. J. Sanford, Reune Martin, R. S. Cooke, Pierard & Ellis, Nathan Trotter, Thomson & Company, Annette A. Ellis, D. Stanton, Mrs. Cornelia A. Suydam, and Doremus & Nixon.

At the July 29, 1845, directors meeting of the Thompsonville Carpet Company, it was decided to sell Henry Schoonmaker two building lots on Church Street for his personal use. A parcel of property near the sawmill on the south side of the brook was sold to the Enfield Manufacturing Company, which would construct its manufacturing facility there.

Understanding the challenges the carpet company faced in housing the early Scottish emigres in 1828, the new stockinette company purchased four and a half acres from Henry Warner, bordering the plot recently deeded to them. The new owners had the property properly graded to address the steep slope toward the river to the west. They contracted to have small Gothic Cottages, designed by Alexander Jackson Davis, erected on the grounds, planting numerous maple trees to add interest and appeal to the

---

[131] It is possible that Steiger Enz was no longer in the partnership due to legal troubles as to the contested ownership of three pieces of knitted wool manufacturing equipment they had allegedly stolen. John C. Allispatch claimed in a lawsuit that the machines were his rightful property and should be returned.

landscape.[132] As the mechanized industry was heavily reliant on imported skilled labor from the British Isles, the effort to construct and provide comfortable accommodations was welcomed by the immigrants.

For the less skilled, yet still essential, emigres, the company built long brick tenements on Prospect and Spring streets to house workers and their families.

By early 1846, the business was up and running, with 35 knitting machines in place and the requisite carding machines.

As the numerous stockholders were mainly New York merchants, they placed their faith in local men: Henry G. Thompson as president of the firm, George Burgess as secretary, James Wallace as bookkeeper, and William Gibbons Medlicott as agent.

Of these men, Medlicott was the most interesting. He was born in Bristol, England, in 1816, his father being a shipping merchant in that city. After leaving school, he followed in his father's footsteps as a seaman sailing aboard ships carrying brokered cargoes.[133] In 1836, at age 21, one vessel he was aboard was wrecked on Rockaway Beach, Long Island, and the youth barely escaped with his life.

It seemed to be a turning point.

Once recovered, he continued his life on the American side of the Atlantic, securing a position in business as a clerk in a large warehouse, possibly in the fledgling wool industry, in New York. While there, he established himself well enough to marry Marianne Dean on September 6, 1842, in New York City. Although it is unclear how he came to know

---

[132] The area is presently known as Cottage Green
[133] Historic Nantucket, Summer 2003, Vol. 52 No. 3, June 1, 2003. Page 8.

the Thompsons, he was offered the position in 1845 as an agent with the Enfield Manufacturing Company, settling first in Thompsonville and then in Longmeadow, Massachusetts, where he purchased a mansion in 1851.[134]

The Medlicott house at 720 Longmeadow Street in Longmeadow, Massachusetts. Image courtesy of the Longmeadow Historical Society, Paesiello Emerson Collection.

In addition to his industrial interests, Medlicott was fluent in Latin and French and was a rare-book collector specializing in early English literature. He eventually amassed one of the world's most extensive collections in these fields, comprising about 20,000 volumes. He made the books available to researchers from Harvard, Yale, Cornell, and other universities who traveled to his home in Longmeadow to conduct their studies.

---

[134] In 1863 Medlicott purchased a small shoddy mill in Windsor Locks to pursue stockinette manufacturing on his own.

William Gibbons Medlicott (Image courtesy of Stephen Forbes via Longmeadow Historical Society)

In addition to its Thompsonville factory, the company rented space in Manhattan, where cuffs were manufactured for the shirts and briefs woven in Connecticut. The knit pieces were shipped from Thompsonville to Manhattan, where the disparate parts were assembled. It was an unworkable situation.

Seeking a better solution, the company realized it needed a reliable water source to complete the processes required to finish knitted goods, such as scouring. Such a location was found downstream from the Gowdy Gin distillery on the Scantic River in Scitico, where the firm acquired a piece of land with water rights, erected a manufacturing building, built a tenement for workers, and constructed a dam to facilitate production.[135]

Twenty-two cuff looms were shipped up from New York and installed in the Thompsonville facility. The English workers who had manned the equipment in Manhattan established themselves in both Scitico and Thompsonville.

As cuffs began to fly off the looms, local women from the surrounding communities of Somers, Longmeadow, Suffield, and Enfield came to the village and took with them as much assembly work as they could manage. After completing the stitching, the goods were returned to the stockinette factory and forwarded to the new mill in Scitico for scouring and finishing under the direction of William Tansley, the site's superintendent.

The completed goods were shipped to New York for sale.

All in all, the new arrangement streamlined production and proved to be much more profitable. The monthly payroll for the Scitico factory workers alone—$4,000 [$165,000 in 2020] — helped the financial outlook for that small hamlet as well.

The good vibes of Thompsonville were spreading, and everyone was benefiting.

---

[135] In January of 1868 a California Miner traveled to Scitico to a spot a little west of the stockinet factory along the Scantic River in search of Pirate Gold.

7: POWER LOOMS

Not engaging with Erastus Bigelow had been a mistake, and Orrin Thompson's error in judgment was becoming clear as the Lowell Manufacturing Company forged ahead, setting new carpet production standards by employing Bigelow's patented power loom technology.

The original agreement struck between the inventor and Lowell had the carpet manufacturer bear the cost of building Bigelow's experimental equipment, as well as fronting the expenses for patenting the machinery.

To maintain these rights the company had to give notice before July 1, 1841, that it would install the looms and then put in enough of them by July 1, 1842, to weave 400 yards a day and by July 1, 1843, 1,000 yards a day. Royalty payments to the inventor were set at 2 cents a yard, and until they reached $18 a week, Bigelow was to receive that amount as a salary.[136]

On October 8, 1842, the Lowell board authorized the construction of enough power looms to produce the 1,000 yards of carpeting per day stipulated by their contract with Bigelow. The equipment was constructed by the machine

---

[136] Broadlooms and Businessmen. Page 17.

shop of the Amoskeag Manufacturing Company in Manchester, New Hampshire.

The first looms were still imperfect and workmen in the Amoskeag machine shop had to aid Bigelow in ironing out the difficulties. Alterations delayed the delivery of the first loom until December 1843, and another eleven months elapsed before all the looms were in the factory. Changes also increased the cost, the final bill being $31,771, or $653 a loom.[137]

As the equipment was being revised and assembled, Lowell revised its agreement with Bigelow so that the inventor assigned to Lowell all ingrain patents granted or to be granted to the innovator.

The first iteration of Bigelow's power looms proved its worth rapidly.

An audit projected an operating profit of about one thousand dollars per loom (50 looms had been built or were under construction) with a savings of six cents per yard on weaving 2-ply and a savings of 12 cents per yard on 3-ply. This revelation led to an expansion of ingrain production and the order of and installation of Brussels power looms, which had been designed by Bigelow as well.

After careful review of the cost figures and estimates for future returns, the Lowell directors voted to further increase ingrain production capacity to over 4,000 yards per day and to employ the new Brussels looms to increase the output of that line to 500 yards per day. This move required adding 150 ingrain and 50 Brussels looms at the Massachusetts site.

The market and business repercussions could be felt by the carpet board in Thompsonville.

The Enfield carpet manufacturer had already invested

---

[137] **Broadlooms and Businessmen. Page 17.**

over \$400,000 in capital improvements at both the Tariffville and Thompsonville sites over the previous year and was now facing stiff competition from Lowell, not only in terms of production but also at significantly reduced costs.

In 1839 Erastus Bigelow permanently reshaped the carpet industry with the invention of the power loom for weaving ingrain carpets.

Henry Thompson saw the writing on the wall and withdrew from the organization.

To meet the immediate threat from Lowell, Thompson ordered wages to be cut by 25 percent in 1846. This was met with massive, yet ineffective, pushback from the weavers.

He then began to search for a power loom that could compete with the Bigelow looms, the same automated technology he had decided against adopting only a few years earlier.

No other technology was mature enough to compete with Bigelow's.

On August 31, 1847, Thompson signed a contract to license Lowell Manufacturing Company technology for between 125 and 150 power looms, for a term of three years, to the Thompsonville Carpet Company, with a provision for an extension. This arrangement required Thompsonville to pay a royalty of two cents per square yard on two-ply and four cents per square yard on three-ply to Lowell. A similar agreement was negotiated for the Tariffville operation.

The installation of new machinery at both sites necessitated the construction of new buildings as well. The old weaving structures could not withstand the increased weight of the power looms. Plans were drawn up for a new brick mill in Thompsonville that would measure 330 feet long and 60 feet wide, including an 'L' on the eastern end. The new building would be two stories tall, except at the west end, where it would reach three stories due to the land's downward slope towards the river.

More money out the door.

To make matters worse, the delivery of the new looms lagged, and the Thompsonville board began to suspect there was a purpose behind the sluggishness. In truth, part of the lag was because Amoskeag engineers were continuing to refine the equipment that had initially been demonstrated to Thompson, which had cost 650 dollars to build. The new and enhanced looms would cost $1,000 each.

On completion of this ambitious program, the whole establishment at Thompsonville was carried on the books *at over $600,000. An inventory of the property made about this time starts with the Old White Mill at the head of the street, with its dam, pickers, cards, and jacks.*

Next to it were wool-washing and drying quarters. Down Main Street on the north side stood the new power-loom mill with 127 ingrain looms, 8 Venetian looms, and shearing machines. Next door was the worsted mill with its cards and combs, pickers and twisters, and 20 Brussels looms.

Closely connected were two small structures for dyeing and winding, and further down on Main Street was the yarn storehouse. At the back of the lot was the chenille and Brussels shop, the Venetian shed, the warping and winding building, the machine and blacksmith shop, another carding and spinning mill, and a collection of small buildings for sorting and storage purposes.

Across the street were the office, the dyehouse, and the Black Mill, in which the three-ply looms had been replaced with cards.[138]

As the new equipment replaced the old, the increased production had a profound effect on wool usage as well, once again growing consumable costs, albeit in support of higher output. In the early 1830s, the mill produced approximately 150,000 yards of carpet. In 1850, despite not having a full complement of power looms installed, carpet output exceeded 250,000 yards.

As power looms were installed, the need for experienced weavers decreased. Some skilled Scots left the village in search of other opportunities, while others remained for supervisory roles.

---

[138] Broadlooms and Businessmen. Page 44.

The unskilled replacement workers lacked the bargaining power of the original Scotsmen and were less challenging to manage and employ. With the dispersal of the hand weavers, the need for the Tread Boys decreased, removing the need to underwrite and to provide an education for them.

Whatever the small savings in labor costs, they were not enough to offset the massive expenditures for acquiring and upgrading the Tariffville operation, constructing new facilities at Thompsonville, or purchasing power looms for both sites.

Hell and damnation.

Sales from an increased stock offering were too slow to replenish the rapidly dwindling coffers.

The beads of nervous sweat began to gather on Orrin Thompson's face as the impossible began to manifest.

The good people of Tariffville and Thompsonville had no clue what was in store for them or their families.

8: FAILURE

What drives a person to become the architect of their own destiny?

This person believes in themselves in an almost religious way, as if they can overcome any challenge as they carve out their future.

There is a Yiddish term that describes this quality, combining confidence, audacity, and impudence – it is called chutzpah. It is a self-assurance bordering on rudeness.

In the comic book medium, there is a character named 'Daredevil' known better as 'The Man Without Fear'. The dictionary defines a daredevil as *a reckless person who enjoys doing dangerous things.* The definition has softened somewhat more recently to present a daredevil in a more favorable light, as *someone calculated, daring, and fearless.*

Atychiphobia is an intense and irrational fear of failure that can impact an individual's ability to function. People with this affliction may avoid or postpone tasks that could lead to success or failure. Successful people rarely, if ever, present themselves as risk-averse.

Individuals with ADHD (Attention Deficit Hyperactivity Disorder) have historically demonstrated specific strengths in creative thinking, divergent thinking,

147

and hyper-focusing. These individuals are less constrained by context when expressing their ideas, which enables them to think more creatively and 'outside the box' while pursuing their dreams.

Entrepreneurs are bold, gregarious risk-takers who share similar qualities as they push the envelope. These individuals stand out in a crowd and naturally attract others simply because of their persona.

It is a common belief that everyone loves a winner.

Winners, though, sometimes lose.

Frederick Hollister was born in Oneida County, New York, in 1825.

His youth was usual for a boy in rural upstate New York. Nothing out of the ordinary occurred that was worthy of being noted in any newspaper at the time.

The first recorded event was his employment as a clerk in the combination drug and grocery store of John Williams in Utica, New York. He worked there with Abijah Lobdell for several years, each honing their skills and learning the intricacies of the business. The duo succeeded Williams upon his retirement, expanding the business. The location was easily recognizable due to its unique black-and-white paint job, earning it the nickname the 'checkered store'.

In 1836, Abijah, in failing health, returned to his native town of Oxford, where he passed away on April 9th of that same year, leaving behind a widow and five children.

Of great activity of mind and body, with broad conceptions, a sanguine temper, and unrestrained ambition, possessed, moreover, of personal magnetism that gave him power over others, Mr. Hollister embarked in projects alien to his legitimate trade, which, at first, eventually wrought his ruin, entailing therewith damage to many who had confided in him.[139]

Paris Furnace was a village situated on the Sauquoit Creek southeast of the center of Paris, New York. The area was named for the Paris Furnace Company, the brainchild of David J. and Sterling A. Millard. The brothers established a scythe manufacturing company in 1835 in a narrow section of the Sauquoit Valley, utilizing a mill built in 1814 for the Cobb and Robinson Shovel Factory. As the company flourished, the area's population grew, and the region first became known as Paris Furnace Hollow, and then simply Paris Furnace.

On the same creek was a small factory called the Sweeting Sawmill, which had been sold to Baker & Gollis by William Barnett. The duo had begun converting the site into a woolen manufactory, but before the conversion was completed, Frederick Hollister swooped in and purchased the mill in 1842, finishing the project and naming it the Empire Mill. Hollister at first met with great success and expanded the single mill into multiple buildings, renaming it, appropriately, the Empire Woolen Company.[140]

In honor of his previous company, Hollister painted the exterior of the new facility in squares of multiple colors, like a checkerboard, and the place came to be known as Checkerville.

Much like Orrin Thompson, Hollister was the prime mover in expanding the manufactory and in erecting housing.

He purchased the land on the west side of the road from this point down along the creek to the old Avery carding mill, where the creek crosses the odd north of the present

---

[139] Utica, NY: From Settlement to the Present Time. Page 220.
[140] History of the Town of Paris, and the Valley of the Sauquoit

Empire Mill (his purchase extended west across the creek and partly up the hillside,) which gave him a good water-power below, and the west side of the highway for building lots, and he also opened a road across the creek at the upper mill, thence along [the] north, skirting the foot of the western hillside and intersecting the main road at the old carding mill below, on which new street, (called Canada) he erected seventeen double tenement houses, and about the same number on the west side of the old main road, also erecting the block of stores near the upper mill, the upper story of which (at the south end) he occupied as an office.

In the year 1843, he commenced the erection of the stone factory, (Empire Mill) 157 feet in length, and four stories, and an attic in height. This was completed and ready to place the machinery therein, in September 1844, and being the year of the Henry Clay campaign, a housewarming, in the shape of a rousing Whig mass meeting, was held in the upper story before the machinery was put in.

Mr. Hollister also erected a large wooden block for hotels and stores, (Hollister House) with a public hall in the upper story, of a seating capacity of three hundred, and the first house of public worship there the beautiful brick Episcopal church (St. Johns) house, and also a tire-engine house, for the hand engine near the upper block of the stores.[141]

Over the years, Hollister's mills burned down twice. Both times, the buildings were uninsured, but the wool magnate rebuilt them, hiding the loss to protect his credit. After the second conflagration, Hollister rebuilt and

----

[141] History of the Town of Paris. Page 286-287

renamed the factory Washington Mills.

The Empire Mills (before the second fire), where Hollister employed, at its height, about 230 people.

These mills manufactured a great variety of Kerseymeres, Sattinets, and narrow clothes; a good proportion of which go to the interior of Ohio, where he has opened a large warehouse, under the charge of his brother, and where large quantities of his goods are exchanged for wool. These factories are well-known in the New York City market.[142]

Hollister founded another operation, the Standard Silk Company, as well as a bank in Buffalo, New York, appropriately named Hollister Bank.

The man was nothing if not energetic.

The philosopher Voltaire notes that little infirmities are characteristic of great minds, and Hollister was no exception. The wool manufacturer had a penchant for

---

[142] Statistics of the Woolen Manufactories in the United States. Page 74.

traveling to New York City to indulge in the game of faro.[143]

An article appeared in the New York Sunday Dispatch of April 21, 1850, detailing a gambling event whereby Hollister was able to use the courts to save him the tidy sum of three thousand dollars (~$130,000 in 2020], which he had borrowed from Samuel Suydam, who ran a gambling organization on Barclay Street in Manhattan. Hollister refused to repay the money to Suydam, and Suydam filed suit to recover. However, as gambling was illegal, the court ruled in Hollister's favor, thereby saving the businessman from having to return the ill-gotten funds.

So much for honor among gamblers.

As a well-known magnate, Hollister was well-connected, with Henry Clay among his acquaintances, who, as a U.S. Senator from Kentucky, ran for president in 1844. Returning to the Senate in 1849, Clay visited Hollister at his home in Utica, sharing dinner with the wool magnate on September 10 of that year while on his way to Syracuse to attend the New York State Fair.

That day, the Washington Mills bore a large banner across its facade bearing the message 'Welcome Henry Clay' as the statesman was borne on a carriage, as a focal point of a parade past the factory on his way to church the following morning.

---

[143] Faro, Pharaoh, Pharao, or Farobank was a late 17th-century French gambling game using cards. Winning or losing occurs when cards turned up by the banker match those already exposed. It is not a direct relative of poker, but Faro was often just as popular due to its fast action, easy-to-learn rules, and better odds than most games of chance. The game of Faro is played with only one deck of cards and admits any number of players.

Henry Clay, United States Secretary of State, was known as the Great Compromiser (Library of Congress, 1848).

In a letter sent to Frederick Hollister and his wife after the event, Clay noted:

In reviewing the incidents of my late visit to New York and the eastward, I should be wanting in heart & gratitude if I failed to express my great obligations to both of you for the kind and hospitable entertainment which I received at your hands and under your auspices, at your house. I can never forget it. My visit to Utica & Oneida is an epoch in my life never to be forgotten. And I shall cherish, with peculiar affection, the variable souvenirs which you presented to me.

I hope that you will be able, some day or other, to visit us in our quiet retreat at Ashland. I need not assure you of the very great pleasure it would afford Mrs. Clay and myself to receive and entertain you here.

May God preserve, prosper, and bless you![144]

Perhaps God was distracted and took his eye off the ball as Frederick Hollister engaged in business with the firm of Austin [sic Austen] & Spicer, who had gotten themselves into trouble in California.

Originally a dry goods import partnership between John Haggerty and David Austen in New York City, the duo morphed into the auctioneering business.

At that time auctioneers were appointed by the Governor, and it was very difficult in those days to get an auctioneer commission, unless the person applying belonged to the party in power, then the Democrats. David Austen was the Democratic partner of Hagerty Austen, and he held the commission for the firm. They were by law required to pay a duty or percentage on sales, and there Was always a competition as to who would pay the largest duties.

In 1830 David Austen was second among fifty-nine auctioneers, paying $42,113. 16. In 1833 the duties paid by David Austen were $52,244.82, the highest of the forty-nine auctioneers who reported.[145]

---

[144] **Papers of Henry Clay: Candidate, Compromiser, Elder Statesman.**
[145] **Austin Families Genealogical Society. Page 230.**

The duo seemed to have unlimited resources. If the East India Company had teas or silks worth $2,000,000 [$80 million in 2020], Haggerty & Austen could advance all that was needed, and could even draw a single check for a million if it was required.

When Haggerty & Austen dissolved, Austin partnered with Henty Augustus Wilmerding to establish the auction house of Austen Wilmerding & Company, which performed successfully for many years until Wilmerding left to found a business with his sons.

David went into business with his father, David Embree Austen, brothers John and George Austen, son David, and partner Charles Spicer, in the firm of Austin & Spicer at the corner of Williams Street and Exchange Place in Manhattan. Haggerty, the former partner, invested heavily in the new concern.

When California was admitted as the 31st state on September 9, 1850, it was declared officially open for business, and companies jumped in with both feet, with opportunities and risks abounding. Flush with cash, Austin & Spicer advanced liberal credit to those companies that had enthusiastically sought to enter the competition on the West Coast. The Hollister Bank of Buffalo joined in as well, opening lines of credit to businesspeople - security be damned.

Then it all crashed.

Whether it was Austen & Spicer that failed first, based on their slipshod, unsecured speculations, or Hollister that failed first, due to Frederick and his brother John's engagement in California and their accumulated debts from wool manufacturing losses in Utica, both entities imploded in 1851, reverberating through the financial community.

Newspapers reported that each had caused the other's failure.

> *We regret exceedingly to be forced to announce the failure of the Aucton House of Austens & Spier, an event which was produced, it is understood, by the failure of Messrs. Hollister of the Empire Mills near Utica. The liabilities of the House are about a million dollars, and the stoppage has not been unexpected for the last forty-eight hours.*[146]

> *A large endorser of Austen & Spicer's paper - to the tune of $600,000 [-$2MM in 2020,– has suspended payment. He is an individual not engaged in business, but is in the habit of endorsing large risks for large considerations.*[147]

As to the failure of Austen & Spicer, the *Baltimore Sun* reported that:

> *It is stated that they have sustained heavy losses from heavy acceptances of accommodation papers, without sufficient security. The immediate cause of their failure was that of Mr. Frederick Hollister, of Utica, proprietor of the Empire Mills, who has been a large speculator, and was engaged last year in those heavy operations of wool, in connection with Messrs. Austins Co., which excited much at the time.*

Fingers pointed left and right, with seemingly plenty of fault to share among all connected individuals, companies, and events.

---

[146] Hartford Daily Courant March 7, 1851, Page 2. Hollister reported liabilities near $1,800,000 [$725MM in 2020]
[147] New York Evening Post March 6, 1851. Page 3. The investor was later revealed as Isaac Storms, a retired tobacco merchant.

Even with the failure of their businesses, these men were cast in a gentle light by reporters.

The failure of Austens & Spicer, today, will cast a gloom over many of our citizens. There seems to be no one universal feeling of sympathy and regret. No man in this community has earned a more honorable reputation than David Austen. He is a liberal, active, intelligent merchant, who has devoted more than forty years to his business as ardently and as honorably as any may could. This catastrophe has been brought upon him by reckless speculators, who should have no influence with him whatsoever. We hope that a little time will bring him to a quiet and honorable repose, with sufficient provision to secure him and his family a happy future.[148]

Frederick Hollister, of the checkered store. Nothing could hold thy ambition in check. A man who, in the quiet Utica of that day, could sum up his indebtedness at merely two million, must have the confidence of the community, and a rare ingenuity for incurring obligations. You were bold to audacity in your conceptions; with an energy vast in their consummation; and a sublime faith in your star; which, however, ultimately dropped below the horizon's verge, in cloud and darkness.[149]

Unfortunately for Thompson & Company of New York, when Austen & Spicer failed, the auction house owed the carpet manufacturer 183,000 dollars [$7,370,000 in 2020), which put Thompson in more than a difficult position, especially after the magnate had spent so much to update

---

[148] Hartford Daily Courant March 7. 1851. Page 2.
[149] The Unresponsive Roll Call at Tattoo May 9, 1893. Luther R. Marsh. Oneida Historical Society. Page 40.

the equipment in the Tariffville and Thompsonville manufactories to power looms while at the same time paying licensing fees to the Lowell Manufacturing Company for the technology.

As both Hollister and Austin & Spicer ceased to be viable companies, their assets were sold, and payments were made to noteholders. Thompson recovered about $30,000 of the outstanding debt from the Auction House.

Hicks & Company and Brown, Brothers and Co. attempted to step into the breach, believing that the carpet manufacturer was solvent and that the company, with access to adequate capital, could continue as a viable organization. Each party looked to secure bonds totaling $750,000 from overseas investors.

Those funds were never secured.

And so, on Saturday, September 18, 1851, Thompson & Company, and their wholly owned subsidiaries, the Thompsonville Carpet Manufacturing Corporation and the Tariffville Carpet Manufacturing Corporation, closed.

Doors padlocked,

Villages and villagers were stunned.

9: QU'ILS MANGENT DE LA BRIOCHE[150]

Psychology shows us that, for men, their job is a significant part of their identity. Traditionally speaking, men have derived a considerable amount of self-esteem, meaning, and views of their competency from work, more so than from other environments, such as home life or social interactions.

Even more so, consider men of the 1850s, who were the sole support system for their families. Women were still classified as property in that era, as the first National Woman's Rights Convention had not yet been held in Worcester, Massachusetts.

Consider also the pride of the skilled Scotsman, who had traveled with his family to a new land—a country less than 100 years old—where he had established a new life for himself and his family based on his knowledge and work ethic. He had helped build a village, create neighborhoods, erect schools and churches, and attract businesses that provided him with the goods and services he needed to sustain himself.

---

[150] Attributed to Marie-Antoinette. Traditionally translated as 'Let them eat cake" it references the plight of the starving French peasants during the French Revolution.

Hard work and perseverance had fostered peace and tranquility for him and his neighbors.

And then it was taken away.

Not because he had done something wrong.

He hadn't.

He had played by the rules.

But the mill had closed.

His job had disappeared overnight.

What was going to happen?

Perhaps a clue could be taken from the workers of Tariffville, eighteen miles southwest of Thompsonville.

By 1840, the population of Tariffville had grown to 200 residents. In that year, Orrin Thompson, who soon after 1825 had established a carpet mill nearby in the Thompsonville section of Enfield, came into control of the Tariffville operation as well.

Rapid growth ensued.

By 1852 the population was 2,000.

The community became a center for trade as well as a mill village. The street pattern took form and, in 1850, the Canal Line Railroad came to the village.

Then, in 1852, a calamity occurred.

Orrin Thompson went bankrupt, partly because of over-expansion at Tariffville. ***The population plummeted to 600****, the Scottish Presbyterian Church closed its doors,* *and hard times were rife.*[151]

Unlike Tariffville, population numbers are unavailable for Thompsonville during the same period. Early Carpet Mill records do note the population of Thompsonville for the years 1837 through 1841. Using the trend established for those years, we can estimate that the population increased at a rate of 110% per year, meaning the population of Thompsonville in 1852 would have been approximately 2,042 people.

This aligns with the approximate population of Tariffville, 2,000 residents, for the same period.

According to the 1850 census, the Thompsonville Carpet Mill employed 300 men and 350 women at the time, numbers which would have remained relatively stable in 1852, which meant 650 people in or around the village of Thompsonville were out of work at the same time when the mill suspended operations, with options of employment elsewhere limited.

Thompsonville, though, unlike Tariffville, was not a 'one-trick commercial pony' of a town.

The village had other businesses like the Stockinette factory (which employed four hundred), the Thompsonville Scale Manufacturing Company (number of employees unknown), the Brickyards of William [sic Welcome] Cady[152]

---

[151] United States Department of the Interior – National Park Service – National Register of Historic Places - Tariffville

[152] Welcome Jedediah Cady settled in Agawam Parish, West Springfield, Mass in 1839 where he bought real estate and began life as a brick maker. In 1845 he moved to Thompsonville, Conn., where he purchased land, built a house, and continued brickmaking. In 1855 he began the manufacture of wines from native fruits, which increased in

(who employed seven) and Talcott Mather[153] (who employed eight), and the Tinsmith Works of David Woodruff (who employed thirty).

Some might have found employment with some of the village businesses mentioned, but certainly not the majority.[154]

When the carpet mills began in Thompsonville, it was the skill of the Scottish laborers that established the business's reputation through the quality of the product. With the move to the power loom, carpet mills no longer required tenured handweavers to operate the equipment, as the only difference in quality from one mill to the next was the marketability of the carpet design *programmed* into the machinery.

> *Some male workers took notice of these lower wages paid to women; not so much out of a sense of social justice as from a fear that their own wages were declining to the level of those paid for women's work.*

> *One carpet weaver from Thompsonville, Connecticut, wrote about the coming of the Bigelow power looms in*

---

quantity and quality. In 1885 he had a stock of several thousand gallons on hand, which was the largest in Southern New England at the time. *Descendants of Nicholas Cady of Watertown Massachusetts Page 225*

[153] Resident of Windsor Locks passed away in 1856. Owned several businesses with his brother Timothy. Unclear as to when he began brickmaking or if he had perhaps bought out another concern.

[154] From the notes of Albert S. Gordon (1930) - *William [Gordon] worked as a weaver for the [Thompsonville] Carpet Works until its failure about 1852, then as a foreman for a stockinet [hosery] firm in Scitico for about 15 years.*

1846 and their impact on the skilled men's work and wages.

The machine, the presence of women in the workplace, and the deterioration of earnings all seemed to be linked in this man's mind. Once the new looms were installed, this weaver warned, 'if we are allowed to work with them at all, we shall have to work at very low wages, probably at the same rate as girls.'

The mechanized carpet mill would put men and women in competition for jobs; and the women, who were accustomed to working for lower wages, would undermine the men's wage scale. It is not certain whether this man resented or felt threatened by the arrival of women weavers or saw both male and female workers being set against each other by management.[155]

The incremental installation of power looms in Thompsonville slowly reshaped the mill's employment landscape, with the male-to-female worker ratio shifting as some Scottish weavers moved into managerial positions. In contrast, others migrated to other locales where the power loom had yet to find a home.

The male workers were not alone in their unhappiness with the lower wages that came with the new power loom reality in carpet manufacturing.

It was the female mill workers, however, who usually voiced the most vehement criticism (as they often did) of what they saw as their own meager and declining wages. The threat of wage cuts was decried by operatives throughout antebellum New England.

Maria Grout, working in Three Rivers, Massachusetts,

---

[155] Aspirations and Anxieties. Page 182.

wrote about the demoralizing effect of lower wages: 'I am not to work in the factory now. The wages have been reduced by more than twenty-five cents on a hundred. Poor encouragement to work. Cannot tell whether I shall go on here to work again or not....'

Workers were often especially disturbed by what they saw as a trend toward lower wages despite higher corporate profits.[156]

The financial impact of the mill closing on the Scottish village was similar to that in Tariffville to the southwest. Although exact population figures are elusive, the census shows that the number of Scots decreased from 409 in 1850 to 198 in 1860, with the majority of that decline occurring in the aftermath of the mill closure. The majority of Scots lived in Thompsonville, and in 1850/52, they accounted for approximately 20% of the population. During the following years, the number dropped to less than 10%.

The Irish population in Enfield, on the other hand, increased from 690 in 1850 to 900 in 1860 (15% to 18%), with the English percentage remaining stable at around 9%.

The population decline of Scots indicates a 'reverse migration' for that group after the 1852 mill closing, with a substantial impact on the village's ethnic makeup. Thompsonville could no longer be considered a 'Scottish Village'.

Most mill workers were still housed in mill-owned tenements as the company had been more than reluctant to sell off land to private individuals. The remaining contract employees were housed in hotels or privately owned

---

[156] Ibid.

multifamily homes. These people suddenly found themselves without a landlord, and the failed company's assets, including the tenements, were scheduled for sale or auction to cover the business's debts.

Mill workers had not only lost their livelihood but, if they were the head of the family, were about to lose the roof over their heads.

It wasn't just a few people in a village of about 2000 who found themselves out of work at the same time; it was approximately 650 people. Almost 30% of the village's residents were simultaneously unemployed, and most were on the verge of losing their homes.

300 men were idle.

Many of these had moved their families to this hamlet 24 years earlier, leaving their native country behind in search of a better life. And for the majority of those 24 years, life had been better. Now, the same troubles they faced years ago in their native land came back to haunt them.

How could they comfort their neighbor when they faced the same troubles?

The possibility of employment to the south at Tariffville was out of the question as Orrin Thompson also owned that manufactory.

But the connections that bound Thompsonville neighborhoods together were strong—those who had shared with those who did not. Years later, in 1875, a young German philosopher, Karl Marx, captured that sentiment famously in his quote, 'From each according to his ability, to each according to his needs'.

Families suffered, as did churches, but each survived on the other's good graces. Their actions and the sentiments of brotherhood would influence the village for decades to follow.

Even after the failure, work still needed to be completed, and a select few were chosen to do so. A company cannot close with the flick of a switch.

A list of assets needed to be compiled for sale or auction to try to repay the numerous investors.

Completed goods needed to be packed and sold to help offset the enormous outstanding debts. All of this was under the guidance of Nathaniel Shipman, a Yale University Law School graduate who had only entered private practice in 1850. He had been empowered to oversee the sale of:

..all the estate, both real and personal, of the Thompsonville Manufacturing Company, assigned for the benefit of the creditors of said company.[157]

Shipman oversaw the organization's Connecticut-based assets, while the firms of Brown, Brothers & Company, and Hicks & Company handled the New York-based assets.

Shipman designated Jabez Taylor and Wait N. Hawley commissioners to review all claims against the organization to determine their validity and establish a 'pecking order' for investor repayment from asset sales.

The trustees assigned the responsibility for selling the equipment, buildings, and property at auction, or in individual purchases or parcels, to William S. Wetmore, James Brown (of Brown Brothers), and John W. Hicks (of Hicks & Company). Of particular interest is that Hicks, Brown, and Wetmore were elected as Directors of the Thompsonville Carpet Manufacturing Company on August 20th, 1851, to secure their losses.[158]

---

[157] Connecticut Courant July 16, 1853. Page 3.
[158] It is fairly clear that the financial challenges of the organization were clear thirty days before the dissolution of

There seemed to be plenty of meat on the bone for the attorneys to piece out the organization's assets.

Nathaniel Shipman graduated from Yale University in 1848 and Yale Law School in 1850. He resided and practiced in Hartford, CT.

the company as a mortgage was executed on all the real estate and machinery in Thompsonville to secure corporate bonds and notes of $375,000 held by Hicks, Brown, and Wetmore.

Orrin Thompson was also personally vulnerable, as individuals lined up to file suit after suit against the former carpet magnate.

James Brown and John H. Hicks sought to recover funds by selling six properties Thompson owned in numerous wards throughout New York City.[159]

John Ward, Henry H. Ward, and Nathan T. Carryl filed a complaint against Thompson seeking to recover thirty thousand dollars in damages and costs associated with the filing of the action.[160]

David Leavitt, President of the American Exchange Bank, sought to recover over thirty thousand dollars with additional interest and costs associated with the filing of the action.[161]

The firm of F. S. and D. Lathrop of New York City was owed approximately $300,000.

An unnamed Hartford bank held $200,000 in Thompsonville paper when the company failed.

Ripley & Cameron, wool dealers in New York, sold 100 bales of African wool to Orrin Thompson on or about September 19, 1851. The wool was in transit when the Thompsonville and Tariffville Companies failed three days after the purchase. Both parties claimed the wool was theirs as delivery had not been made, with Ripley & Cameron ultimately prevailing in court.

All in all, there seemed to be plenty of pain to go around.

Some, though, would profit from the pain.

---

[159] New York Evening Post August 9, 1852. Page 4.
[160] New York Daily Tribune November 10, 1851. Page 4.
[161] New York Evening Post November 3, 1851. Page 4.

The vultures circled in the secondary markets as Thompson and Company offloaded merchandise to cover their massive debt load.

William E. Sugden, who continued the New York carpet reselling firm of Caitlyn & Co. after it dissolved in 1849 as Sugden & Co., boasted in regional advertisements that he purchased large lots of Thompsonville carpets at less than agents' prices, which he would gladly sell at below-market prices.

The chutzpah of free market profiteering.

Historically, it is the worker who bears the brunt of a business's failure. A company can declare bankruptcy and leverage the law to protect itself against damage beyond the closure of operations.

While they may not be made whole, financial investors can expect to recover some of their losses.

Workers, though, have no options to protect themselves or their families when a company dissolves, as their years of hard work gain them nothing but emotional anxiety and financial pain.

The investments of skill and allegiance that secured the reputation and market position of the Thompsonville Carpet Company were not honored in the same way as were the purchased stock, bonds, or credit of the well-to-do.

Workers were simply flotsam and jetsam.

Orrin Thompson had failed them as well.

Since the failure of Thompson & Co. the great carpet manufacturers, the factories at Thompsonville and Tariffville, Conn., have been closed, all the mechanics discharged, and those villages so lately flourishing, are left desolate.

Such are the benefits which the policy of 'the democracy' confers upon the workingmen.[162]

---

[162] Poughkeepsie Eagle Oct 21, 1851. Pg 2.

10: ANTI-FIDDLERS

In the early morning hours of April 15, 1912, a septet orchestra played a variety of genres and styles from the White Star Line's music book, including classical, hymns, and opera, on the tilting deck of the sinking Titanic. The music was an attempt to calm the passengers and block out sounds that might increase anxiety.

Some resources report that the passengers asked the bandmaster to play hymns, and that 'Nearer, My God, to Thee' was the last song the band played. The hymn, written by Sarah Fuller Adams in 1841, is a retelling of Jacob's Dream from the Bible. Other sources state that the musicians' decision to play music reflects the human spirit's resilience and art's ability to transcend tragedy. The playing of music may also have served a purpose for the musicians, allowing them to dissociate from the approaching tragedy and retreat to a more comforting environment.

Mothers are well-known for using music to comfort and soothe their children's souls, singing lullabies to their newborns to help them relax and perhaps fall asleep.

This makes the actions of some First Presbyterian Church congregants in 1845 more difficult to understand.

Although it was the Thompsonville Carpet Company's money that funded the construction of the First Presbyterian Church, it was one mistake by the same firm that had the most impact on the sect. That error was in not deeding the land upon which the house of worship was constructed to the church. It was an unfortunate oversight that would play out in the 1850s to the dismay of reverent villagers.

Aside from that deed error, a musical issue within the Presbyterians' ranks in 1845 led to a split within the congregation.

A letter of reflection from James R. Hamilton, written to the Connecticut State Librarian in 1924, detailed the issue that became a divisive matter.

Among the earliest of my recollections is one of attending service in the Presbyterian Church in the little factory village of Thompsonville, Connecticut.

On a bright sunshiny Sunday morning walking along the brookside, holding to my Mother's dress, I saw a small mud turtle in the path and captured it. I wished to return home that I might play with it, but my mother would not allow that and compromised the matter by permitting me to carry it to church with me.

I liked to go to church early so that I might see the minister climb the stairs to the high pulpit which seemed very high to me, and I could see the Precentor[163] who sat in a little closet-like place under the pulpit.

The minister, Dr. Harvey, appeared to my eyes as very

---

[163] A precentor is a person, usually ordained, who is in charge of preparing worship services. This position is usually held in a large church. Most cathedrals have a precentor in charge of the organization of liturgy and worship.

tall and stern, and I was very much afraid of him when he made his yearly round of calls on each family in the parish, and the children were assembled to answer the questions in the Westminster Assembly's Shorter Catechism.[164]

The village population was largely made up of Scottish families who worked in the factory. There was but one church [at the time] in the village, but there were three taverns, and every grocery store had not only West Indian molasses[165] *but a supply of New England rum for sale.*

The singing in the church was led by the Procentor, who took the pitch from the tuning fork, or from a sort of whistle with a moveable stopper, called paddock.[166] *Those were the only musical instruments allowed.*

The words used in the worship were the Psalms of David

---

[164] The Westminster Shorter Catechism is a catechism written in 1646 and 1647 by the Westminster Assembly, a synod of English and Scottish theologians and laymen intended to bring the Church of England into greater conformity with the Church of Scotland.

[165] West Indian molasses is a by-product of sugar cane refining in the Caribbean that was a key player in the triangular trade system from the 1600s to the early 1800s. In this system, New England slave traders would bring rum to Africa to purchase enslaved people, who were then sold to sugarcane plantations in the West Indies. The plantations used the sugar to make molasses, which was then shipped to the colonies to be distilled into rum for the traders to take back to Africa to buy more slaves. This trade was known as the Colonial Molasses Trade".

[166] Although resources seem nonexistent on this as a musical term, it seems as if the writer was referencing something like a slide whistle.

in meter with, on very special occasions, a few paragraphs of Scripture … that I was required to commit to memory with many of the Psalms and the Ten Commandments. The two that I remember are 'Oh God of Bethel by whose hand' and 'Oh God our help in ages past'.

We children were taught that the building was a House of God and that 'He could not look upon sin with any degree of allowance'.

The two commandments that were most firmly fixed in my memory are the fourth and the fifth. We were taught to 'Remember the Sabbath day and keep it holy. Six days shall thou labor and do all thy work', and 'Honor thy father and mother that thy days may be long in the land that the Lord they God giveth thee'. My parents believed that the second part of the fourth commandment was just as binding as the first part, and at ten years of age, I was working in the factory about thirteen hours a day, six days a week.

When I was about seven or eight years old there were some in the church that were not satisfied with the congregational singing and insisted on having a choir, and soon, owing to the lack of men singers, wanted a bass viol added to give more solid harmony to the music.[167] It seemed to many in the congregation that it would be a desecration to permit the use of an instrument of that sort

---

[167] The nineteenth century saw the reintroduction of accompanied music into the Church of Scotland. Organs began to be added to churches in large numbers and by the end of the century, roughly a third of Church of Scotland, over 80 per cent of kirks, had both organs and choirs. The Free Church that broke away from the kirk in 1843 in the Great Disruption, was more conservative over music, and organs were not permitted until 1883.

in the House of God. I do not know how long the matter was discussed in the Sessions, but there came a day when a big bass viol was in the choir gallery, and Dr. Harvey arose in the pulpit and said:

'Let us fiddle and sing to the praise of God, Psalm Number...' [and] immediately about one-half of the congregation rose up and left the meeting, among them my father with his family of eight, my Uncle James Ronald with his family, and others.

They went down to one of the schoolhouses near, and one of the Elders – I think it was Hugh Richmond – read a sermon. It was not long before the seceders had organized a church as the Associate Reformed Presbyterian Church, secured a piece of ground, and a 'the people had a mind to work' they had a building of their own in which to worship, with a minister named Peter Gordon.

There was much ill feeling manifested between the fiddlers and the anti-fiddlers which continued for years.

On September 15th, 1845, the separatists formed themselves into a society for worship. They reached out to the Associate Reformed Presbytery of New York, which identified December 22 of that year as the official date of organization. Sixty-four membership certificates were presented, and ten additional people were admitted based on their 'profession of faith'.

Robert Galbraith, William Liddell, Hugh Richmond, and Robert Davidson were chosen as church elders. The presbytery appointed Reverend Peter Gordon, and he preached in the Main Street schoolhouse second-floor space from January of 1846 until May of that same year.

Funds were raised to erect a new church on land gifted by the carpet mill for the price of one dollar. By August of

1846, a church had been built for $4,500 [$180,000 in 2020].

A call was made that summer to Reverend Peter Gordon, asking him to ascend to the full-time pulpit, at a salary of $500 per year [$20,000 in 2020], which Reverend Gordon accepted on June 18, 1846.

It would take a year before the official installation would take place on April 5, 1847, with an article in the Hartford Courant commemorating the event on the following Friday.

Agreeably to [the] appointment of the Associate Reformed Presbytery of New York, Rev. Peter Gordon, formerly of the James Street Church, New York, was on Friday last, 2d inst., regularly installed in the Pastoral charge of the Associate Reformed Church of Thompsonville, Rev. Joseph McCarroll, D. D., of Newburgh, presiding. On this occasion, the Reverend gentleman preached to a large and attentive audience, from Gen.iii.24; 'So he drove out the man; and he placed at the east of the garden of Eden, Cherubims, and a flaming sword which turned every way, to keep the way of the tree of life'.

The discourse was a masterpiece, worthy [of] the high character of the venerable and learned Professor; in its progress, the typical representation contained in the text, of the ministry of reconciliation that was to dawn upon the world at the commencement of the Christian era, was beautifully illustrated, and the arduous and important duties that devolve on the Christian minister, were eloquently and clearly delineated.

At the installation, the charge both to [the] Pastor and people, was in keeping with the sermon, and altogether the services were of a very interesting and impressive character.

In the evening, the young men of the congregation gave a

Soiree in the church, where a numerous assembly met, and during the entertainment, several of the songs of Zion, selected from the 'Psalms of David', were sung with devotional spirit; and thrilling addresses were listened to from Rev. Mr. Gordon, Rev. Mr. Robbins, of Enfield, and Rev. Dr. McCarroll - the latter of whom pronounced the Apostolic Benediction, and the audience retired about 9 o'clock, highly gratified with the proceedings of the day.

Thompsonville, April 5, 1847.[168]

Reverend Gordon's connection with the church terminated in March of 1851, and the pastor later traveled, of all places, to Australia. The Reverend passed away shortly after he returned to the United States.

In the same year (1851) the carpet company failed, the mills being closed nearly two years.

Business was dull and many went elsewhere to seek work. Though 30 were admitted to the church from 1851 to 1854, these were more than offset by deaths and removals, and the financial and spiritual condition of the church was unpromising.

However, notwithstanding the general apathy, many remained loyal to the church and their Master and their prayers were answered when, on September 12, 1854, a new pastor, Reverend James McLaughlin, was installed. In spite of their financial embarrassment, the congregation did not hesitate to promise a salary of $600 yearly.[169]

Various church records reference the difficult times in

---

[168] Hartford Courant April 9, 1847. Page 2.
[169] One Hundredth Anniversary of the United Presbyterian Church, Thompsonville, Connecticut. Nov. 7-11, 1945. Pg 12.

the village in terms of attendance, contributions, and general malaise of the village during the two-year aftermath of the carpet mill shutdown. Still, the actual reduction or fluctuation in member numbers, in either Presbyterian Church, is either nonexistent or not available.

Membership aside, religious services continued to tie the community together and to provide a place of solace and hope for a challenged village.

And that faith was about to be rewarded.

11: REBOOT

William Henry was born in Hartford, Connecticut, on January 25, 1780, to William and Mary (Nevins) Imlay.

His father was a self-made man, successful in every venture that attracted his attention. W. H. wanted for nothing as he matured, inheriting his father's business acumen and sense of adventure.

By 1799, he had partnered with Charles Seymour (Charles Seymour & Company) in a venture marketing West Indian goods, crockery, and iron—an eclectic assortment of products one would not naturally associate. The two prospered for two years, then separated, each continuing in business, selling the same products, with W. H. adding paints and dye-stuffs to his product mix.

In 1829, he purchased the upper grist mills in Hartford (near the site of the present State Armory), renaming them the Imlay Mills, and set about producing and marketing rye flour, buckwheat, and corn meal under the business name William H. Imlay & Co.

But he was a man of many interests beyond his core business, holding timberland in Michigan, owning a large merchant store in Clinton, Georgia, sitting on the Board of Directors of the Connecticut River Banking Company (where he would later assume the presidency), and sitting on the Board of Directors as a stockholder in the Connecticut Life and Trust Company.

In 1843 he closed his partnership with Zephaniah Preston and John Wright, reopening the firm under the same name and adding a new partner, his son-in-law, Daniel Buck, Jr. It was a move that would later become a costly embarrassment in early 1851, as a series of events forced the magnate to declare a form of 'temporary insolvency' as young Buck ran into financial difficulties, Michigan timberland management became onerous, heavy investments in local railroads failed, and a costly association with the Atlantic Shipyards in Brooklyn took their toll.

For Imlay, it was a temporary setback, as it became clear his paper value of over one million dollars easily allowed him to deal with his half-million-dollar liabilities.

It was at that time, in the latter days of that year and trickling into 1852, that the static carpet mills in Thompsonville and Tariffville attracted his attention. He began discussing with the company's creditors the possibility of reforming and restarting the business by issuing a new round of stock and allocating the existing creditors' shares based on their losses.

Whether it was due to the financial challenges W. H. Imlay had recently faced that same year or not, the stock swap proposal never gained ground.

But the idea itself would prove to have merit.

Cyprian was born in Hartford, Connecticut, on May 4, 1773, to George and Eunice (Lord) Nichols.

In 1786, Cyprian's father, George, died, leaving the thirteen-year-old—the only child of the marriage—alone to help his mother care for the family.

Thomas Tisdall, born in 1757, marketed various goods from his store in Hartford until he partnered with John McNeight in 1790 to open a soap and candle factory within the city limits. By all indications, the partners took in young Cyprian to apprentice in the factory, which enabled him to provide for himself and his mother.

By 1794, his mother, Eunice, had died, and the young man was left with no parents at the age of twenty.

McNeight and Tisdall parted ways in 1796, paving the way for young Cyprian to partner with Thomas Tisdall in the manufacture of soaps and candles.

TISDALL and NICHOLS,

MAnufacture and offer for fale at their Soap and Candle manufactory, on the Little River Bank, weft of Main Street, Hartford,

Mould Candles of different fizes by the ton or lefs.

Dipt   do.   do.   do. by do. or do.

Shaving Soap (that is old) by the grofs or dozen cakes.

Marbled Soap in bars.

Soft Soap by the barrel.   Alfo,

A few cafks Providence Stone Lime.

The above Goods they warrant to be of the firft quality, and may be obtained on very reafonable terms for Cafh or Tallow.

A high price given for TALLOW, either rendered or in the raff.

Hartford, Dec. 25.

The partnership continued until 1804, when the duo announced in the Hartford Courant that their partnership had come to an end and that all matters should be settled without delay.

However, the partnership continued despite the announcement until another announcement in the American Mercury newspaper noted that the partnership had been dissolved in May of 1807.

However, the partnership continued despite the announcement until another announcement in the Connecticut Courant noted that it had been dissolved in May of 1809.

This time, the dissolution stuck.

WILLIAM H. IMLAY having disposed of his stock in trade to the subscribers, they will conduct business at the store lately improved by Wm. H. Imlay & Co. under the firm of

NICHOLS & TINKER.

They have recently received from New York, fresh supplies of Groceries and other Goods, which with those on hand, composing the stock of the late firm of Wm. H. Imlay & Co. renders their assortment very extensive.—They respectfully solicit the patronage of the public, and particularly of those who have heretofore been customers at said Store, assuring them that the prices and qualities of their Goods shall be satisfactory.   CYPRIAN NICHOLS,
                SAMUEL TINKER.
Hartford, April 13, 1813.   2w16

Nichols, now flying solo, erected a new building on Maiden Lane, just west of Main Street in Hartford, where he would continue to produce soaps and candles of all types.

He seemed to expand his offerings at the location to include stoneware, brown sugar, and rum.

By 1813, Nichols crossed paths with William H. Imlay, purchasing Imlay's store in Hartford as W. H. moved on to other ventures. Nichols found a new partner in Samuel Tinker, and the pair conducted business under the name Nichols & Tinker.

The business expanded far beyond Nichols's comfort level, including a wide range of products, from wines and hard liquors to tobacco, foodstuffs, household goods, and even equipment.

The partnership was short-lived, most likely due to Nichol's unease with managing the product mix, as the duo broke apart in October of 1814, divesting themselves of the business.

Tinker would die 7 years later.

Nichols refocused on the soap and candle business, taking on new partners, Henry Sooter and Lemuel Humphrey, shortly thereafter, and continued the company as C. Nichols & Company.

By 1819, the unexpected death of Sooter reconfigured the firm as Nichols & Humphrey.

NICHOLS & TINKER,

OFFER FOR SALE

(At the Store formerly occupied by the late firm of Wm. H. Imlay & Co.) a general assortment of GOODS, on accommodating terms, among which are the following articles, VIZ.

14 Pipes, half pipes, and qr casks old Madeira, Vidonia, Teneriffe Mamora, Malaga and port } WINES.

16 Chests Hyson, Young Hyson, Hyson Skin, Souchong & Bohea } TEAS.

29 Hhds. Lump,
7 do. Loaf,
8 do. and 15 bbls Muscovado
10 Boxes white & brown Havana } SUGARS.

13 Hhds. W. I. Rum,
6 do. New-England do.
5 do. Old Spirit.
2 Pipes Cogniac and Naples Brandy.
2 do. Country and Pierpont's Anchor Gin.
6 Hhds. Molasses.
20 bags green and Bourbon Coffee,
20 do. Pepper.   400 lbs, Cassia,
15 Kegs Ginger.
Cloves, Mace, true Cinnamon.
Nutmegs, Chocolate.
400 quart, pint, and half pint Tumblers.
50 Kegs Harris' first quality sweet scented Tobacco.
10 bbls. Leipers and Lorrillard's bladder Snuff.
200 Bushels Rock Salt.
100 Do. blown do.
4 Tierces Glue. 40 bbls, Tar.
13 do. Rosin.
London White Lead.
do.   Red   do.
Paris Wite.   3 Hhds. Whiting.
Spanish Brown, Venetian Red.
Spruce Yellow.   Verdigrise.
A general assortment of fine Paints.
Spirits of Turpentine, Ship Varnish.
Linseed and Lamp Oil
Sheet Lead. Painters Brushes. Chalk.
Spanish flote Indigo,
Copperas, Allum, Logwood.
Nicaragua, Fustic, Camwood.
35 Casks cut and wrought Nails, assorted sizes.
10,000 feet 8 by 6, 7 by 9, 8 by 10, 12 by 10, and 16 by 12 English Crown Window Glass.

LIKEWISE,

An extensive assortment of Iron, comprising Russia, O. Sable, Square, assorted sizes; 2 3-4 1 3-4 and 1 1-2 inch flat Sweeds. 6 Tons 1 1-4 inch do. light drawn, suitable for one horse waggon tire; Bloomery, Rockwells refined, Axletree drafts, Share moulds, Nail rods Spike do.

ALSO,

German Steel, warranted genuine.
American blistered do. made from Swedes Iron.
Cart, waggon, and chaise boxes.
April 21.   tf8

183

NICHOLS & HUMPHREY,
CONTINUE to carry on the Soap and Candle business, and have on hand mould and dipped Candles of all sizes in common use; yellow Bar Soap that is old; Shaving and Soft Soap, warranted of the first quality and offered for sale on very accommodating terms.
Tallow, family Ashes and Grease, and damaged Butter and Lard wanted as usual.
Hartford, Aug. 31.   3m 49

The partnership held firm for almost twenty years and was underscored by the birth of Lemuel's second son, whom he named Cyprian Nicholas Humphrey.[170]

Cyprian, then a wealthy man, began seeking additional challenges to hold his interest.

In 1826, he was elected auditor of the Hartford County Agricultural Society. The following year, he is assigned as an assessor for his home city. In 1828, he became a city alderman and served until 1830, when he was elected a Representative from Hartford to the Connecticut State House, along with Henry Ellsworth.

Cyprian was appointed by the Connecticut General Assembly as a trustee of the newly formed Connecticut Life and Trust Company in 1833, a group presided over by W. H. Imlay. The well-to-do traveled in the same social and business circles.

In 1836, Cyprian was elected vice president of the Hartford Savings Society, while serving as a Justice of the

---

[170] By 1838 Nichols had withdrawn from the partnership, and the business was carried on by Lenuel Humphrey and George Seyms. Seyms had been an employee of Nichol's for 25 years and had most likely bought out his interest in the soap and candle business.

Peace for the city and as a member of the Hartford Civil Authority.

In 1838, he ran again for a seat in the state legislature as a representative of Hartford, but lost.

At the meeting on Thursday evening, the Democrats nominated

CYPRIAN NICHOLS, and
THOMAS H. SEYMOUR,

as their candidates for the Legislature. The meeting was large, and there was a resolution and determination manifested that is honorable to freemen. The Spirit of Independence was there. Men who are not to be terrified or brow beat by the threats of "no Bread," from an unprincipled Bank aristocracy.

Cyprian continued to influence local politics and remained on the board of directors for the Phoenix Bank (of Hartford) and continued as a Vice President of the Society for Savings Bank (of Hartford).

Still active in his 80th year, he, along with others, petitioned the State Legislature, possibly influenced by W.H. Imlay's failed attempt, to 'resuscitate' the Thompsonville Carpet Works.

HOUSE.—Committee on Incorporations other than Banks reported favorably to granting petition of Cyprian Nichols and others, for incorporation of New England Carpet Company; report accepted and bill in form passed.

Committee on Military Affairs, to whom

The petitioning group, as noted in the Litchfield Enquirer report (above), consisted of Orrin Thompson, Cyprian Nichols, John L. Bunce, William R. Cone, Frederick

Tyler, Thomas Belknap, James M. Bunce, and Henry Keeney. These men had petitioned the State Legislature:

> ... *praying for an act of incorporation...[to make] and [establish] a body politic and corporate, by the name of the New England Carpet Company, for the purpose of manufacturing carpets, wool, cotton, and other manufactures materials...[171]*

However, something happened after the petition was submitted and approved. The New England Carpet Company never materialized, and no reason can be found in any resources as to why it never did.

Shortly thereafter, the following petition was presented before the same governing body and approved.

> *Upon the petition of Cyprian Nichols and others, praying for an act of incorporation: Resolved by this Assembly, Sec. 1.*

> *That Orrin Thompson, Cyprian Nichols, George Beach, William Hungerford, Edmund Grant Howe, David Nichols, David Clark, Charles Boswell, Timothy M. Allyn, Richard D. Hubbard, Gurdon Trumbull, with all others who are or shall hereafter become associated with them, be and they hereby are, with their successors and assigns, made and established a body politic and corporate, by the name of the Hartford Carpet Company, for the purpose of manufacturing carpets, cotton and other manufactures and goods....[172]*

---

[171] Act for Incorporating the New England Carpet Company, Resolutions and Private Acts of the General Assembly of the State of Connecticut May Session 1853

[172] Act for Incorporating the Hartford Carpet Company, Resolutions and Private Acts of the General Assembly of the State of Connecticut May Session 1853

Only **two** of the individuals from the New England Carpet Company petition were **also included** in the Hartford Carpet Company petition.

Thompson and Nichols.

Within two months, on August 18, 1853, the tireless engineer of BOTH initiatives, Cyprian Nichols, died.

That left Orrin Thompson, once again, in a position to restart the carpet mills.

12: THE SPACE INBETWEEN

The Free Banking Era in the United States was a period from 1837 to ~1866, during which individual states granted charters to banks, allowing anyone to open a bank and issue currency.

That's correct.

Banks could issue their OWN currency. It's not unlike the Wild West of Bitcoin today, where anyone can design their version of cryptocurrency and cater to market demand through 'initial coin offerings' (IPOs for cryptocurrencies).

In 2024, there were more than 1,600 cryptocurrencies available for purchase, investment, and use.

Three-dollar bills had a short-lived history during the

Free Banking Era and could only be redeemed at the issuing bank, not used as 'legal tender'.

The limitation on the notes didn't stop their use.

On December 8, 1852, Colonel Robert Morrison Abbe of Thompsonville, arrested four men in nearby Holyoke, Massachusetts, for passing $3 counterfeit bills, drawn on the Bank of Hartford, to several merchants in Abbe's home village in northern Enfield.

Lyman Houghton, Asa Pease, Frederick Wright, and Arthur Horregon were brought before the Massachusetts magistrate and sent to the local jail for holding, where they awaited transfer to the State of Connecticut after the governor of the state filed the necessary requisition.

Abbe owned an Inn on Enfield Street, just south of Bridge Lane, where he welcomed individuals seeking shelter for the night. It is unknown whether his establishment served liquor, as the previous owner, Robert's father, Daniel Abbe, Jr., had been denied a liquor license there years before, when a local tavernkeeper, Peter R. Field, was the recognized innkeeper and taphouse.

On July 26, 1851, at approximately 11 a.m., Abee's Hotel on Enfield Street caught fire and burned to the ground, essentially driving Abbe from the business, at least at that location. The establishment had cost $5,000 to construct, but was insured for less than half that amount, so the smart business move was not to rebuild the inn.

Instead, it seems as if R. M. Abbe either subsequently purchased or leased the Globe Hotel along the Connecticut River in Thompsonville, thereby maintaining his interest in keeping an inn or tavern. The timing was somewhat questionable as, with the carpet manufactories shuttered, there would have been a lull in hosting activity.

*Quite possibly the ONLY photo of the **Globe Hotel** in Thompsonville in existence. The arrow points to the backside of the hotel, which was situated on the Connecticut River side of the railroad tracks.*

Abbe held steady through the lean years, though, as he was identified in various newspaper articles as *proprietor* of the Globe Hotel from 1852 through 1858. Whether the proprietor equated to the owner, though, is unknown.

> **FOR SALE.**
> THE ABBE PLACE in Enfield, containing 26 acres of the very best of land, a dwelling house convenient for two tenements, two barns, tobacco sheds sufficient for nine acres of tobacco, ice house, horse sheds, two good wells, soft water in abundance and handy. In short, it is an exceeingly desirable place, and no one can examine it without liking it. Apply to the subscriber, proprietor of the Globe Hotel, at Thompsonville. ROBERT M. ABBE.
> Thompsonville, May 17, 1852. tfd&w48

Article in the Hartford Weekly Times October 9, 1852. Page 4.

FOR SALE. The Abbe Place in En-
field, containing 26 acres of the very best of land,
a dwelling house convenient for two tenements,
two barns, tobacco sheds sufficient for nine acres of tobacco, ice house, horse sheds, two good wells, soft water
in abundance and handy. In short, it is an exceedingly
desirable place and no one can examine it without liking
it. Apply to the subscriber, proprietor of the Globe
Hotel, at Thompsonville. If not sold by the first of
April, it will be otherwise disposed of.
                                        ROBERT M. ABBE.
Thompsonville, March 12, 1858.   1fw90

Article in the Hartford Weekly Times May 27, 1858. Page 4.

The announcement of the establishment of the
Thompsonville Scale Manufacturing Company appeared in
the April 28, 1852, edition of the Hartford Courant.

The names of the new company's members were
familiar to the villagers, and the establishment of the
business was welcome news for a village in need of good
news.

Although familiar, the members, except for Horatio
Osgood, lacked even basic knowledge of the manufacturing
process for their chosen product, which brought into
question the makeup of the board.

Horatio Osgood (29) was listed on the 1850 census as a
'scale manufacturer', so he seemed well-suited for the
venture. Osgood had also been granted a patent in 1852 for
'attaching pieces of metal by casting', so his skills and
knowledge were unquestionable.

As for the others:

The Scrimgeours had owned a store in Thompsonville
for many years, and the family was well-respected.

Joseph P. Converse (49) was a physician in town, while
Wait Hawley (23) was an attorney, and William McCrone,
Jr. (27) was a weaver.

Hartford, and State of Connecticut.
Dated at Thompsonville, this eighteenth day of March, A. D. 1852.
(Signed) Joseph P. Converse................40 Shares.
      Warren Terry......................40 do
      Samuel A. Stillman..................40 do
      Edwin H. Andrews..................40 do
      E. J. Scrimgeour...................20 do
      Jeremiah V. Allen.................20 do
      H. S. Belcher & Co...............20 do
      Hugh Richmond ....20 do
      George H. Barber.................20 do
      William McCrone, Jr.............20 do
      W. N. Hawley......................20 do
      Horatio B. Osgood.................50 do
      John O. Raynolds..................50 do
  Published by order of the President and Directors,
ap 27   3d   W. N. HAWLEY, Secretary.
    Times copy.

Samuel Stillman (29) was a farmer in Enfield, as were George H. Barber (33) and John Raynolds.

Edwin Andrews (24) had no trade specified in the 1850 census, so his particular skill sets remain unknown.

There were two Jeremiah Allens – the father (48), a carpenter, and his son (17) – and neither had any history in the scale business.

Hiram Belcher (49), of H. S. Belcher, was a merchant in the village. Initially located in Enfield Center, the store had relocated to the village, but location rarely has anything to do with production competency.

Hugh Richmond (51), an émigré from Scotland, was a skilled weaver.

The purpose of the organization, as detailed in their Articles of Association, was to manufacture, sell, and traffic in all kinds of counter and platform scales.

Soon after the business was established, a clause in the agreement caused the shareholders to take legal action against Osgood, the only owner with scale manufacturing experience, seeking an amendment to the contract.[173] It seemed that Osgood was attempting to extract himself from the agreement – perhaps it was a late case of buyer's remorse or perhaps fallout from the demise of the carpet business.

Whatever the reason —whether it was due to the board's legal action OR having only one owner experienced in the business —two years later, the operation closed. The property, machine shop, foundry, offices, and a five-tenement dwelling house were put up for sale.

Osgood was the only shareholder from the group to continue in the weights-and-measures business, but not in Thompsonville. He relocated to New Haven and continued to receive patents for improvements to his scale business.

Continuing the theme, Thomas Watson closed his doors in 1852. He had operated his tailor shop in the small village for 9 years, handling repairs and custom tailoring.

On a brighter note – and just in time for the carpet mill to cease operations - the double track of the New Haven, Hartford, and Springfield Railroad was completed from Springfield to Thompsonville in early November of 1852. The portion remaining to be completed the following year would connect Thompsonville to Windsor.

As 1853 opened, the Hartford Courant's March 26 edition reported the suicide of Joseph S. Harvey, Postmaster at Thompsonville. The article stated the government employee had taken his own life in a fit of insanity by shooting himself with a musket, living for five hours before succumbing to the injuries. Given the recent upheaval in the village, who could question the anxiety that might have led to his demise?

---

[173] Thompsonville Scale Manufacturing Company v. Osgood

Apparently, his father could.

In a heartfelt response to the newspaper report, and possibly colored by a parent's desire to put his son in a more benevolent light, Joseph Harvey Sr. posted the following.

The facts are these; My son resigned the office of Postmaster sometime last fall, and made a journey to the South on business, hoping to benefit his health; and returned about the first of February last. He suffered from Neuralgia in the head but has at no time been insane except temporarily some years since during the continuance and effects of a brain fever.

He had a short time previous to his death, felt much relieved from the bodily pain with which he had been afflicted, and his friends and himself were anticipating his entire relief. He was making preparations for a journey to the West with the intention of remaining there; and after eating a hearty dinner and reading the newspaper, commenced arranging his things for a journey by packing his trunk.

Taking up a fowling piece he proceeded to clean it, and fired it once at the rear of my house, and remarked that 'it did not go well", and went to his room and reloaded it again to shoot at the mark, as is supposed.

A person in another room heard his un fall from the bed, on which it was lying, and explode. On rushing to the spot it was found to have discharged its contents into his body. When asked how it happened, he, with difficulty, articulated 'before I knew it.' He lingered a few hours, and after taking an affectionate leave of his relatives, breathed in his last peace, animated with a Christian's hope.

The kindly tendered and efficient sympathies and services of the community of which he had been a member, were very grateful to his surviving friends, and have a lasting impression in their memories.

The exertions and attentions of the surgeons called to render assistance were everything that could be wished.

Respectfully Yours,

J. Harvey[174]

Often, the disparity between those who have and those who don't is magnified during times of financial stress. While Thompsonville residents struggled to rebuild their lives after the closing of the carpet mill, south along Enfield Street, in a mansion erected by the King of the Scantic, Augustus George Hazard, the gunpowder magnate held a dinner party—for those who lived above day-to-day economic struggles.

On June 17th, 1853, forty invitees from Massachusetts and Connecticut joined A. G. Hazard at his sprawling estate on Enfield Street to celebrate the anniversary of the 'first great battle of the Revolution'.

Assembled there were:

Governor Seymour of Connecticut, the Honorable George Ashmun, the Honorable George T. Davis, the Honorable A. H. Bullock, the Honorable George Dwight, Colonel Ripley (from Massachusetts), the Honorable A. N. Skinner (mayor of New Haven), the Honorable William J. Hamersley (mayor of Hartford), the honorable James Dixon, the honorable William W. Eaton (Speaker of the House of Representatives), the

---

[174] Connecticut Courant March 26, 1853. Page 2.

Honorable Henry C. Deming, and John Cotton Smith, Esquire.[175]

Surely many *honorable*, if not influential, people.

In attendance as well was Orrin Thompson, who was individually cited at the proceedings. Speaking of how Enfield had progressed during the years since the Revolution, the article recalled:

> *-- to the many changes which had taken place within its borders since that period – the building up of the manufacturing village of Thompsonville through the enterprise of a gentleman present (Orrin Thompson, Esq.,) and the more recent starting into life and activity of another village (Hazardville,) through the spirit and wealth of the gentleman who presided at the festive board.*[176]

At the time, Orrin Thompson was deep in negotiations to restart the mills in his namesake village. He must have felt somewhat conflicted to be highlighted so soon after his company's recent failure.

In a nod to those unfortunate souls in Thompsonville, perhaps in return for a meal and possibly food to take home to their families –

> *…the company [was] entertained with Scottish songs by gentlemen from the village.*[177]

After all, since medieval times in England, it was customary for hungry singers who arrived at local inns, bars, or saloons to offer to sing a song or recite poetry in exchange for a meal.

---

[175] Hartford Courant June 20, 1853. Page 2.
[176] Hartford Courant June 20, 1853. Page 2.
[177] Ibid.

What better way to help the men of Thompsonville?

One month later, a notice appeared in the Hartford Courant posted by William Patrick of Thompsonville asking for help in retrieving his *brown hair trunk with a rope around it* that had been stolen from the sidewalk near George Welch's State Street drugstore in Hartford. It contained almost the entire 'wearing apparel' of the poor man, and the person returning it would receive the 'thanks of the owner'.

Perhaps Patrick, an unemployed Scotch weaver, could've taken comfort in the fatal mistake made two months later by village resident Thomas Lawler while working at the Stockinette factory, which opened up an immediate employment opportunity.

On October 21, 1853, Lawler found himself caught in winding machinery…

…by the shafting, which made one hundred revolutions a minute. He was first [noticed] by a boy as he was revolving with the shaft. He was literally torn to pieces, and his boots and stockings were thrown across the room.

One of his hands [had been] torn off last spring by the same shafting.[178]

Prospective employees, including William Patrick, could apply for the open position at the company's office.

The year ended on a high note for Alva Chapin of Thompsonville, as he butchered a young hog on December 19th. At least the Chapins would have enough to eat.

The pig, only fourteen months old, weighed in at 588

---

[178] Norwich Courier November 2, 1853. Pg 2. (reprinted from the Hartford Times)

pounds…a true Christmas miracle.

As Tiny Tim had said, 'God bless us, every one!'

Perhaps 1854 would prove more hopeful.

Isaac Pease was born in Longmeadow, Massachusetts, in 1809. He relocated to Thompsonville, Connecticut, where he owned a successful wool mill. In the 1830s, Pease began manufacturing clock cases in his wood shop, purchasing the mechanical movements from firms like Terry and Hoadley, and installing them in his finely carved cases.

As Spiritualism began to sweep the region in the mid-1850s Pease, already a *traveling agent* for the Spiritual Telegraph newspaper, became inspired by dial telegraphs, popular in the 1840s and 1850s, and came up with the idea of constructing a similar sort of dial face, with an alphabet, numerals, and some simple responses to questions marked around its perimeter to enable communication with the deceased.

> *We learn from the N. Y. tribune that Mr. J. [sic I.] T. Pease, of Thompsonville, in this state, has invented a 'Spiritual Telegraph Dial'. An apparatus has been contrived with a dial plate containing the letters of the alphabet, the words Yes and No, the numerals, and some other signs. The index is a movable one, so that the spirits can turn it to point to any letter, etc., they may choose. This is a great improvement over the old clumsy modes of rapping and table tipping. We trust this gentleman will receive the proper encouragement for his ingenuity.[179]*

> *I.T. Pease of Thompsonville (Conn.) has succeeded in inventing a machine which he denominates the Spiritual*

---

[179] Hartford Courant January 13, 1854. Pg 2.

A Spiritual Machine.

We learn that Mr. J. T. Pease, of Thompsonville, Connecticut, has succeeded in inventing a machine which he denominates the Spiritual Telegraph Dial. This apparatus is contrived with a dial face, on which are marked the letters of the alphabet, the Arabic numerals, the words Yes and No, and some other convenient signs. A moveable hand, or pointer, is fixed in the centre; and when a ghost wants to communicate with its pupils and friends in the body, all that is requisite is for it to give a gentle twitch to the pointer, and the revelation is accomplished. Mr. Pease states that with a good tipping medium to facilitate the movements of the pointer by agitating the table, letters will be indicated to the dial as fast as an amanuesis can write them down. There is also an arangement by which the dial may be concealed from the sight of the medium, so that he cannot know what it is that is being said by the ghost.—[Exchange.

[Will Mr. P. interrogate his machine respecting the future of the Ericsson, and send us the result of his observation. If he will foretell the destiny of this ship we are ready to endorse his invention, but until we see some such evidence of its skill we must remain chary of it.

Telegraph Dial. This apparatus is contrived with a dial face on which are marked the letters of the alphabet, the Arabic numerals, the words Yes and No, and some other convenient signs. A moveable hand, or pointer, is fixed in the center, and when a ghost wants to communicate with its pupils and friends in the body, all that is requisite is for it to give a gentle twitch to the pointer, and the revelation is accomplished. Some Yankee ought next to invent a visible ghost and take out a patent.[180]

On February 4, Scientific American reprinted the Boston Investigator article, replacing the smarmy endnote with a clarifying quote by Pease (*see previous page*).

Nonplused, Pease offered a more robust description of his invention in the June 3, 1854, edition of the Spiritual Telegraph publication.

The dimensions of the instrument are only eight inches square, average thickness two inches, which makes only a small package, and can be sent by express to any part of the United States for a small sum. The face of the instrument is similar to a clock dial; a pointer is attached to the center wheel pivot, on this dial is printed, with a beautiful copper-plate engraving, the twenty-six letters of the alphabet, all the notes and characters in music, the Arabic numerals, and a number of short communications, such as 'yes,' 'no,' 'don't know,' 'I think so,' 'a mistake,' 'I'll spell it over,' 'a message,' 'done,' 'I'll come again,' 'I must leave,' 'good-bye,' etc. which may thus be given without repeating the whole alphabet to get one letter.

---

[180] Boston Investigator December 18, 1853. This article got the inventor's first name correct.

Perhaps the device would be used to contact, communicate with, and resurrect the spirit of the village, which had been depressed for two years.

With the closure of the Thompsonville Scale Manufacturing Company, Samuel Stillman offered his Enfield farm for sale, as he was no longer listed in the 1860 Thompsonville census, having moved to other locations. His action would be the last bad news for the village and a precursor for welcome, good news for the former hamlet.

> **FARM FOR SALE**—Situated in Enfield, three-fourths of a mile from the Thompsonville Depot on the Hartford and Springfield Road, containing about 80 acres, well fenced and suitably divided into meadow, pasture, tillage and wood land. On the farm there are large, well finished buildings, convenient and in good repair; also plenty of never-failing pure water, and plenty of fruit of all kinds and varieties. The location is one of the pleasantest in the valley of the Connecticut River. The farm, with the stock and tools and a well established milk business, will be sold cheap if sold soon. For particulars, inquire on the farm of
> mh 16   18d 52   S. A. STILLMAN.

Like manna from Heaven, the announcement appeared in the April 8, 1854, edition of the Hartford Courant.

Brown, Brothers & Company of New York City gave notice that they would pay on demand the final dividends on the mortgage bonds of the Thompsonville Manufacturing [Carpet] Company, paving the way for the reopening of the plant under the guidance of the new owners.

THOMPSONVILLE

Within a few weeks, new life has been infused into this fine village, or rather city — for it bears more strikingly the appearance of a city than a village.

The immense carpet factory of this place has been idle for two years, and all efforts to start it into full operation failed, till a company of gentlemen, principally of this city, raised a capital sufficient to purchase the whole concern at the Assignee's sale; and procuring a charter from the General Assembly of last year, they have been able to set the machinery in motion Most of the machines are now at work, and one a week will be started until the whole number, 147, are in full operation. The larger portion of the old hands have again been employed, and are now at their posts, and Thompsonville is really herself again.

The new Company has purchased all of this valuable property for a sum not exceeding $500,000, and having no debt or embarrassment, they cannot fail to realize large sums of money in profits from their investment; and by starting these great works a market is opened to all the town around, and much wealth is added to the place in which the Factory is situated.[181]

The New London Daily Star provided some additional information.

Instead of a man and boy to operate each loom, the new invention [requires] the services of only one girl to each loom, producing 25 yards per day, or 5 times as many yards as the handloom.[182]

On June 13, 1854, an advertisement appeared in the Springfield Republican looking for…

…Several active and intelligent girls to attend Carpet Power Looms at the mills of the Hartford Carpet

---

[181] Hartford Times May 27, 1854. Page 2.
[182] New London Daily Star June 1, 1854. Pg 2.

Company at Thompsonville.

By July 6th, sales outlets began promoting the arrival of new carpets from Thompsonville Mills.

On October 19, the stockholders descended en masse to the manufactory grounds. Free tickets were offered to anyone who wanted a tour of the facilities.

On December 1st, the final installment of the capital stock, $500,000, was completed.

Thompsonville was back in business.

13: RESURRECTION

Edmund Grant Howe was a director on the board of the Connecticut River Railroad Company, a director on the board of the Connecticut Mutual Life Insurance Company, a director on the board of the Connecticut Fire Insurance Company, and the President of the Hartford County Savings Association.

He was a driven man.

He was also elected as the first President of the Hartford Carpet Company in 1853, serving for only a short time.

In 1854, Edmund's wife, Frances, aged 36, passed away from an unreported illness.

On February 20, 1854, Howe resigned his position as the figurehead of the resurrected carpet company, yielding to fellow board member Timothy Mather Allyn. Howe retained his positions as a board member and stockholder and assumed the additional responsibility of treasurer for the company.

It was clear that his wife's passing had no impact on his thirst for business.

NOTICE.

THE subscribers have entered into Copartnership to transact the mercantile business in the city of New-York, and in the city of Hartford. The business in New-York will be transacted by TIMOTHY M. ALLYN and ANSON LOOMIS, under the name and firm of ALLYN, LOOMIS & CO., and in Hartford by JOB ALLYN, Jr. and MICHAEL MARSH, under the name and firm of ALLYN, MARSH & CO.

TIMOTHY M. ALLYN,
ANSON LOOMIS,
JOB ALLYN, Jr.,
MICHAEL MARSH.

Hartford, June, 1827.

ALLYN, MARSH & CO.

Have taken the Store on Main-street, one door south Mr. St. John's Tavern, and three doors north of the Episcopal Church, formerly occupied by Charles Sigourney, Esq., where they are receiving an extensive New Stock of Goods, comprising a general assortment of

Dry Goods, Groceries, Crock-

ery and Hard Ware, which they offer for sale at as low prices as they can be obtained in this city for cash, approved credit, or most kinds of country produce.

The above arrangement will enable them to take advantage of the markets and consequently to sell on as favourable terms as others. The inhabitants of the city and country are invited to call and examine the goods.

All orders from the country punctually attended to.

FOR SALE,
40,000 Merchantable Brick.

Hartford, June 30, 1827.   58

Timothy Mather Allyn was descended from one of the oldest families in New England, with their roots traced back to colonial times. In 1638, Mather Allyn purchased one-sixteenth of the Town of Windsor, Connecticut, where his family, which had emigrated from Braunton, England, lived for many years.

In 1827 a post in the Connecticut Courant announced the multi-state partnership between Timothy Allyn and Anson Loomis (in New York City doing business as Allyn, Loomis & Company) and Job Allyn, JR (Timothy's older brother) and Michael Marsh (in Hartford doing business as Allyn, Marsh) where two separate mercantile companies would be established to address the dry goods needs of each city.

ALLYN, LOOMIS & CO.

ARE now opening, from the latest importa-
tions, (at their store, 255 Pearl-street,) a
general assortment of British, French, and American DRY GOODS, which they offer at Wholesale on the most favorable terms.

New-York, March 14, 1828.   6w96

Five months later, the Allyn & Loomis partnership broke apart for undisclosed reasons.

Loomis had been a resident of Windsor, as had Allyn, so the decision to close the New York operations may have been influenced by the challenge of operating a store in another city or by the reluctance of one party to relocate there.

As for Anson Loomis, he opened a store in Windsor, selling dry goods, though he never achieved the same level of success as his former partner.

In 1830, the (Job) Allyn & (Michael) Marsh partnership

invited Timothy Mather Allyn, late of Allyn, Loomis & Co., to join their company. As a result, the firm was formally closed and reopened under a new business name.

NEW ARRANGEMENT.

ALLYN & MARSH have associated T. M. Allyn, of the firm of Allyn & Loomis, New-York, with them, for the purpose of establishing (in connexion with their present business) a Wholesale Dry Goods and Commission business, under the firm of ALLYN, MARSH & CO. Hartford, Jan. 1, 1830.

NOTICE.—In consequence of the above arrangement, all accounts with the late firm of Allyn & Marsh, must be closed, and all debts that are due at this time, must be paid by the 1st February next.

ALLYN, MARSH & CO.

Have just received from New-York a general assortment of

Staple and Fancy Foreign Piece

GOODS, which they offer at Wholesale, at the lowest New-York prices.

Goods retailed as usual.

Store Exchange Buildings, West Front.

Hartford, Jan. 1, 1830.   90

The partnership continued for another three years, until Marsh and Allyn went their separate ways. Marsh then partnered with John G. Litchfield to open a dry goods store in the capital city, operating under the name Marsh & Litchfield. The duo expanded on Marsh's previous business, adding groceries to the dry goods mix.[183]

Timothy and Job reformed their partnership in 1833 as

---

[183] Marsh & Litchfield would break their partnership in 1835.

T.M. & J. Allyn. They continued their dry goods business while adding jobbing and commission services to their product mix, all of which were provided from the same Hartford location as before.[184]

Seven years later, in 1840, Timothy bought his brother out of the business and continued the firm on his own at the same location.

Allyn continued in his business until he sold out in 1848, having amassed a fortune at the age of 48, which allowed him the luxury of pursuing other interests.[185]

Although Allyn was not schooled in the art of carpet-making, he was a very successful businessman and well-suited to take the reins of the Harford Carpet Company in 1854.

The only thing he couldn't control was the whims and fluctuations of the economy.

The Missouri Compromise of 1820 admitted Missouri into the Union as a slave state and Maine as a non-slave state at the same time, so as not to upset the balance between slave and free states in the nation. The law also outlawed slavery above the 36° 30' latitude line in the remainder of the Louisiana Territory, which had just been purchased

---

[184] A commission business is import/export whether carried on regionally, nationally, or internationally. Jobbing was where a company bought from manufacturers and sold to retailers.

[185] Allyn built the Allyn House in 1908 recognized as one of the city's premier hotels. He donated 100,000 dollars in 1875 (3MM in 2024) to build an industrial school for boys and girls in Hartford. He served as Hartford Mayor from 1858-60 and was a Director of the Connecticut Fire Insurance Company. He left an estate worth 2MM in 1882 (57MM in 2024).

from France.

This provision lasted for 34 years, until it was repealed by the Kansas-Nebraska Act of 1854, proposed by Stephen Douglas of Illinois.

The bill, originally known as the Nebraska bill, proposed organizing the Territory of Nebraska, which encompassed the present-day states of Kansas, Nebraska, Montana, South Dakota, and North Dakota.

The nation was driven to settle the Western territories, and a transcontinental railroad seemed the most appropriate method to move large numbers of people westward. The issue at hand, in the early 1850s, was where to lay the iron line. Douglas wanted a northern route, while a group of influential southern senators led by Missouri's David Atchison favored a southern route.

As these political discussions continued, President Franklin Pierce sent James Gadsden, the new U.S. Minister to Mexico, to renegotiate a border with the Mexican government that would provide a route for a southern railroad. The new treaty, known as the Gadsden Purchase, promised a $10MM payment to Mexico for 29,670 square miles of land south of the New Mexico Territory. It was then *game on* in the Senate.

In the end, the Senate voted at 5:00 a.m. to pass the legislation 37-14, and the proposal became law on May 30, 1854.

The Kansas-Nebraska Act effectively undid the Missouri Compromise, created two new territories, and allowed for popular sovereignty insofar as slavery.

The action effectively led to the creation of the new Republican Party and, in the process, contributed to the prelude to the Civil War.

The push to build the transcontinental railway, spurred

by the Kansas-Nebraska Act, fueled massive speculation in railroad securities as investors sought to cash in on the initiative.

The Free Banking Era created a disconnected banking system in which banks chartered *before the institution of free banking coexisted uneasily with private banks.*

In the summer of 1854, a discovery of fraud in the stock accounts of the New York and New Haven Railroad Company and the Harlem Railroad Company triggered a disturbance in the Stock Exchanges. Both companies had issued 50,000 shares of stock -- 20,000 shares above their legal limit. In addition, the Harlem Railroad Company was found to have issued 4,131 unauthorized shares of stock.

These over-issues amounted to $2,000,000 ($75 million in 2024) for the New York and New Haven Railroad Company and $276,000 ($10 million in 2024) for the Harlem Railroad Company.

> *The discovery of the above frauds created a universal panic that for a while threatened to break up the railroad system throughout the country.*

> *Stocks precipitately declined, and were unsaleable even at a mere nominal price; while those who had borrowed money upon railroad stocks or bonds, subject to the call of the lender, were required to make immediate payment. This twofold operation created much distress in every commercial community.*

> *The rapid decline in stocks ruined a great many whose chief investments were in this species of property; and the impossibility of borrowing upon these securities at any price, obliged all who were carrying any considerable amount to fail in their obligations, or obtain an extension*

from their creditors.[186]

Shortly thereafter, in September 1854, a banking panic broke out. The panic was geographically concentrated in the interior West and Northwest but reached as far east as New York and as far west as California.

A panic began in the interior, and especially in the West and Northwest.

In Ohio, Indiana, Illinois, Michigan, Wisconsin, Iowa and Missouri, and to some extent in the States on the south of the Ohio, a large circulation of bank notes, mostly of the free banks, had been obtained through expenditures for railroad purposes, and the general expansion of business.

When the contraction began, this circulation came in rapidly, and found the banks wholly unprepared to meet it. As the difficulty became known, the excitement increased, and every effort made for relief only heightened the panic.

All the banks that had balances at the East drew from them, and borrowed to the extent of their credit besides, while between twenty and thirty, perhaps more, of institutions which were really solvent, were compelled to suspend payment.

A large number of private bankers were carried down in the crash, and the distress became general.[187]

---

[186] "Commercial Chronicle and Review," Merchants' Magazine and Commercial Chronicle, Aug 1854, Pgs. 207-208.
[187] "Commercial Chronicle and Review," Merchants' Magazine and Commercial Chronicle, Dec 1854, Pgs. 716-717.

During the panic, banks in Ohio relied heavily on their correspondent banks in New York City, resulting in a decline in deposits. It was into this financial climate that the new Hartford Carpet Company began anew.

Allyn proved up to the task.

At the annual directors meeting of the Hartford Carpet Company held on January 12, 1855, the net earnings for the previous five and a half months were reported as over $12,000, or an eight percent return.

This speaks of first-rate management on the part of the officers of the company, during these hard times.[188]

It was, as they said in Scotland, 'Mony a mickle maks a muckle.'[189]

---

[188] The Connecticut Courant January 27, 1855. Pg 3.
[189] Roughly translated - If you look after the pennies then the pounds will look after themselves.

14: GOOD & EVIL, DARK & LIGHT

Though inextricably intertwined with the challenges and successes of the many iterations of the carpet company, this tale is about Thompsonville, its identity, and how successive waves of immigrants shaped it.

Not to be forgotten were the native characters and passersby who added their eccentricities to the village of émigrés.

In February of 1855, Reverand Dr. Joseph Harvey, pastor of the 'old school' Presbyterian Church of Thompsonville, did something unusual for a preacher. He accused a brother minister, Rev. Dr. Bennet Tyler of East Windsor, of

> *...preaching heretical, anti-scriptural and dangerous doctrines, opposed to the Westminister [sic Westminster] catechism, the Saybrook platform, and various other ancient and indisputable authorities which have long marked out and staked off the boundaries of safety and propriety in matters of religious belief.*[190]

---

[190] Litchfield Enquirer February 22, 1855. Pg 2.

Born in Middlebury, Connecticut, on July 10, 1783, Tyler was

> ...*a man of humble and sincere piety, and of a genial and sympathetic nature. In his theological opinions he did not embrace pure Calvinism, but as modified by Edwards and his school.*

> *He was in full sympathy with the traditional theology of New England, and was a straightforward controversialist, avoiding metaphysical speculations and verbal subtleties. In forming his system he began, not with mind, but with the Bible, and he looked for no advances in theology except such as come from a richer Christian experience.*[191]

The sermon that not only drew the attention of Dr. Harvey but also his ire was found in 2 Corinthians 8:12.

> *'For if there is a willing mind, it is accepted according to that a man hath, not according to that he hath not.'*

> *The doctrine of the ability or inability of the sinner to repent is the bone of contention between them. The Presbyterian thinks that 'it requires no strength for a man to fall down'. The Congregationalist contends that 'God does not require of men what they have no power to do.'*

> *This splitting of hairs by these divines is poor business. They would be much better employed in preaching the gospel to the poor.*[192]

The issue caused a great uproar in the gospel

---

[191] The Cyclopedia of Biblical, Theological, and Ecclesiastical Literature.

[192] Hartford Courant February 24, 1855. Pg 2.

community, to the extent that Ira Case, Minister of the Gospel, wrote an entire book on the subject and published it by the Dartmouth Press in April 1855.

Truly, a nerve had been struck in the clergy as to **whether Man was predisposed to sin** and **whether he had any control over doing so or in truly repenting**.

In Thompsonville, in the opinion of the right Reverand Harvey, it was clear that Man not only could repent but that he must – free will be damned.

Regardless of doctrinal spats, the flavors of religiousness continued to expand in the little village:

A Baptist Church was organized on January 13, 1858, with 17 members.

That same year, 100 or more residents joined the Methodist Church in just three months.

An Episcopal sect had been organized three years earlier, in 1855, and a church was constructed in 1860. That same year, a Roman Catholic church was built for the adherents of that branch of religion.

Certainly, by 1860, there was enough preaching to keep the residents aware that God was not only watching the people of Thompsonville but also had expectations of them.

David Frisbee Woodruff was born in Farmington, Connecticut, on September 10, 1800, to Eldad and Eunice (North) Woodruff. He was the second of six children, preceded only by his brother, Hiram, who was born four years earlier.

By 1829, Woodruff was embedded in Enfield, as he was added to the eligible voter rolls as an elector on April 6 of that year, along with eighteen others. William Dixon, Town

Clerk at that time, had the applicants recite an oath designed to complete the process, which may have reflected the *oath of fidelity* that used to be a requirement to segregate the *ne'er-do-wells* from upstanding citizens.

Two requirements for white men to vote were land ownership and payment of property taxes. David Woodruff must have met those requirements before the 1829 town meeting to be added as an *elector* in the town.

Woodruff was included in the 1830 census for Enfield, as was his wife, Emiline Allen, whom he had married in Farmington ten years earlier, further proving his residency.

Recreated 1836 Map of Thompsonville based on later maps of village and newspaper accounts

Although Woodruff's original land deed has yet to be recovered, all indicators point to his original home and place of business as they appear on the 1836 map.

In addition, 1846 and 1847 land deed records mention the sale of Thompsonville Carpet Company properties to Woodruff, using Woodruff's existing property lines on North Main Street and Main Street as borderlines for the transferred lots. This verifies his residency at that location before the land purchase.

Agents.   a25 WaS6mal3teow

The American Cooking Stove is manufactured with certain improvements secured by letters patent, under date of May 5, 1863, and December 5, 1865. One of these improvements covers the arrangement of fitting a portable ash pan in the hearth of a Cooking Stove, to receive the ashes as it passes down from the grate. All persons are cautioned against manufacturing, vending or using other Stoves made in *imitation* of the *American*, as suits have been commenced for infringement of these patents, and all persons manufacturing, selling or using said *imitations*, will be liable for damages for infringement on these letters patent.

SHEAR, PACKARD & CO.,
17 and 19 Green street,
Albany, N. Y.

The American is for sale by
DAVID WOODRUFF,
el3 WaS6m   Thompsonville, Conn.

American Women.—America is justly proud of his

Not only did Woodruff hand-construct articles, he seemed to represent/sell pre-manufactured products as indicated by this 1866 advertisement in the Springfield Republican.

By 1850, Woodruff's tin smithing business was a growing concern in the village, employing an average of thirty men manufacturing pans, pails, stove pipes, and roof tinning materials among other products during that period.

Unfortunately, most of the 1860 industry records for Enfield have been lost, so there is no data on how his business fared during that period.

By 1870, however, the company had contracted to an

average of four men employed—a stark reduction. The reduced workforce reflected increased competition in the industry and greater employment opportunities in the carpet manufacturing sector.

On February 18, 1856, late in the evening, the tin manufacturing establishment of David Woodruff on Main Street in Thompsonville erupted in flames, the cause of which was unknown. The fire raged for hours, consuming the entirety of Woodruff's manufactory, but not his home. Thankfully, it was insured, and the establishment was quickly rebuilt.

As indicated in the 1870 census, Woodruff's business had severely contracted, as the metal worker was seventy years old by that time. Yet, the tinsmith continued to run advertisements in local papers well into the summer of 1872, seeking peddlers for his wares, a clerk, and a bookkeeper for his business.

FOR SALE AT A BARGAIN—The fine two story mansion and the two fine stores of David Woodruff, Esq., with barns and sheds, all in fine order, situated on the main street, within three minutes walk of the depot, with about one acre of land, in the center of the flourishing village of Thompsonville, being the best and most desirable piece of property in the place. Terms easy. Apply to J. H. MILLER, Real Estate Broker, No. 251 Main street, Hartford; or DAVID WOODRUFF, on the premises. ap 16 1md

By May of 1873, though, old age accomplished what competition and fire could not – David Woodruff, a manufacturing mainstay in the village, almost from its inception, offered up his residence and business for sale *at a bargain*. He had mentored numerous people in the trade, who had gone on to either start their own enterprises or utilize their skills in the employment of others.

By July of that year, Thomas Mansley purchased Woodruff's store and began to make modifications to the building.

Mansley had been born in Halifax, England, on January 15, 1831, and emigrated to Thompsonville in 1857. Initially unable to find work in the village, he secured temporary work in Hartford as a marble polisher, a trade he had learned in his home country. Within a few years, he was offered a position at the carpet company as an apprentice dyer.

To better their station in life, Mansley's wife, Susan Noble, was hired on as a weaver at the Hartford Carpet Mill, manning a power loom, while Thomas peddled dry goods from house to house in the evenings. After five years of hard work, Thomas rented space at the corner of North Main and Main Streets, where he operated a dry goods store for 15 years.

Outgrowing that location, the Woodruff property became available, and Mansley purchased it, reconfiguring the building to better accommodate his dry goods business. Beyond acquiring Woodruff's land, Mansley purchased the entire North Main Street block of buildings from Main Street to Church Street, as well as seven other houses scattered around the village and an additional three tenements in Springfield, Massachusetts. By 1879, Mansley had added two stories to the block of buildings on North Main Street, increasing the rentable space by threefold.

In 1871, Mansley purchased the four-tenement dwelling house then known as *the hair factory* from John Young, adding to his collection of properties.

The hair factory building was erected by James Wallace, who relocated to Thompsonville in 1833 as an assistant to George Martin while setting up the original carpet manufactory for Andrews, Thompson & Company. After exiting the carpet business, Wallace partnered with others to open a general country provision store, and soon thereafter expanded into the butchering business.

During that same period, around 1844, Wallace branched into the manufacture of haircloth, hair mattresses, felt, and other hair-related products in a building he erected on Young Avenue, which became widely known as the *old hair factory*. When Wallace and his partners faced hard times, the property was auctioned off to John Young, signaling the end of horsehair product manufacturing in the village. Of interest is that, by 1880, the road leading from South Main Street to the Hartford Carpet Company's mills was locally referred to as the *Hair Factory Road*.

Further west, along the Connecticut River, in the November 11, 1859, issue of the Springfield Republican, an article reported that

> *...Charles Mathews & Co. of Thompsonville are erecting a large building to be used as a brewery. A 12-horsepower steam engine is to be used in the building, and the works will go into operation in a few weeks.*

The Connecticut Courant agreed in an article in their November 19 issue of that same year

> *...A brewery is being built in Thompsonville, by Messrs. Charles Matthewson & Co., for the purpose of brewing a superior kind of ale. The arrangements are for a large business, and the building is already completed, so that the operations may be commenced soon. A 12-horsepower steam engine will be employed in the works.*

One problem with the reports is that there was neither a Charles Mathews nor a Charles Matthewson living in Thompsonville at the time.

There was, though, a *John Matthewson*.

John Matthewson, born in Battle, England, on November 16, 1812, emigrated to the United States at Ellis Island aboard the Switzerland, arriving on September 1, 1845, soon after his marriage to Ann Turvey in Surrey, England, on July 21, 1845.

The pair made their way to Thompsonville, Matthewson securing a job as an overseer at the Hazard Powder Mill in nearby Hazardville. Although his previous experience is unknown, he may have worked at the Chilworth Gunpowder Mills on Blacksmith Lane in Surrey, England. The East India Company constructed mills along the Tillingbourne River in the 1600s. It was the sole legal producer of gunpowder for the King in England during the first half of the 17th century.

As Matthewson was hired on as an overseer upon his arrival,

it seems as if some previous experience in the powder-making process would have been a requirement.

By 1850, Mathewson and his wife already had three children, John Jr, Edwin, and Anne. By the time the brewery opened in 1860, the couple had added Albert (who died in his first year), Florence, and George. Their last son, Charles, would be born four years later in 1864.

Mathewson's original partner in the business was Daniel Gray[193], who had been born in Newport, Rhode Island, in 1805, and had moved to Enfield by 1835, before the birth of his only child, James Phillip, with his wife, Marcella Woodward Gray.

Gray was a successful and skilled carpenter with a personal estate valued at $15,000 in 1860 (~$570,000 in 2024), making him wealthy at the age of 55. By all accounts, Gray had no experience running a brewery, but neither did Mathewson. How the duo expected to be successful in brewing ales and porter beer is best left to speculation, but they succeeded together until 1872, when Gray withdrew from the business, returning to his carpentry roots at the age of 67. By that time, his worth had risen to $20,000 (~$760,000 in 2024).

Left to his own devices, Matthewson continued the business until he died in 1879.

The business lived on, managed by his estate, and continued to produce ale and porter until the formal assumption of the company by two of Matthewson's sons, Albert and George, who, in 1885, renamed the concern as Matthewson Brothers & Company. By that time, the primary business had expanded, and the production

---

[193] Sometimes spelled Grey

machinery had been updated. Based on the manufactory's location along a major river and its railroad access, two other wholesale businesses were added: coal and ice.

As the old Irish proverb goes:

There are more worlds than one, and in many ways they are unlike each other. But joy and sorrow, or, in other words, good and evil, are not absent in their degree from any of the worlds, for wherever there is life there is action, and action is but the expression of one or other of these qualities.[194]

It was the same in Thompsonville from 1860 to 1880. Good and Evil coexisted in a constant tug of war to see who might prevail and imprint itself on the identity of the village.

In 1857, years before the Civil War began, 22 slaves escaped from the South in barrels on a ship headed north, arriving safely at the Port of New York. Once there, the barrels were opened, and the former slaves headed north in smaller groups to evade capture.

Six of them —a mother and five children —made their way through Hartford and Thompsonville, with the good people of the village contributing $30 (~$1,200 in 2024) to help them make safe passage to Canada.

...they obtained funds enough to carry them as far as the Suspension Bridge [Niagara Falls].

They were a hard looking set, and appeared as if they had been barreled up thought the winter, but the children were bright, and will make the Canada woods ring one of these

---

[194] James Stephens, Irish Fairy Tales

days.[195]

The benevolence of the residents was demonstrated through their giving, many of whom were immigrants themselves and opposed to the concept of slavery. Here, then, was the good.

The following year, John Sullivan of Thompsonville was brought before Origen Seymour in the Superior Court of Hartford to face charges stemming from an assault with a razor on his wife, Catherine, with murder the intent of murder. Johnson claimed he was *bereft of reason* at the time and so was not responsible for the act. The jury agreed and sentenced Sullivan to be confined at the State Prison based on a finding of temporary insanity.

Released the following year, Sullivan returned to Thompsonville, where he attacked Patrick Wallaham[196], his wife Bridget, their two children, and, as noted in the report, *unnamed others* as well.

The arresting constable was also attacked, but Sullivan was finally taken in on seven charges of battery, charged $70, which he was unable to pay, and sentenced to thirty days in jail.

A seemingly light sentence based on multiple assaults.

Dennis Myers and his wife, both of Thompsonville, were each convicted of assault and battery in 1861, just five days before the Civil War broke out. On their way to jail, the wily Dennis escaped the officer, who had stopped to take his evening repast, and headed to Springfield, Massachusetts, leaving his wife behind.

---

[195] Connecticut Courant May 2, 1857. Pg 2.
[196] Misspelled as Wollahan in the Connecticut Courant October 22, 1859. Pg 2.

Finding a blacksmith shop in the city, he paid to have the shackles removed, which he summarily tossed into the nearby Connecticut River.

The woman was taken to jail, however, and if the odious husband will keep away the community around Thompsonville recommends commutation of his sentence.[197]

Seems as if the village was less enamored of the wife.

At that time, there was no permanent jail in Thompsonville to house miscreants. It seems as if the Town leased any available spaces for the temporary housing of criminals before they were sent to Hartford.

The selectmen of Enfield have rented the room formerly used as a barber's shop over the Market in Thompsonville. For a lock-up to accommodate criminals and traveling vagrants.[198]

Three hots and a cot didn't seem to be sufficient punishment for either Mr. Sullivan or Mrs. Myers, but such was justice as it was handed out in 1860.

Over the following years, evil deeds seemed to infect the little village, not the actions of Thompsonville residents, but those of visitors or passersby.

On the afternoon of November 2, 1866, a man and a woman passing through Thompsonville as they headed north came upon the Shakers. They attempted to talk them into taking an infant who was three weeks old, bundled, and traveling with them.

Surprisingly, the Shakers demurred, the couple leaving

---

[197] Connecticut Press April 6, 1861. Pg 1.
[198] Hartford Evening Post November 14, 1865. Pg 2.

with the baby.

The following morning, local huntsmen came upon the newborn, their hounds locating the child in a shallow hole, covered with leaves. The baby had marks about its head as if it had been stomped and left for dead, but the child had survived, and due to the goodwill and actions of the hunters, he was brought safely back to town.

The report concluded:

The miscreants are still at large.[199]

The following year, another tragic tale.

A young man from abroad, of good and favorable personal appearance, stopped at the Thompsonville Hotel last Tuesday. He proved to be a hotel burglar, and ransacked the chambers and stole from the trunk of the servant girl seven dollars. He was arrested, and confined in the lock-up, and duly tried and convicted.

His youthful and innocent looks and deportment elicited much sympathy, and then he seemed to be open to confession, and took moral lecture from the justice so gracefully, that the sentence was mild — seven dollars and thirty days in Hartford.

But when the constable went to his cell to take him to jail, the bird had flown. With a jack-knife he had cut his way out, where older reprobates had failed.

Somebody was sold.[200]

---

[199] Connecticut Courant November 10, 1866. Pg. 2.
[200] Connecticut Courant February 2, 1867. Pg. 1.

At times, some activities were due to a wee bit of the drink and less malicious than others.

The fourth passed off quietly at Thompsonville, no special demonstrations being made. Two ladies of the Hibernian persuasion[201] got too independent, and a chivalrous constable caught them and made the court happy in mending the breach of the law with a fine of $1 and costs.

A more general row and fight occurred at the Globe Hotel, but no officer was around, and no arrests were made.[202]

Some evil brought upon the village was baser.

Frances Haythorn, the 15-year-old intellectually compromised daughter of Joseph Haythorn, overseer of the carding department at the Thompsonville Stockinet factory, was reported missing on Sunday, August 9, 1868, and was found wandering the streets of Bristol the following Tuesday, disheveled and forlorn.

Albert Potter, of Warehouse Point, just to the south of Thompsonville, was arrested and charged with her abduction, as well as other crimes.

The offense charged is enticing a female underage from her parent or guardian, with the intent to seduce or commit fornication, and the penalty is a fine of not more than $1,000, and imprisonment not longer than one year, or both.

There was intense excitement in Thompsonville, and a crowd of more than one thousand gathered about the court, though few could hear, and the girl's testimony was taken

---

[201] The Ancient Order of Hibernians (AOH) is an Irish Catholic fraternal organization – so in this case Irish lassies
[202] Connecticut Courant June 132, 1867. Pg. 1.

at her father's house. Mr. Haythorne is a citizen of excellent character, and much respected. The daughter, Frances, fifteen years old, is of rather feeble and simple mind and defective memory. Potter is about twenty-two years old, a joiner and carpenter by trade, and rumors of previous affairs have damaged his reputation for virtue.

The newspaper report recounted specifics of the assault, how the young man had first met the young girl and had driven her around in his buggy.

Returning towards Thompsonville, he left the main road and drove into a piece of woods, where, under his persuasion and commands, the simple girl submitted to the scoundrel's purposes.

He took her to Freshwater Bridge, near Thompsonville, and left her.

She walked down Enfield Road and was overtaken by a stranger who said he was a baker. He took her to East Hartford, outraging her person on the way, and lodged her either in Hartford or East Hartford, at what her description is probably a house of ill-fame.

Monday morning, she wandered about Hartford desiring to go home. She took the railroad track and walked in the wrong direction, on through New Britain, reaching Plainville at night.

Another stranger overtook and accompanied her, and for a third time, she was the victim. About daylight Tuesday morning she entered Bristol in his company.

It was there that the 'couple' ran into someone who recognized the young girl, chased away the offending party, and returned the girl to Thompsonville.

Medical testimony was not called, but physicians were

ready to testify that she had been most infamously treated.
It is enough to convert one to the most ultra doctrines of
depravity.[203]

As if one assault wasn't enough.

Was the success of the village, the good and forgiving hearts of the residents, somehow inviting the less moral to prey upon Thompsonville?

The Presbyterian, Episcopalian, Catholic, and Methodist Churches in the village created an oasis of God-fearing people who, in turn, built supportive neighborhoods of residents who respected not only each other but those merchants and employers who brought services and jobs into the village.

Residents saw prosperity.

Outsiders saw opportunity.

On June 16, 1870, two burglars broke into the store of Morrison & Reynolds by prying open the front door with a crowbar. They then set upon the safe, blowing it open with a powder charge and removing a large cache of money and important documents.

An attentive local woman, who was attending to a sick neighbor, heard the activity and notified an officer, who assembled a group of like-minded citizens to intervene, but the criminals had already made off toward Springfield.

Pursuing the pair, the Thompsonville faithful caught up to them along the train tracks in the city, and shots were exchanged. The duo split but were captured and returned to Hartford, where James Willis and George Warner, both out-

---

[203] Connecticut Courant August 15, 1868. Pg 4.

of-towners, were sentenced to four years in the State Prison.

The following month, Benjamin Bright's meat market in the small village was burglarized, although only a small amount of money was taken. Bright offered a $100 reward for the capture and conviction of the thief or thieves.

They were never found.

If nothing else, Thompsonville remained resilient, hopeful, and optimistic as if the evil actions of others held no sway over them.

As 1870 ended, Robert McCrone, the market gardener of the village, began the erection of one of the largest greenhouses in the country within the borders of Thompsonville. McCrone had purchased the massive greenhouse of the Miller Brothers, located in Sunderland, Massachusetts, and had contracted to have it moved south, by rail, to the Connecticut village. He would expand operations, hiring an additional seven employees to cultivate vegetables throughout the winter months over the next decade.

Still, the carpet company was the engine that powered the village, and the organization's fate was buoyed by a determination of the Commissioner of the United States Patent Office, William Bishop, in February of 1860.

The power loom patent held by Erastus Bigelow had expired. All arguments put forward by the inventor to extend patent protection were set aside, and the management at the Hartford Carpet Company could only rejoice.

Since the restart of the Thompsonville mills in 1854, the company had paid $25,000 per year in royalties to license the technology. As the power looms in Tariffville were about to restart, the company would be facing additional costs there as well.

By not extending the Bigelow patent, the Hartford Carpet Company would save approximately $300,000 in licensing payments over the next five years for the equipment in Thompsonville and Tariffville.

What to do with the windfall?

Perhaps it was time to help shine some light on the village to deny scoundrels protection from the dark.[204]

The Springfield Gas Light Company was incorporated in 1848, with a capitalization of $500,000.

The Springfield Gas Company, also known as the Gasworks, was initially located on the banks of the Connecticut River. The massive building had four gigantic smokestacks, and when it was in operation, the belching smoke emitted a foul odor.

Springfield had followed other towns like New Haven,

---

[204] The Influence of Street Lighting on Crime and Fear of Crime.

Hartford, and Bridgeport, which had opened private manufactured gas companies before 1850. Long before methane, ethane, butane, and propane were produced, gas was **manufactured** in plants using heated, anaerobic vessels called retorts[205]. These units would usually source coal, which would be carbonized (super-heated but not burned), yielding volatile gases. These gases would then be collected, cooled, and purified, yielding solids (coke), liquids such as coal tar and/or water, and gases. These gases would be piped to homes for cooking and lighting, and piped to streets to light walkways and roads.

The treasurer of the Springfield Gas Light Company was George Dwight, who had partnered with his brother-in-law, Homer Foot, in running the Dwight family mercantile business in Massachusetts, founded by George's father around 1800. The partnership was cross-bound as George had married Homer's sister Mary Skinner Foot, and Homer had married George's sister Delia Dwight.

By January 29, 1849, the Springfield Republican reported:

> *The first Gas Street Light in Springfield has been located on the south corner of State and Main Streets. It began its philanthropic efforts on Friday evening [January 26], and diffused its brilliant light, like a patient star, through the live-long night.*

In 1852, Dwight was selected by the Town of Springfield to petition the state to declare the municipality a city. The appeal was granted on May 25 of that same year, and the former town was anointed as a city. By 1853, Dwight had been elected to the State Senate representing Springfield.

On February 1, 1854, an announcement in the

---

[205] Retorts are closed ovens used to produce manufactured gas by heating coal to drive off volatile gases.

Springfield Republican reported the notice of an alliance between George Dwight, Nathaniel Treadwell, and Henry Chapin where the three had formed a co-partnership under the name Chapin, Treadwell & Company to design and erect coal gas works and to lay the requisite delivery infrastructures as well as provide the pipe, fitting, and fixtures for the same.

Who originally contracted with the firm to *gasify* Thompsonville is unknown, but the Republican noted in an article in the September 21, 1854, issue that:

Messrs Chapin, Treadwell & Company of this city have just finished, and set in operation, gas works in Thompsonville, CT., which, including the carpet factory and other mills there, with the stores, already supply about 200 lights.

The article noted that the same company had nearly completed a similar gas works project in Milford, Massachusetts, in Worcester County, and had received a contract to build another gas works in Norwich, Connecticut.

Months before, in May of 1854, Wait Hawley, William Osgood, Horace King, Manning Wheelock, and James Nichols had incorporated the Thompsonville Gas Light Company to manufacture and sell gas, to be made from rosin, coal, oil, and other materials, to furnish gas to the town of Enfield to light streets, stores, and other facilities.

The Thompsonville Gas Light Company, initially capitalized at $20,000, was empowered to:

…lay down their gas pipes, and to erect gas posts, burners, and reflectors in the streets, alleys, lanes, avenues, or public grounds, of the said town of Enfield, and to change and alter the same from time to time, as occasion

might require, and to do all things necessary to light said
town and the dwellings, stores, and other places situated
therein.[206]

On September 20, 1854, the Thompsonville Gas Light
Company purchased the entirety of the gas generation and
delivery infrastructure, already deployed in Thompsonville,
from Chapin, Treadwell & Company [with George
Dwight[207] representing the '& Company'].

The sale included:

Buildings Generating Apparatus, Gasometer and Tank.
Street mains, Service pipes, meters, tools, fixtures, and all
the apparatus and appurtenances connected with said gas
works.[208]

Almost one year later to the day, Homer Foot, Dwight's
brother-in-law and former work partner[209], acting as a
representative of George Dwight and Henry Chapin,
entered into a strangely constructed agreement to
repurchase the Gas Works from the Thompsonville Gas
Light Company. The reason the company agreed to the
terms of the pseudo-sale document remains unclear, as the
Gas Works had been in operation for only 12 months.

Foot had, according to the agreement, essentially
promised to buy back the works for $10,000 in cash and
$10,000 in bonds[210] floated to the Thompsonville Gas Light
Company. If the bonds were repaid by August 1, 1860, then
the repurchase of the factory would be null and void, and
Foot, Chapin, and Dwight would relinquish their promise

---

[206] Special Acts & Resolutions: May Session, 1854

[207] Dwight signed the property transfer papers along with
Chapin and Treadwell.

[208] Land Records Thompsonville 1854.

[209] Dwight left his mercantile partnership with Foot in 1854.

[210] Basically, a short-term loan at 6% interest.

to purchase, with the works reverting in toto to the Gas Light Company. If, though, any of the semi-annual interest payments due each February and August were missed, or the bonds not repaid by the due date, then Foot, Chapin, and Dwight would have the right to auction off the assets of the company to recover their losses, with any overage from the sale beyond the losses remitted back to the Thompsonville Gas Light Company board.

Until the bond due date, the Gas Light Company retained oversight of the operations.

The document was signed by George Dwight and Henry Chapin and recorded on September 19, 1855.

Two years later, the Chapin, Treadwell & Company was dissolved, with George Dwight[211] identified to settle the final affairs of the organization. Dwight was authorized to continue the business as a sole proprietor as well as use the company name in any future business dealings.

> COPARTNERSHIP NOTICE. — The undersigned have this day formed a copartnership under the style of *DIMMOCK, DWIGHT & CO.* The business to be conducted by said firm being Gas Engineering and contracting for the Erection of Gas Works.
> Offices, No. 135 William st., New York.
> "   "   2 Elm st., Springfield.
> GEO. M. DIMMOCK, Springfield.
> GEO. DWIGHT, JR.,   "
> WILLIAM L. SCHOENER & CO., New York.
> GEO. DWIGHT,
> H. A. CHAPIN.
> Springfield, Dec. 31, 1859.   j10 6d

---

[211] George Dwight remained as the treasurer of the Springfield Gas Light Company, which was interesting as he would have influenced expansion contracts for the gas distribution for the city and most likely award the contracts to himself.

Right on the heels of that announcement came the sale of the firm to George Dimmock, who purchased the entire steam and gas fitting business from George Dwight, with Dimmock taking over the same space that Chapin, Treadwell & Company [thereafter Dwight] had occupied.

At the end of 1859, right before the bond payment from the Thompsonville Gas Light Company was scheduled to be made to Homer Foot, as the representative for George Dwight and Henry Chapin, an announcement of a partnership between Dimmock, Dwight, Chapin, and others appeared in the Springfield Republican.

But something happened on or before August 1, 1860.

The record may be elusive, but the results are not.

Auction Sales.

AUCTION SALE — THOMPSONVILLE GAS WORKS.—The undersigned will sell at public auction, by order of the Court of Probate for the district of Bridgeport, Ct., on Tuesday, the twenty-third day of February, 1864, at eleven o'clock a. m., unless previously disposed of at private sale, "The Thompsonville Gas Works," situated at Thompsonville, Ct., in complete running order, including all street mains, meters and fixtures. Said works are capable of producing, storing and distributing about 15,000 cubic feet of Gas per day, and are now in successful operation.

For further particulars inquire of C. Briscoe, Esq., Thompsonville, James E. McIntire, Esq., at Springfield, Mass., Ira W. Ford, at Hartford, Conn., or of the undersigned at Bridgeport, Conn.

W. H. PERRY,
R. T. CLARKE,   } Trustees.
JAMES WILSON,

Bridgeport, Feb. 13, 1864.   f 16 6d

Either the principal repayment on the Foot loan *or* the interest payment on the same was defaulted on by the Thompsonville Gas Light Company, inviting either Homer Foot, George Dwight, Henry Chapin, or the newly formed

Dimmock, Dwight & Company to enforce the loan/purchase agreement from 1855, thereby setting in motion the sale of the gas works by auction.

Dimmock retired from Dimmock, Dwight & Company on March 1, 1861, so his role in enforcing or benefiting from the 1855 agreement is suspect, as the firm continued without him as George Dwight & Company.

And, for whatever reason, the auction of the gas works business, conducted by the auctioneering agency of Ford & Levett, located at 9 Central Row, Hartford, took place *four years after* the expiry of the 1855 agreement.

If the auction sale was successful, there seems to be no record of any transaction by the auctioneers in 1864. Four years later, though, on September 15, 1868, an article appeared in the Springfield Republican announcing the sale of the Thompsonville Gas Works to the Hartford Carpet Company, on whose property the works were located, and with whom Chapin, Treadwell & Company had signed a land agreement to lease the property for 12 years in 1854.

George Dwight, the agent for William Dwight, facilitated the sale[212], which indicates that Dwight, either George or William, had purchased the property at auction or had assumed ownership through other legal means.

In any event, by 1868, the Hartford Carpet Company was involved in the gas generation and lighting business, not only for itself but also for as many residents and businesses that had been connected to the service through its delivery infrastructure.

Owning the operation helped Hartford Carpet's bottom line by lowering its fuel costs, but it also presented additional management and maintenance challenges.

---

[212] It is unclear the connection between George Dwight and William Dwight. It could be a mistake in reporting.

And perhaps it suggested a new tagline for the carpet manufacturer—The Hartford Carpet Company—we'll keep a light on for you…[213]

The remaining question, though, was - why did the mill purchase the gas works?

What was the motivation?

The answer was rooted 11 miles southwest of Thompsonville, in the village of Tariffville.

---

[213] Apologies to Tom Bodett and Motel 6.

15: SHADOWS OF FUTURE SUFFERING

At the start of the 1860 presidential campaign, a handful of fired-up young Northerners appeared as bodyguards to defend anti-slavery stump speakers from frequent attacks. The group called themselves the Wide Awakes.

Soon, hundreds of thousands of young White and Black men and women, working-class Americans in their twenties, were organizing torch-bearing, uniformed brigades of their own to push back against slavery.

Within a year, the nation would be at war with itself, and many on both sides would point to the Wide Awakes as the mechanism that got them there.

In Thompsonville Hon. Dwight Loomis spoke to a crowded house, and at the fine collation afterward, Messrs. Thompson and McCrone were called out. The Wide Awakes were all out, and a most cheerful fact was the presence of 40 well-organized and uniformed Wide Awakes from that shockingly sham democratic town, Windsor Locks.[214]

---

[214] Connecticut Press, September 22, 1860. Pg 2.

In November of 1860, at a closing ceremony of the national campaign held in Hartford, Connecticut, a massive procession wound through the capital city, including four divisions of Wide Awakes from all over the state and even Rhode Island.

CITY INTELLIGENCE.

The Closing Scene of the Campaign!

THE REPUBLICAN JUBILATION!

A GRAND DISPLAY!

Extensive Illumination!

Fireworks, Music, Speeches!

A BIG THING!

EVERYBODY COULD SEE IT!

LINCOLN & HAMLIN.

The Glorious Wide-Awakes!

A group of 40 men from Enfield and Thompsonville, led by Captain Jabez King, carried banners inscribed with the statements *We Vote For Honest Men* and *Old Abe Splits Rails But Not Parties.*

Abolition was alive and well in Thompsonville.

Indeed, there were benefits to having the New Haven-

Hartford-Springfield Railroad run alongside the Connecticut River in Thompsonville, but it also posed potential hazards to people and property.

On Sunday, December 26th, the day after Christmas, the night train from Springfield sliced an **_unnamed Irishman_** in two as it passed southward through the town.

He was killed instantly.[215]

At least the Connecticut Courant on September 21, 1861, included the name of the individual killed on the railway. Matthew McCrone, additionally identified as a Scotsman, was run over by the express train at eight o'clock in the evening, dying immediately.

At the time, the railway along the riverside in Thompsonville was not elevated where Main Street terminated, making crossing the tracks a _dicey_ proposition, whether one was on foot or in a carriage.

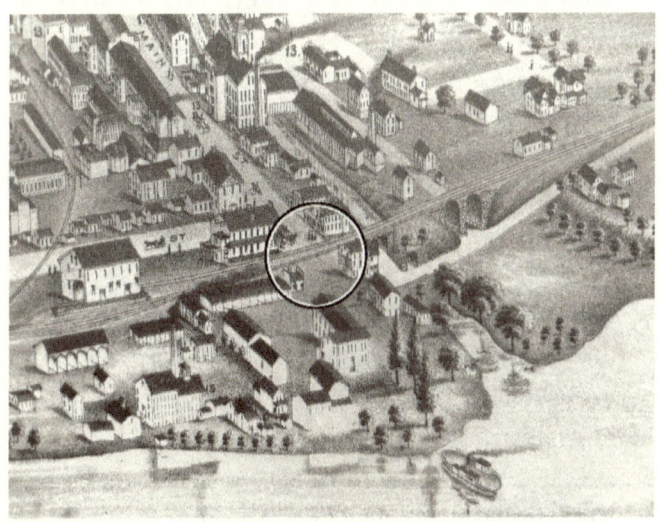

---

[215] Springfield Republican December 28. Pg 4.

The railway **was** elevated farther south, but not from the west end of Main Street to Lovejoy's Ferry or northward along Scotch Row. This provided easy access to the multiple tracks as they headed north/south past the Carpet Factory, on the east side, and the Globe Hotel, Mathewson Distillery, and tenement housing on the west side.

Without the benefit of a crossing gate, deaths continued.[216]

On February 8, 1864, the Hartford Courant reported:

The afternoon freight train from this city [Hartford], Saturday, ran over a little son, aged three years, of Mr. Smithson, at Thompsonville.

He was playing on the track, when the train came suddenly upon him and crushed his head in such a manner that he survived but a few moments.

Twelve days later, reporting on February 20, 1864, the paper picked up the thread again:

Within a few years, nine persons have been killed and two injured by the cars at and near the Thompsonville depot.

It wasn't just the lives of residents that were being taken, but property was being destroyed as well.

A nursery of young trees, valued at three hundred dollars, in Thompsonville, owned by Robert McCrone, was destroyed by fire recently, caused by a spark from a locomotive.[217]

---

[216] In fact, the first U.S. patent for a railroad crossing gate wasn't awarded until 1867, and even then the crossing gates were operated manually with a crank mechanism.
[217] Hartford Courant April 13, 1864. Pg. 2.

That same month -

The barns of Benjamin Bright in Thompsonville, near the railroad track, were destroyed by fire last night (Sunday) evening – supposed to have caught from a locomotive spark.

Several buildings nearby caught fire, and were only saved by great exertions. The loss of Mr. Bright is about $2,000 – insured $900.

Mr. Steiger[218], a butcher, occupied one of the barns. Five beeves[219], slaughtered and ready for market, five live fat hogs and a lot of hides, etc. were burned up. His loss is about $1,500 – no insurance.[220]

The Hartford Daily Courant reported the Thompsonville fire could be seen from the capital city.

accounts of their predecessors.

The Hartford and New Haven railroad has just been compelled by the Connecticut courts to pay to Benjamin Bright $3700 for the destruction of his barn at Thompsonville, some three years ago, by a spark from one of their engines. Heretofore, this company has always settled such claims by gift, not admitting a legal obligation, but from a sense of justice. This is the first case of the kind ever tried in Connecticut, and establishes an important precedent.

Unlike others, Bright brought suit against the Hartford and New Haven Railroad for his losses, winning a judgment of $3,700 against the company. Bright's case set a legal

---

[218] George Steiger worked a slaughterhouse in a Bright owned barn alongside the railroad tracks.
[219] Plural for beef
[220] Litchfield Enquirer April 21, 1864. Pg 2.

precedent at that time.

The railroad appealed the verdict to the State Supreme Court, but the court refused to hear the case, thereby assuring Bright's win.

Beyond accidents and fires there was one other curious class of injuries associated with the railroads in Thompsonville – people leaping from moving trains.

Three of these incidents occurred in 1864.

Two Irishmen belonging in Thompsonville, made an attempt to get off the express rain from New York to Boston, at Warehouse Point, Tuesday evening. One jumped off just before reaching the station, on an embankment, and losing his equilibrium, was precipitated to the bottom, some forty feet, touching terra firma only at long intervals.

The other attempted to jump on the platform, but was caught between the car and platform and rolled along the length of a car. Mr. J. T. Hass, depot agent, instantly caught him, and threw him on to the platform.

But for this timely assistance he must have fallen on the track and been killed. As it was, he received severe bruises.[221]

You'd think they could have waited until the train pulled into the station. Their efforts weren't unique.

As the midnight train from Boston last night passed through Thompsonville, a man was seen by several passengers to jump from a car and strike upon his head. The train, which was going at full speed at the time, was

---

[221] Hartford Daily Courant February 19, 1864. Pg 2.

stopped as quickly as possible and backed to where the man lay.

He was taken up insensible and brought to this city [Hartford]. Doctor Jackson was called and examined the wounds, finding the man's skull broken in the back part of his head, a terrible gash having been made, so that the brains ran out.

From letters found in the pockets of the victim it was learned that his name was James Colleran and that he lived in Thompsonville. One letter from his father in the old country cautioned him against using liquor now that he was married.

It was probable that he had been drinking or he would not have committed such a reckless act.[222]

He should have heeded his father's advice.

At other times, there was an apparent reason for leaping from a moving train, as was recorded in the Litchfield Enquirer on September 14, 1865, where a prisoner from Thompsonville, on his way to a Hartford jail cell, leaped from the saloon window[223] as the car passed Windsor at about 30 miles per hour. The report failed to mention whether the criminal survived, but at least the reason for exiting the train was clear and valid.

By 1868, it seemed as if some individuals in Thompsonville had it in their minds to turn the tables on the railway, as the December 21 edition of the Springfield Republican reported:

---

[222] Hartford Daily Courant July 16, 1864. Pg 2.

[223] A saloon window is a window on a metro saloon car, which is a type of railway car for sleeping, dining, or parlor.

Additional villainy appeared Friday night, obstructions being discovered on the railroad, consisting of a wooden fence rail and an old iron rail from the track, placed so as to make terrible destruction for the train which should strike them.

Thankfully, four fires (if one could truly be thankful for fires), which had been set throughout the village earlier that evening, had caused the discovery of the obstructions, and they were removed without any damage.

Although the railroad had been saved, the fires had impacted buildings and livelihoods all over Thompsonville.

The first fire was discovered in the barn owned by the Hartford Carpet Company in the northern part of the village, where the teams of working horses were kept. That fire was quickly put out.

The second occurred at two in the morning in Henry Thompson's barn, which quickly spread to a woodshed and Thompson's dwelling, then jumped to engulf James Cooper's wood residence. The firemen saved Thompson's home but not Cooper's.

Soon afterward, at six in the morning, the store of F. E. Ely was ablaze but soon extinguished.

The final assault was a fire set in the barn of Richard Conroy's widow, destroying the structure.

Constable J. P. Davis claimed that all efforts would be made to locate the firebug, but that never seemed to occur, and the arsonist, having had his fill, reached a sort of détente with both the good people of Thompsonville and the New York and New Haven Railroad.

But fires would still shape the village.

On January 16, 1864, building Number Three at the

Hartford Carpet Company mills in Thompsonville went up in flames. The brick building, two stories high, 80 feet long, and 30 feet wide, had been used for wool spinning and carding. The fire spread so quickly that several employees were forced to leap from the second floor to the ground, a distance of about 40 feet, to escape.

Three employees, Andrew Sloan, Timothy Sullivan, and Charles Young, were among the more severely hurt, with Sullivan injuring his head and shoulders, and Sullivan breaking his ankle.

Although the monetary loss to the company was approximately $33,000, with only $13,000 covered by insurance, the financial markets seemed unconcerned, as Hartford stock rose from $177 to $180 per share.

The company presented the Springfield department with a monetary gift of $100 (~$4,000 in 2024) for their assistance in fighting the inferno. Unreported was the company's gesture of thanks to the local firefighters.

Three years later, on June 14, 1867, at 6:45 in the morning, a fire erupted in the picker room of the one-story, 100-foot-long by 40-foot-wide wool spinning and carding brick building at the carpet mill in Tariffville, Connecticut. Reminiscent of the fire that occurred three years earlier in Thompsonville, this one differed in that the building was full of both lint and oil, which helped fuel the blaze.

The chief force pump[224] was in this building, and on account of the spread of the fire was soon rendered useless.

---

[224] The force pump was originally developed by Ctesibius, a Greek inventor and mathematician living in Alexandria, Egypt. It used TWO cylinders that alternated their up-and-down movement, meaning the transport of water was continuous.

Power loom brick mill, two stories, 230 by 80

Carding and spinning mill, three stories and basement of brick, 100 by 40.

Carding mill, three stories and basement, of stone, 100 by 40.

Worsted spinning mill, four stories of brick, 150 by 40.

Wool room, basement and two stories of wood, 100 by 40.

Several dye houses and store houses, cheaper low, wooden buildings.

The Old Tavern, wooden, three stories, about 60 by 85, used as a boarding house.

Engine house with drying rooms above, three stories, 150 by 40.

Self-acting "jack" mill, two stories, of wood, 150 by 40.

Machine shop, two stories; carpenter shop above, and blacksmith shop adjoining.

The large picker room, a two story wooden building, 40 by 60.

Store room, two stories, 40 by 60.

Five tenement buildings near the Old Tavern.

A store, brick foundation, with four tenements above, about 25 by 40.

Another store about 25 by 70, occupied up stairs as a Methodist chapel. Also four other tenement houses containing fourteen tenements and one other similar building badly damaged.

A water pipe connecting with the second force pump was severed so that, too, was rendered useless. A smaller force pump worked by the donkey engines[225] was not of sufficient power to overcome the fire, which soon spread to the power loom mill, a large building 220 feet by 80. This too was soon completely in a blaze, and the fire commenced catching in the buildings adjoining.

---

[225] A steam donkey or donkey engine is a steam-powered winch style engine. Named "donkey" as these engines replaced horses as a power source.

The buildings were dry, and contained much flammable material, and the wind blowing in gusts fanned the flames to a terrible fierceness. There was no fire engine near, and no telegraph office in the village.[226]

The article listed the number of carpet company-owned buildings and the property destroyed in the fire. Private buildings lost included a four-apartment tenement and a joiner's shop owned by Edward Pease.

At the time, fire engines were horse-drawn, typically traveling at speeds of four to twelve miles per hour, which made their ability to respond to a crisis questionable. If this scenario didn't underscore the need for local fire departments, then nothing would.

Unfortunately, it was too late for Tariffville.

The village then found itself in a situation similar to that of 1851, sixteen years earlier, when the mill shut down due to economic problems.

By the burning of the dwelling houses, thirty families were deprived of homes, and much of their furniture either lost or broken. By the burning of the mills, about 650 hands are thrown out of employment, and probably three times as many deprived of their ordinary means of support. The village was built up just about the mills, and depended for its support chiefly on them.

The aspect of the unfortunate village yesterday at noon was very striking.

Crowds of men and women and children filled the streets, some of whom had been burned out of house and home,

---

[226] Connecticut Courant June 15, 1867. Pg 3.

and nearly all of whom now saw their sole means of livelihood suddenly destroyed.

As the spectator walked along, he could hear, now in the shrill tones of provincial English, now in the shrill accents of Irish dialect, words of complaint and despair from women who already felt the shadows of future suffering and anxiety resting upon their hearts.[227]

The losses in terms of human pain were incalculable, but in terms of company property, losses were estimated at $900,000 to $1 million, with only $332,000 covered by insurance. The coverage could have been almost $100,000 more, as the buildings had been readjusted only a few months earlier, but the president of the Tariffville operations had refused to pay the premium increase.

Rebuilding was speculated on, and the benefits of doing so were discussed, but ultimately the idea was rejected.

As if the people of Tariffville had not suffered enough, the Hartford Courant followed up with an article calling the actions of the village residents into question.

A few of the villagers worked willingly [in support of the fire departments battling the blazes], but as a general thing they were indifferent and unwilling to work, and nearly every one seemed discouraged, and thought the fire could not be stayed.

Some of the buildings might have been saved by proper efforts on the part of the villagers, by the use of fire buckets. If the brussels carpet building had not been saved undoubtedly the fire would have extended across the street and swept off the entire village.[228]

---

[227] Connecticut Courant June 15, 1867. Pg 3.
[228] Hartford courant June12, 1867. Pg 8.

How dare the residents succumb to the shock of the moment and all that it meant, and how easy it was for the reporter to criticize the good people of Tariffville from the comfort and security of his workplace, far removed from the horror of the event.

Two months later, the iron from the remains of the carpet site was sold to S. T. Hammond & Company, junk dealers from Springfield, Massachusetts.

At least someone profited.

But what had prompted the fire?

Months before, on the evening of January 3, 1867, there had been a meeting of factory workers at Tunxis Hall in Tariffville, where Dr. Isaac Harrington spoke to workers on the labor initiative called the *Ten-Hour Movement*[229].

Four Resolutions followed the opening statement on which the labor document was constructed, which read:

Whereas. *It is enacted law of this State that ten hours constitute a day's work, yet the same is openly and systematically violated by the woolen, cotton, and other mills of this state, running their mills and working women and little children from 8 to 9 years of age, eleven hours per day, therefore —*[230]

The resolutions supported the idea that the state should enforce the ten-hour workday rule, elect only men who would work to write laws supporting workers, workers would only support politicians working on their behalf, and that disparate and disconnected *Ten Hour League* groups

---

[229] A movement to reduce work hours from eleven to a ten-hour workday.

[230] Hartford Courant January 8, 1897. Pg 8.

within the state should work together to

> ...*[select] candidates for the legislature, and other important positions, whose past lives and sacrifices in behalf of labor, will be a guarantee of their future integrity. Such men are to be found in the rank of labor, and should be pushed forward and sustained by the toiling masses, where they would simply display those dormant talents for legislation, which have only been too much engrossed in designing and executing those monuments of our industry and skill that adorn and are the pride of this our common country.*[231]

Was the labor threat of the Ten Hour League enough to incite someone to take incendiary action against the Tariffville carpet business? It would seem an extreme response to this type of labor unrest.

Before the 1867 Tariffville meeting, mill workers from both Thompsonville and Tariffville had petitioned management in November 1866 for a reduction in labor hours from eleven to ten, reflecting the actions of other workers in other fields in Connecticut.[232]

The Labor Question

The operatives in Thompsonville organized a Ten Hour League, with Elder A. Sloan, president, and Alexander Richmond, Esq., secretary. The character of its officers are a guarantee that it is conservative in purpose and considerate in action.

A large and enthusiastic meeting was held last Tuesday evening, and was addressed by a gentleman called Dr. Harrington. His lecture has been variously criticized, but

---

[231] Ibid
[232] Litchfield Enquirer November 15, 1866. Pg 2.

generally commended.

Whoever is conversant with the labor of operatives cannot fail to appreciate their designs in lessening the hours of employment. Ten hours labor in the present carpet work is more exhausting than were twelve hours on the hand loom. Then the weaver could stop his shuttle at will. Now he is compelled to keep step to the motion of the engine almost aa unceasingly as the belt runs upon its accustomed pully [sic pulley].

Ten hours of such confinement and labor is enough for the physical man, while it does not furnish any too much spare time for the proper culture of the intellectual and moral man.[233]

Clearly the concerns of the Thompsonville workers reflected those of the Tariffville workers, insofar as a general desire to spend less time at work and more time with their families as well as pursuing other wholesome activities. The labor interests of both mills predated the Tariffville fire, indicating the fire was most likely just an unfortunate event and not some extreme response to quell a labor uprising.

In fact, the Thompsonville operatives were even more committed to the labor movement than their counterparts to the south in pushing the ten-hour agenda. By January 1867, Thompsonville had established not only a branch of the Ten Hour League but also a regular meeting schedule and elected officers.

At the January 31, 1867, meeting in the Enfield village, congratulatory letters were read from all over New England, and a list of resolutions was passed, one of which encouraged the involvement of local clergy in pushing

---

[233] Hartford Courant December 22, 1866. Pg 4.

forward the labor-sensitive agenda.

Surprisingly, given the previous iteration of the company's willingness to establish evening schools to educate the Tread Boys in the early days of the carpet mill, there was no such initiative during this period to address the workers' concerns.

> *They know full well that labor is and must be a matter of an agreement, and the most that legislation can do is to prevent the capitalist from taking advantage of their necessities and rendering their labor oppressive, even to servitude. The employment of children, without regard to age, in utter disregard of their educational condition, and in open violation of our school laws, and compelling them to work as unceasingly as the adults – this is not labor – it is a servitude but little less than slavery.*

> *The great tendency of corporations is, to give little heed or care to the moral, physical, and education condition of those dependent upon them for labor. It is thus that they prolong the hours of labor, allow the children to enter the workshop and subject them to unceasing toil, and take the privilege of making rules to which the laborer must assent or leave, according to his necessity or choice.*[234]

In these labor actions and newspaper reports, we hear the echoes of Karl Marx and Frederick Engels, who had written and published their Communist Manifesto in 1848, which exposed the challenges between the *bourgeois* and *proletariat* classes.

Even more so though, the underlying themes of the Ten-Hour Movement recalled the British Ten Hour's Bill which was enacted in 1847 and summarily rejected by the British government in 1850. In an article written by

---

[234] Hartford Courant February 5, 1867. Pg 4.

Frederick Engels, published in the Neue Rheinische Zeitung Politisch-Ökonomische Revue No. 4, 1849, Engels provided some historical context to the reasoning behind the bill, reflecting many of his and Marx's beliefs at the time, as well as those of the labor class.

> ...with the rise of large-scale industry, there arose a quite new and infinitely callous exploitation of the working class by the factory owners. The new machines rendered the labour of grown men superfluous; their supervision demanded women and children, who were much more suited to this occupation than the men and simultaneously cheaper to employ. Thus industrial exploitation at once took possession of the whole of the worker's family and locked it up in the factory; women and children had to work day and night without a break until they were overcome by utter physical exhaustion.

> The callously brutal exploitation of children and women at that time-an exploitation which did not let up so long as there was a muscle, a sinew or a drop of blood left to extract profit from-still remains a vivid memory for the older generation of English workers, and not a few of them bear this memory in the form of a crooked spine or a mutilated limb, and they all bear their thoroughly ruined health with them wherever they go. The fate of the slaves in the worst of the American plantations was golden in comparison with that of the English workers in that period.

The workers of Tariffville and Thompsonville were clearly in good international company.

Until they weren't.

The labor movement had been undermined by a force of nature, where fire erased the employment of 650 workers and required the carpet makers to the north to work even longer hours to make up for the production loss.

So much for a hoped-for reduction in work hours.

Two months after the Tariffville fire, the Hartford Carpet Company purchased a steam fire engine from the Amoskeag Works[235] in Manchester, New Hampshire, and presented it to the Thompsonville Fire Department.

SINGLE PUMP HARP FRAME ENGINE.
Built by the Amoskeag Manufacturing Co.

A day late and a dollar short[236] for Tariffville, from where the company had withdrawn its business for the second time in history.

---

[235] The Amoskeag Manufacturing Company originated with Benjamin Prichard's construction of a small cotton mill at Amoskeag Falls in 1804. Between 1840 and 1876 they produced textile equipment, steam locomotives, steam fire engines, sewing machines, and firearms.
[236] An idiom thought to have originated in the United States in the mid-20th century - too little too late. At the time, the dollar was very powerful, so even a small shortfall could have serious consequences.

16: BONESHAKER

The Merriam-Webster dictionary defines the velocipede as a lightweight wheeled vehicle propelled by the rider, such as a tricycle, a three-wheeled railroad handcar, or a bicycle.

The Encyclopedia Britannica describes it as -

a version of the bicycle reinvented in the 1860s by the Michaux family of Paris. Its iron and wood construction and lack of springs earned it the nickname "boneshaker."

It was driven by pedaling cranks on the front axle. To increase the distance covered for each turn of the cranks, the front wheel was enlarged until, finally, in the ordinary, or penny-farthing, bicycle, the wheel would just go under the crotch of the rider.

The "penny-farthing" nickname came from the smallest and largest British coins of the time, in reference to the disparity in the size of the wheels.

Wikipedia, the dictionary of the internet, goes a bit further, defining it as –

a human-powered land vehicle with one or more wheels. The most common type of velocipede today is the bicycle.

The web resource continued –

VELOCIPEDE.

The earliest usable and much-copied velocipede was created by the German Karl Drais and called a Laufmaschine (German for 'running machine'), which he first rode on June 12, 1817. He obtained a patent in

January 1818.

This was the world's first balance bicycle and quickly became popular in both the United Kingdom and France, where it was sometimes called a draisine (German and English), draisienne (French), a vélocipède (French), a swiftwalker, a dandy horse (as it was very popular among dandies[237]) or a Hobby horse. It was made entirely of wood and metal and despite the condition of the roads at the time was sometimes ridden for long distances.

Wikipedia agrees with the other resources that –

Velocipede came into common usage as a generic term, with the launch of the first pedal-equipped bicycle, developed by Pierre Michaux, Pierre Lallement and the Olivier brothers in the 1860s.

The Michaux company was the first to mass-produce the velocipede, from 1857 to 1871. That French design was sometimes called the **boneshaker**, *since it was also made entirely of wood, then later with metal tires. That in combination with the cobblestone roads of the day made for an extremely uncomfortable ride.*

In 1868, Thompsonville had its version of the velocipede, designed and built by James Alfred Lakin, a Civil War veteran, born on October 7, 1841, in Boston, Massachusetts.

Lakin most likely arrived in Thompsonville around 1865 as the village experienced exponential growth. If anyone was

---

[237] A dandy was a man who was known for his refined language, personal grooming, and interest in fashion and physical appearance in Britain in the late 18th and early 19th centuries.

interested in starting a business, then this village was the place to be, as ready customers abounded, cash in hand.

Primarily a jeweler, with a successful store located in the village[238], Lakin was inquisitive, possessing an active mind.

James Alfred Lakin – Thompsonville jeweler, watchmaker, inventor, and velocipede builder and enthusiast.

With his jewelry business firmly established by 1866, Lakin

---

[238] The location of the Thompsonville store is unknown.

submitted the paperwork for his first patent in March of that year— a delicate piece of machinery (a lathe) used to fashion watch gear parts. So popular was the item that he received seventy-five orders within a week of patent approval.

As proof of his social standing while conducting business in the village, Lakin employed a servant girl to assist his wife, Henrietta Jane Wolcott, with household chores and various other tasks, as his young wife had her hands full caring for an infant son, Henry Alfred Lakin.

Unfortunately, the young servant girl absconded with clothing and jewelry lifted from Henrietta on the morning of October 15, 1867, and lit out for greener pastures. Jabez Davis, a newly elected town constable (with two years of experience in Michigan), worked together with the New Haven Police to locate and capture the thief and recover the stolen items.

One year later, in March 1868, Lakin was awarded a second patent. This patent was granted for creating a spring-foil dial wheel washer to keep the dial wheels of a watch in their proper place, so the face hands do not catch each other as they pass. So popular was the item that he received seventy-five orders within a week of patent approval.

TO WATCHMAKERS.—
Spring Foil Dial-wheel Washers for keeping the Face, Wheels, and Hands of Watches in their proper place. Best thing in use. No Watchmaker should be without them. Price 50 cents per gross. Sent by mail to any address. The Trade supplied. Address   J. A. LAKIN,
20 os2]   Thompsonville, Conn.

On July 29, 1868, Lakin was at it again, this time with another patent for his *Heat Radiator*. The new award surprisingly had no connection to Lakin's other endeavors. In his submission, he claimed

This invention consists of a peculiarly shaped radiator, as

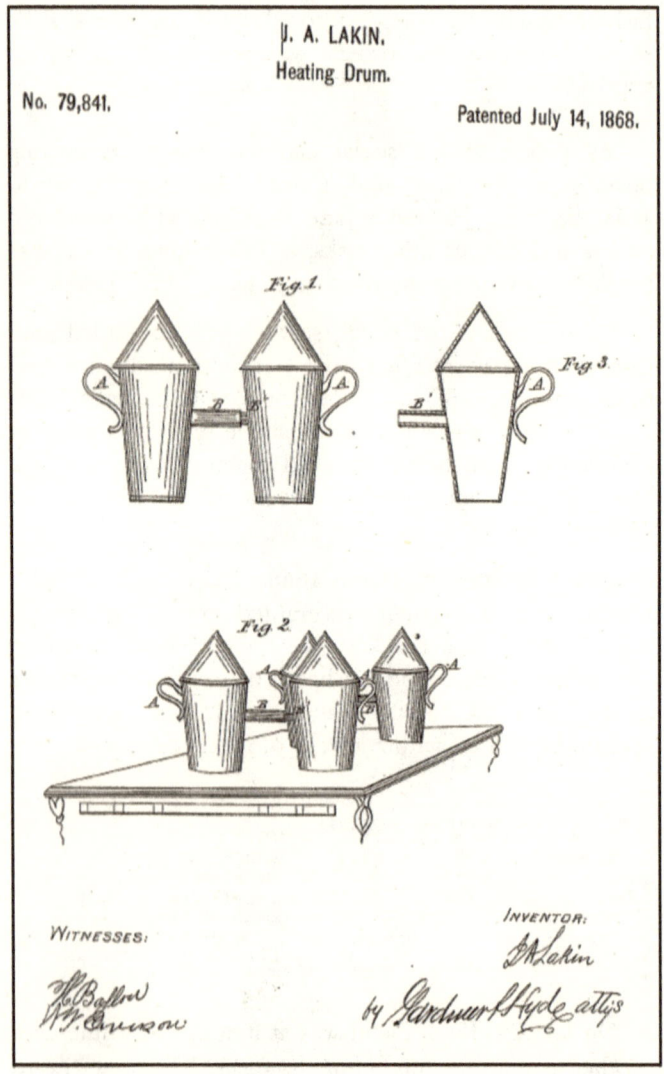

hereafter explained, for the purpose of raising the temperature of a house or room, by means of the increased radiating surface obtained by the application of this device to an ordinary cooking stove, thus employing the latter as a furnace, and saving a large proportion of heat that would otherwise be lost through the chimney.

In his spare time, Lakin became intrigued by the velocipede, which had begun to capture the attention of enthusiasts nationwide. One of the most common complaints about the early bicycle was its weight, which made the vehicle difficult to balance, maneuver, and pedal.

With his knowledge of metal tubing, threading, and coupling, Lakin improved the velocipede, creating a lighter and nimbler version.

Restored Lakin Velocipede at the Connecticut Historical Society (2024).

By February 1869, Lakin was manufacturing and selling

his velocipede as a kit by mail, as if he were the 19th-century Amazon of bicycles.

VELOCIPEDES

OF THE

LAKIN PATTERN.

The best Machine yet offered to the public. It embraces all the best points of the American and French Machines and cannot be surpassed for beauty. Manufactured by J. S. LAKIN,
Thompsonville, Ct.

N. B.—A complete set of castings for making this beautiful machine, including the Forks, Sockets, Boxes, Crank, Turntable, &c., &c., ready for any blacksmith to fit up in one day, sent to any address on receipt of $10.00. f16 Cd

By April, Larkin was adding custom parts, such as improved foot stirrups, for safety and security.

VELOCIPEDES

OF THE LAKIN PATTERN,

Acknowledged by all riders to be the best Machine in use. Send stamp for cut and circular of this beautiful pattern.

We furnish many of the parts of this machine to those who wish to manufacture this beautiful pattern. We send our best gun metal castings, with the threads all cut, and ready for any mechanic to put together in a day, including the forks, sockets, boxes, tiller bolt and turn table per, set $12. Our improved Stirrups, which keep the foot of the rider from getting into the wheel, per pair $2.50. Our new American Saddle, $3.50. Address, J. A. LAKIN,
m25 12d Thompsonville, Conn.

At the end of April, a copartnership of William W. Cowles & Herbert C. Dean signed a licensing agreement to manufacture Lakin's Vecilopedes in their Chicopee, Massachusetts, facility, promising to complete orders *with neatness and dispatch.*

At the end of that same month, J. A. Lakin put on a public demonstration of his Thompsonville bicycle by riding from his home village to Springfield and back in one hour and thirty minutes. Accompanied by referees to ensure there was no cheating, Lakin rode the entire trip except for two or three hills, which required him to walk to crest them.

In view of the fact that the road is extremely sandy and unfavorable to velocipede riding, the time made was very good.[239]

Following the success of the cycling adventure, the April 30, 1869, edition of the Hartford Courant reported –

J. A. Lakin, the Thompsonville velocipedist and manufacturer, is now practicing for a race of one hundred miles, to be made in ten hours, exclusive of a two-hour stop at the end of fifty miles, or the two hours to be used at intervals of fifteen minutes each. He will ride his 35-inch wheel machine.

On the heels of his successes, Lakin needed a new adventure to garner his interest, so, on May 18th, the intellectual gadabout put his Thompsonville store up for sale.

WATCH and JEWELRY ESTABLISHMENT FOR SALE

The well-established Watch, jewelry, Cutlery, Stationary, and Fancy Goods business, now in a flourishing condition and with a good run of watch work. I will sell my entire stock of fixtures. The store has 33 feet of counter,

---

[239] Litchfield Enquirer April 29, 1869. Pg 1.

showcases well stocked, and now employs three men to run it. To the right man this is a rare chance. Reasons for selling is Western Fever.[240]

A modified advertisement was published in the Hartford Daily Courant one month later, disclosing the store's sales of $40k per month—an astronomical figure for the time. Lakin stated that any potential buyer could review his books to support his sales numbers.

By November of that same year, Lakin had sold his Thompsonville store and opened a new shop at 221 Main Street in Springfield, Massachusetts. Despite his proclaimed bout of *Western Fever*, Lakin had chosen to head north six miles, no more than he had pedaled on his earlier velocipede adventure. To expand his business, Lakin purchased the jewelry store of F. A. Grover in Westfield, Massachusetts.

Lakin seemed to receive a good bit of ribbing from the local press concerning his bicycling interest, as reported in the Springfield Republican of April 1, 1870.

*Our neighbor Lakin, the jeweler, who used to be as notable a master of that fiery steed, the velocipede, as Rary was of the horse, actually **sold** one yesterday.*

He did, upon our honor! And the man rode off upon it.

Have any of the asylums lost a lunatic?

Journalistic sarcasm notwithstanding, May 5, 1870, marked the date when Lakin disposed of the entirety of his remaining velocipedes, except for the *historic cycle* he had ridden from Thompsonville to Springfield.

And then, eight days later, possibly due to the caustic reporting by the Springfield media, J. A. Lakin sold his Springfield jewelry store to a buyer from Boston and moved

---

[240] Springfield Republican May 18, 1869. Pg 1.

to Westfield, Massachusetts, where he had purchased a branch store only a few months earlier. By 1875, Lakin completed a contentious sale of his Westfield store to an employee, J. H. Lockwood, who had been planning to open a jewelry store of his own.

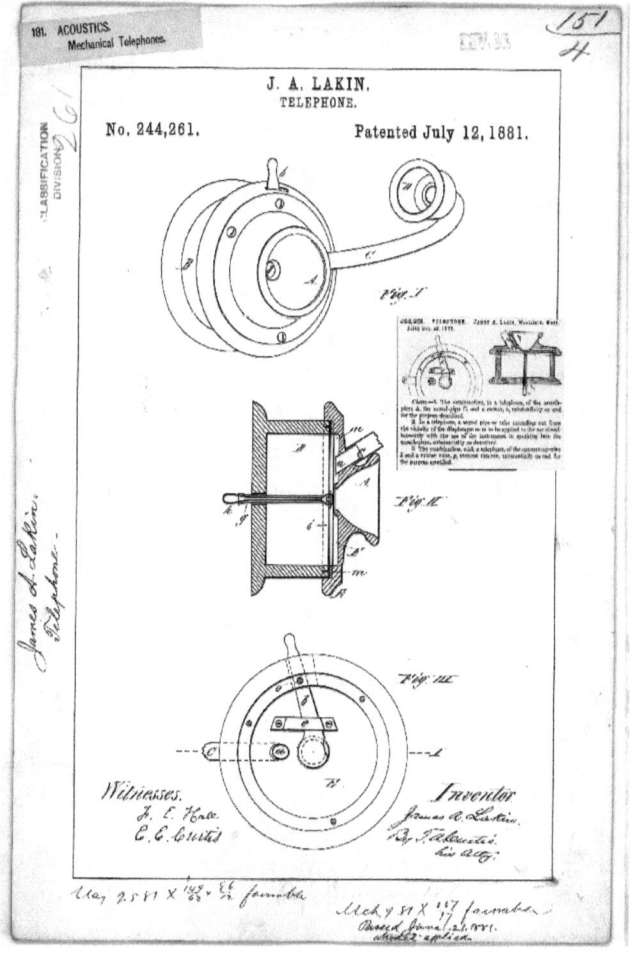

Five years passed, and James A. Lakin upended the

immature telephone industry with a new transmitter that extended the distance over which sound could be transmitted. In his *Acoustic Telephone* patent application, he claimed that –

> *The object of my invention is to increase the volume of sound transmitted between two connected telephones, to facilitate the hearing of the transmitted sound without removing the mouth from the mouth-piece of the instrument, and to permit the Wire or connecting medium to extend out through the room or building in any desired direction from the instrument without changing the location of the latter...*

The Thompsonville Press, in its November 30, 1882, issue, reported on the former village resident's success.

> *A day or two ago the trunk lines were opened, and operators at Fitchburg, Worcester, New Haven, and other places from 10 to 80 miles away plainly heard the ticking of a watch held near the improved transmitter, and also that of a small lever clock on a shelf several feet away.*

> *Mr. Lakin is confident that the ticking might have been heard over any length of wire, even a thousand miles, under favorable circumstances, and believes that the time is not too far distant when people will talk from Boston to Chicago without difficulty.*

Only two months later, J. A. Lakin sold the rights to his telephone to the People's Telephone and Telegraph Company of New York. The improved equipment was tested successfully over 300 miles, then 500 miles, and finally over 800 miles. Lakin was confident that, with a slight adjustment, the company could complete a call from Boston to Chicago.

Not bad for a Thompsonville jeweler.

17: A BOTTLE IS BETTER

Several names consistently appear throughout the early historical records of Thompsonville. One of these is Benjamin Bright, who has already been featured in some stories and will be mentioned again as this tale unfolds.

The village was built on the strengths, dreams, and eccentricities of numerous individuals, and the 1870s decade welcomed and bid farewell to many of them.

George Steiger was born in St. Gallen, Switzerland, in 1838 to John Ulrich Steiger and his wife Anna Maria. He emigrated to the United States in 1854 at the age of 16, on board the vessel Europa, sailing from Bremen, Germany. He was not listed as traveling with his parents or siblings, and it is unclear whether he intended to meet anyone upon disembarking at Ellis Island. His declared destination was Thompsonville, Connecticut, so the fair assumption is that family or relatives were living there and expected his arrival.

After a short residence in Thompsonville, records indicate that Steiger moved to Hartford, Connecticut, for approximately five years to pursue an apprenticeship or education, returning to the Enfield village at the age of 21.

Although there is little direct research to prove it, it

seems as if Steiger entered the employ of Benjamin Bright in Bright's butchering business upon the young man's return to Thompsonville. Tax records list him as holding a butcher's license, which suggests Steiger learned the trade during his time in Hartford.

In any event, at the start of the Civil War, Bright sold his business to Steiger and entered the cattle brokerage business in New York under the name Bright's and Fagin, buying cattle and shipping them to various New York markets.

As noted in the earlier chapter, Steiger was working in one of Bright's barns along the railroad when a spark burned the buildings to the ground in 1864, causing a substantial loss to the young butcher and a property loss to Bright. Steiger continued his slaughtering business and seemingly caught Marianne Bright's[241] eye while working at the family homestead.

When Benjamin returned home after the war, Steiger asked Bright for Marianne's hand in marriage, and the two were wed in 1867.

Although no photos of the butcher can be located, a detailed description of George Steiger, included on a passport application when the young man turned 40, is included. He was of shorter stature, at five feet six inches, with a high forehead, an oval face and chin, grey eyes, a small mouth, and a straight nose. Although no weight was included in the application, a story in The Descendants of John Rising of Suffield, CT, mentions his girth.

George Steiger, called 'Mr. Staggers', was the fruit and vegetable peddler from Thompsonville.

He was an extremely fat man.

It was said that when his horse and cart boarded the ferry

---

[241] Benjamin's daughter

boat, it scraped the river bottom half way across the river to Suffield.

He was a fast talker and once, when selling squash for six cents a pound, said 'Six times six is sixty-six, take it for half a dollar.'

Steiger's life between his marriage in 1867 and 1878 is difficult to piece together. Local newspaper articles mention Steiger's building in Thompsonville in 1870, indicating that the butcher may have purchased a building in the village to market his meat products. Another article noted that Steiger bought Horace Brainard's fancy confectionery store on Main Street in Thompsonville in 1872. It is unclear whether he purchased it with the intention of moving the same or different merchandise. Years later, a few articles in 1880 mentioned gatherings held at Steiger's Hall in the village, although no exact location was given.

What is clear is that by 1878, Steiger had set up a bottling operation in Thompsonville, on Prospect Street, directly across from the Post Office on Mrs. Murphy's[242] Block. How Steiger had fallen into the bottling business[243] is, like much of his life, unclear, given that his expertise was in butchery. Some of his relatives in his homeland of Switzerland might have been involved in the brewing and bottling business, which could indicate why Steiger chose to return to Eastern Europe in 1878. It may also point to issues Steiger was experiencing in the bottling business, as bacterial infestation in the process continued to spoil batches as they were bottled and capped. To guard against this issue, the

[242] Wife of the deceased John Murphy who had a general store on the corner of Prospect and what was once called Wall Street, Prince Street, and now Asnuntuck Street.
[243] Steiger's Bottling Works was unrelated to and preceded the Thompsonville Bottling Works by some 35 years.

Germans had begun using heated liquids to kill the bacteria before bottling. It is possible that the 1878 trip was intended to allow Steiger to review this process overseas so it could be deployed in Thompsonville.

Steiger had a good relationship with the local constables and justices, as reported in a Springfield Republican article of November 12, 1878, in which a going-away party for the peacekeepers had to be ensured by the same.

George Steiger of Thompsonville is a merry Switzer, who returns today to the stormy crags, perpendicular pastures, and roaring landslides of his native heath.

He promised the boys a 'farewell party' the other night, but at an evil hour on the set day, he went to Springfield and failed to come home in time. On his return the next day, the boys caged him and held a court martial.

Chief Justice George Wilson fixed the penalty at 20 pies[244], and Associate Justice Weising added 12 dozen lager and tonic beers. Steiger ordered them up and the boys laid themselves out so that all was gone in five minutes.

But four pies and eight tonics so unfavorably affected an honored member of this high court that he had paralysis of the stomach, and all Sunday his life was despaired of. However, he will recover.

Envious Windsor Locks folks say they can tell now when the wind is north without consulting the vane because of the smell of pie and beer that comes drifting down the river.

Although Steiger was referred to as a bottler, it seems as if he was a brewer as well, as upon his return in the Spring

---

[244] It's unclear as to whether these were pastries or meat pies. Meat pies would have reflected Steiger's core business.

of 1879, the Hartford Courant, July 18 edition, reported the following.

A comparatively new industry has sprung up almost as if by magic and is now employing a considerable number of persons, and should the business continue to increase in the future as it has done since it was started last year it must become one of the prominent industries of the place. Anyone not a stranger would refer at once to the well-known George Steiger, who at his bottling establishment on Prospect Street makes a specialty of Steiger's tonic and Steiger's lemon beer, besides other articles usually put up in bottles, such as soda, small beer, and sarsaparilla.

He has been taxed to the fullest capacity, employing a set of night hands, and even then could not fill all of his orders. Besides employing several teams to deliver his goods, large quantities are shipped by rail to the more distant places.

The purest water is used in the preparation and the greatest care in mixing the ingredients, so as to have the products uniform. Mr. S. spent the winter in Germany, keeping his eyes wide open in observation of everything that would forward his business.

By all accounts, it seemed as if Steiger had fallen into a profitable business, with more orders than he could fill.

Beyond work, Steiger seemed to be the delight of the village, participating in numerous social events and even leading a musical group referred to as a 'little German band'.

Even when he wasn't performing, he seemed to be at the center of residents' attention, even if humor was shared at his expense.

Duprez & Benedict's[245] *minstrels gave a very good performance at Franklin Hall last Friday evening. The hall was well-filled. The references to Steiger as the fat man and to the Thompsonville post office as the smallest thing in town, were appreciated by the audience and well applauded.*[246]

THEY HAVE COME AND WILL APPEAR TO-NIGHT
DUPREZ & BENEDICT'S
MINSTRELS AND BRASS BAND.

HOW'S DAT!

Most Reliable Popular Troupe Traveling.
INTRODUCING AN ATTRACTIVE ORIGINAL NEW PROGRAMME.
SCHOOL CHILDREN ADMITTED AT 20 CENTS EACH.

Accept a Cordial Invitation.

Union Printing and Publishing Co., (John Hodge, Prop.) Lockport, N.Y.   (OVER)

Content to be the center of attention and always 'ready for a challenge,' Steiger, a very large man, to the delight of the locals, placed a bet with an expressman[247], Samuel Hood, that he could wheel the latter around a square mile of the village in a wheelbarrow.

The wager was the talk of Thompsonville with, in the words of the November 12, 1880, edition of the local paper, *every preparation … made to make the affair a grand*

---

[245] Originally conceived as Carle, Duprez, and Green's Minstrels performing locally in New Orleans. The troupe later became known as (Charles H.) Duprez & (Lew) Benedict's Minstrels, which performed across the United States.
[246] Thompsonville Press December 12, 1880. Pg 2.
[247] a person who worked for an express company, delivering and collecting packages, or managing and packing cargo.

one: a procession made up of a drum corps, Company B of the Boys in Blue, and the Hancock Pioneers, all in full uniform, [were] to accompany the victims, but on account of bad weather and other reasons, the affair [was] given up.

Even while Steiger ran the bottling business, he also ran his store on Prospect Street, selling meats carved by his hand and from his father-in-law Benjamin Bright's slaughterhouse.

Reflective of his personality and his presence, Steiger did everything large—even clambakes, to which he invited locals and regionals, as the Thompsonville Press captured in a September 14, 1882, article.

The clambake at George Steiger's came off according to programme, and was a success. It was slightly past the hour, however, when the spread was set before the guests, on account of the delay in the morning of the arrival from Boston of the clams – but Mr. J. W. Weber, of Springfield, who had contracted to the furnish the entire menu and [supervise] its preparation, was equal to the occasion, and at once posted off to Hartford and secured what was lacking and necessary to make up as fine and palatable a clambake as Steiger ever attempted to present.

In the meantime, Steiger had kept his guests in good humor and what little time was lost in getting ready only added to the appetite, and when they did sit down about 4 o'clock ample justice was done and all did eat and were filled, and there was an abundance.

A large number were present from Springfield, and towns all about, and good order was maintained throughout.

George Steiger epitomized what was good and kind of the village, making up for any perceived shortcomings of Thompsonville as reported by yellow journalism.

On October 9, 1882, Steiger applied for his annual liquor license in the village, requesting permission to sell spirituous and intoxicating liquors, ale, lager beer, Rhine wine, and cider at his Prospect Street location.

Three days later he, along with F. P. Sloane, Peter Clarkin, and John Donovan, was arrested by the local constabulary for selling liquor at a cattle show held in Thompsonville. At the time Connecticut only prohibited the sale of alcohol on Sundays, so the reasoning behind the arrest is suspect as the event was held on a Wednesday. While others pled guilty and paid a ten-dollar fine, Steiger objected, was overruled, and was fined twenty dollars and court costs.

Surprisingly, the next month Steiger quit the bottling business, assigning his equipment, to satisfy his creditors, to the brewing and bottling firm of (Christian) Kalmbach & (Theodore) Geisel, known locally in Springfield as *Come Back and Guzzle*.

Ted Geisel was the paternal grandfather of another

famous Springfield native, Theodore Geisel. Although his name may not ring any immediate bells, most people know him as Dr. Seuss.

Yes, the grandfather of the famous children's author, Dr. Seuss, made his money as a brewer in Massachusetts. Perhaps Seuss's words and drawings are more understandable now that we know his lineage.

In 1876, the elder Theodore Geisel purchased a small brewery on Boston Road in Springfield, MA. After forming a partnership with Christian Kalmbach, the duo opened the Kalmbach and Geisel Brewery. Copyright Springfield Museums used with permission.

With the bottling endeavor capped, Steiger focused on his core business and opened another production operation in the basement of Mrs. Murphy's building, manufacturing Frankfurt sausages[248].   The new product was sold in

---

[248] A Frankfurter Würstchen (*Frankfurt Sausage*) is a thin parboiled sausage in a sheep's intestine casing. A hot dog, an American invention inspired by the Frankfurter, is also a hot dog.

Steiger's merchant store, located on the first floor of the same building. One year later, in 1883, Steiger closed the business again for an unknown reason. It might have been for health reasons (due to his weight), although he was still a relatively young man at 45.

By 1888, the Thompsonville native opened a new merchant business at 20 Pearl Street, where he carried light groceries, canned and smoked meats, pickled lamb's tongue, pig's feet, tripe, ham, and other swine-related foods. The Irish and Scottish in the village seemed to need those offal dishes, and they still held a taste for Crubeen, Skirts and Kidneys, and Coddle.

Three years later, Steiger closed up shop once more, and T. J. Mulligan took over the space. Like Steiger, Mulligan peddled his wares on set routes to other regional towns and kept a brick-and-mortar store.

George Steiger continued without a store, returning to his roots as a fruit and vegetable peddler until 1915, at the age of 77, when he took out an advertisement in the Thompsonville Press announcing he was selling his route, horse, and other business essentials in anticipation of retirement.

The original bottler of Thompsonville died at the age of 84 in 1923.

As the Connecticut Temperance Union stated in an article in the Meriden Daily Republican in their January 1, 1869 edition:

> *Thompsonville is cursed with rum almost beyond any other place that we have seen. The population is largely foreign, and we were told that after pay-day the drunkenness is fearful. Men and women sink in the debasement of drink together.*

Thompsonville and Warehouse Point have been cursed immeasurably by distilleries.

Three years later, a Springfield Republican report reflected the same situation.

A Thompsonville saloon keeper says there never was so much drunkenness and rowdyism in that village as during the past year. He is disgusted with the place and is going to give up the business.

Yet, there was money to be made in that industry, beginning with George Steiger in 1878, when he started bottling ale and other intoxicating liquors.

Steiger was followed by Patrick J. Sullivan, who announced in the Thompsonville Press in the April 16, 1885 issue, that he was about to open a lager beer bottling establishment and had purchased a team of horses to help him deliver the goods. By the next month, the bottling location had been set in Thomas Mitchell's house on North Main Street. Within a year, Sullivan took occupancy of the first floor and basement of a new building constructed on G. L. Nobles's block on Main Street.

At approximately the same time as P. J. Sullivan launched his saloon and bottling operation, Martin R. Maher, the brother-in-law of George Steiger, took the plunge, leaving behind his carpentry tools to cork ale, lager beer, Rhine wine, and cider in a barn and building owned by Doctor George S. Miller[249] on Prospect Street. Maher would purchase that same property one year later.

Maher died on March 17, 1899. By March 23, 1899, Maher's bottling operation was purchased by the Gliesman Brothers. Frederick (Fritz), born in 1852, and his sibling Carl (Karl), born in 1856, would begin a general bottling

---

[249] Miller was born in Nova Scotia in 1834, studied medicine in Boston, and located to Thompsonville shortly thereafter.

business at 31 Main Street in the village, where the pair owned a saloon. Two months later, the pair expanded their operation due to the volume of business they were handling. By September, the Thompsonville Press reported:

Gliesman Brothers have been making a decided success of the bottling business this season. They have recently added new and improved apparatus and are supplying quantities of soda and mineral waters, besides an extensive trade in bottled lager.

Less than one year later, in February of 1900, Fritz Gliesman sold the bottling operation to William E. Wiebe of Springfield, Massachusetts. Weibe's brother Louis, a cigar manufacturer in the village for years, died that same month.

W. E. WIEBE,

SUCCESSOR TO

GLIESMAN BROTHERS,

Manufacturer and Bottler of all Kinds of Soda and Mineral Waters. All orders promptly attended to.

31 North Main St., Thompsonville, Ct.

Five years passed, and Wieber [incorrectly identified a Weids in The New London Day] dropped stone-cold dead while standing at the counter of the Thompsonville Hotel. It was reported that heart trouble, summer heat, and overwork brought on his demise.

He was 29 years old.

Thomas Hayden was born in 1862 to Peter and Bridget

Hayden, both born in Ireland and who had emigrated to Thompsonville to seek work and a better life.

Young Hayden was well known among the local constabulary by his late teens and early twenties, running afoul of the law. In 1882, he went to trial, at the age of 20, along with other village ruffians William Smith, James Conlin, John Nash, John Shaughnessy, and Hugh Steele for causing a disturbance on the railroad – an offense the rail company took seriously.

By the age of 25, in 1887, Hayden was employed by Martin Maher, bottler and brother-in-law of George Steiger. It would be his first initiation into the business.

Still 'rough around the edges,' Hayden married Nellie Pease in 1890 in a compulsory ceremony[250] and found himself in jail the following year due to his wife's complaint of non-support. She filed for and was granted an uncontested divorce from the lad in 1892.

As is often the case, though, as strange as it might seem, Thomas Hayden soon found himself on the right side of the law, working as a constable for the village in 1894. He seemed to have a talent for the job, making a local name for himself and even collaborating with law enforcement from other areas to capture criminals.

By 1900, Hayden was listed as a saloon keeper on the Federal Census, and his location was known as Hayden's Hall at 52 South Main Street. Here, he drew on his earlier experience working with Maher and began bottling ale and lager for sale.

---

[250] A compulsory marriage, also known as a forced marriage, is a marriage that occurs when one or more parties are married against their will or without their consent. The assumption here is Hayden, based on his character, had most likely done something to invite the arrangement.

As with most men in blue, Hayden was a standing member of the Enfield Society for the Detection of Thieves and Robbers and was elected to the position of pursuer in 1901. That same year, he purchased the farm of Patrick Haven, located in the Weymouth district of town. The property held a house, barns, sheds, and 65 acres.

Life had changed for the better.

In 1904, Hayden's uncle in West Virginia passed away, leaving the bottler a small fortune. Flush with cash, Hayden decided to sell the Thompsonville saloon to Alphonse Tradeau of nearby Hazardville. He then retired from business to live on his farm with his brother, Peter.

Samuel Katz arrived in Thompsonville sometime in the 1890s as a peddler of various goods. In one early newspaper report, he is referred to as a 'banana peddler' in the village, and in another, he is charged with 'peddling without a license' in Scitico. A Springfield Republican article reports that he settled in Poquonock, Connecticut, in 1900 to establish a bottling business there, while another newspaper identifies him as a Thompsonville bottler who filed for bankruptcy in 1904.

Of all the reports, the Hartford Courant articles of 1904 are the most reliable, identifying Katz as a Thompsonville bottler who ran into financial trouble due to poor business practices and became insolvent. Whatever the true story, the Goldenthal Brothers, village bakers, bought out the equipment of Katz's bottling establishment in July of 1904 and set up operations in the Chamberlain Hotel as the Tivoli Bottling Works. Two months later, the brothers bought the Hotel.

TIVOLI BOTTLING WORKS,

THOMPSONVILLE, CONN.,

B. GOLDENTHAL, Manager.

Bottlers of Gold Medal Tivoli Beer, Highland and Hampden Ales and Porters. Telephone 93-2.   Chamberlain's Corner.

283

Like William A. Chamberlain before him, the Goldenthal Brothers, or Tivoli Bottling Works, would run into trouble with the law for selling alcohol illegally on Sundays.

In April of 1906, the Goldenthal Brothers sold the Chamberlain to Alphonse Labonte and William Lamontaigne, exiting the bottling business to refocus on their core baking business.

However, liquor had gotten into Bernard Goldenthal's blood, and he and his brother Joseph dissolved their partnership in 1907. Joseph retained his interest in the bakery business, and Bernard took a position working at the Springfield Brewing Company, just north of Thompsonville.

In March of 1908, Bernard is back in the saloon business, purchasing the taproom of John Savage at 42 South Main Street[251], and requesting the transfer of the alcohol license into his name.

One year later, Joseph Goldenthal sold his bakery business to the firm Forst and Lameman of Hartford, turning around and purchasing Martin Broderick's saloon at 3 Whitworth Street. Six weeks later, Joseph sold that same watering hole to George and Jacob Landa of Springfield, Massachusetts, stating that he had decided to move back 'home' to Hartford. He then purchased the bar of Joseph Katz[252] & Company at 270 Front Street in the Capital City.

In April of 1910, Bernard followed suit, selling his saloon to John and William Cochefski of Suffield from across the Connecticut River and returning to Hartford to

---

[251] Savage had purchased the business from John Higgins who had retired in 1907.
[252] No relation to Samuel Katz who had begun the Goldenthal's adventure in beer and bottling.

rejoin his brother.

Goldenthal's Tivoli Bottling Works lived on, though, as Springfield Brewing expropriated the name and worked out of the Thompsonville Hotel, distributing bottled refreshments from its Massachusetts brewery to the village's thirsty citizens.

NOTICE.

KNOW ye all men by these presents: That I, Thomas F Sullivan, of the Town of Enfield, county of Hartford, State of Connecticut, am engaged in the said town, in manufacturing, bottling and selling soda waters, mineral and æra ted waters, porter, ale, beer, cider, ginger ale, small beer, lager beer, and other beverages or mixtures in bottles, cans, jars or siphons, w th the following trade-mark and device on bottles, boxes and siphons:

BOTTLES
The Thompsonville Bottling Works,
Thompsonville, Conn.

SIPHONS
Sullivan & Burke, Thompsonville, Conn.,
also " T. F Sullivan" marked on the
metal neck of siphons.

BOXES.
The Thompsonville Bottling Works,
Thompsonville, Conn.
Sullivan & Burke, Thompsonville, Conn.
Signed and sealed at said Enfield, this
31st day of July, A D 1906
THOMAS F. SULLIVAN
Enfield, Conn., July 31, 1906.

Personally appeared said Thomas F. Sullivan, signer and sealer of the above, and made oath to the above before me, William J. Mulligan, Notary Public.

The above having been filed and recorded in the office of the Superior Court for Hartford county in 1906.

On August 22, 1907, Thomas F. Sullivan, a saloon owner and bottler in Thompsonville, filed a 'notice of record' with the Connecticut State Superior Court, registering his trademarks associated with the name Thompsonville Bottling Works as they were applied to boxes, bottles, and siphons.

Sullivan had worked at his establishment at 47 Main Street in the village since 1888, bottling mineral waters, lagers, ales, and porters. Like many entrepreneurs, he would put money back into his business to streamline operations, which he did in 1901 by installing a five-horsepower boiler and engine to assist with charging fountains, bottling, washing, and hoisting barrels and bottled goods from the basement to the first floor.

The 1907 action was more about addressing the 'repurposing' of the bottles, boxes, and siphons by competing bottlers in the region. The lack of regulations and branded equipment allowed some companies to use assets originally purchased by competitors to produce and deliver their liquors. Sullivan was ahead of his time.

After the death of his brother, Patrick J. Sullivan, the saloon owner and lager bottler discussed earlier, Thomas combined businesses at his Main Street location, inviting his brother-in-law, Patrick F. Burke, to join him in the effort in 1893.

Burke was an interesting choice as a partner, as he was well-known as a drunk around the village, having been arrested multiple times for public drunkenness, breach of the peace, and disturbing the peace. Partnering with his brother Thomas didn't seem to quell Patrick's attraction for lager.

> *Patrick Burke was fined five dollars for drunkenness and disturbance of the peace and sentenced to thirty days in jail by Justice C. F. Morrison Wednesday morning. The arrest was the result of a long-drawn-out family disturbance in which the bottle has been a prime factor.*[253]

> *Patrick Burke was brought before Judge Davis Wednesday morning by Officer Hayden*[254] *and fined $3 for drunkenness, $5 and a sentence of fifteen days in jail for breaking the peace, and twenty days in jail and costs of prosecution for resisting the officers. The costs amounted to $18, about one-half of which goes to the town treasury.*[255]

> *...and last Friday Patrick Burke was sentenced to 30*

---

[253] Thompsonville Press April 11, 1895. Pg 2.

[254] Remember Tom Hayden, former bad boy and saloon owner?

[255] Thompsonville Press July 8, 1897. Pg 2.

days for breach of the peace.[256]

Having had enough of his brother-in-law's antics, the partnership was dissolved in 1901, Thomas retaining the saloon and bottling business. Patrick attempted to open a café of his own, but his alcohol license was rightly denied.

Unfortunately for Burke, his struggles with drinking continued…

Patrick Burke arrested by Bromage, charged with breach of peace, was sentenced to three months in jail.[257]

Beyond the saloon and bottling business, Sullivan was engaged in numerous social clubs in Thompsonville, serving as an officer in the Nonotuck Tribe of Red Men in the Asnuntuck Lodge, on the committee of the Ancient Order of Hibernians, as a Chairman of the local Democratic Committee, as a member of the Court Sumpter of Forresters, and as a fellow in the Holy Name Society of Saint Patrick's Church.

In 1907, Sullivan's mother, Mary, passed away after a brief struggle with pneumonia. Her death seemed to take the wind out of Thomas's sails. Within two years, he sold the saloon and the Thompsonville Bottling Works to Patrick J. Cunningham of Springfield, Massachusetts, and John Hannon of Holyoke, Massachusetts.

When the Massachusetts pair acquired the business, they remodeled the entire building, dedicating the basement to bottling, upgrading the first floor to a more modern bar, and converting the upper floor into apartments. Additionally, new bottling equipment replaced the old, and a new engine was installed to streamline operations. The Thompsonville Bottling Works continued to bottle beer, ale, porter, and

---

[256] Thompsonville Press October 19, 1899. Pg 2.
[257] Thompsonville Press September 10, 1903. Pg 2.

soft drinks.

Four years earlier, in 1905, another competitor arrived on the scene. Julius A. Heinz purchased a complete set of modern bottling equipment from the Crown Supply Company of Boston, Massachusetts, and installed the equipment in his building at 48 North Main Street in the village. Unlike others, though, Heinz was steering clear of alcohol, focusing instead on carbonated tonics, employing tin-lined and triple-silver equipment to ensure the beverages were pure and healthy. He also used a new method of steaming and washing bottles to eliminate all germs, installed a filtration system to purify the source water, and achieved a clarity approaching that of spring water.

Within one year, though, Heinz was exposed as appropriating competitors' bottles for his own use. The practice was not uncommon at the time, as 'empties' were often left at properties other than those from which they were initially purchased, and glass bottles, even registered ones, usually resembled those of another bottler. Heinz

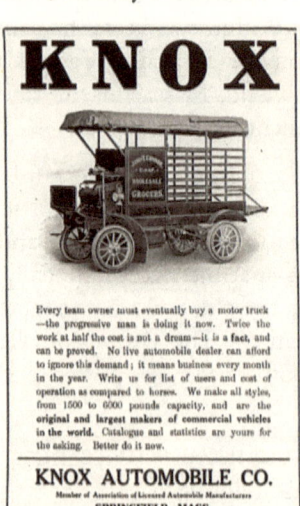

KNOX

Every team owner must eventually buy a motor truck —the progressive man is doing it now. Twice the work at half the cost is not a dream—it is a fact, and can be proved. No live automobile dealer can afford to ignore this demand; it means business every month in the year. Write us for list of users and cost of operation as compared to horses. We make all styles, from 1500 to 6000 pounds capacity, and are the original and largest makers of commercial vehicles in the world. Catalogue and statistics are yours for the asking. Better do it now.

KNOX AUTOMOBILE CO.
Member of Association of Licensed Automobile Manufacturers
SPRINGFIELD, MASS.

claimed, and it was independently substantiated, that his competitors were also using his bottles.

Each business agreed to use greater precautions to ensure the practice did not become commonplace.

As 1909 ended, Heinz became the first bottler in Thompsonville to use an 'automobile truck' to deliver his goods, purchasing a vehicle from the Knox Automobile Company of

Springfield, Massachusetts.

At the time, the truck had an impressive 40 horsepower, enough to carry heavy loads. Heinz modified his building to accommodate loading and unloading products from the vehicle.

A sign at State Line promoted the bottlers' wares:

> ***Drink Heinz's Soda,***
> ***Morning, Noon and Night,***
> ***Then you'll always***
> ***Feel all right.***[258]

On August 17, 1911, Heinz was at it again, accused by Cunningham & Hannon, owners of the Thompsonville Bottling Works, of appropriating glass bottles. Heinz was charged with repurposing bottles and siphons stamped with the registered name of the competitor's company. Constable Thomas Hayden (remember him?) had searched Heinz's property and had found over 100 Thompsonville Bottling Works bottles, 50 of which were filled with soda and ready to ship to Heinz's customers.

The court decided to charge Heinz 5 cents per bottle for the offense. Heinz decided to appeal the ruling.

Before the appeal could even be scheduled, Julius A. Heinz sold his operation to Katz & Company of Springfield, Massachusetts. The sale was misreported as the true purchaser of the bottling works was Harry Squirsky[259] of Springfield. Albert Katz[260] was associated with the firm, primarily as a chemist, and would lead the effort to create new soda drinks for the concern.

---

[258] Thompsonville Press Industrial edition July 1911
[259] Misreported as John P. Squire
[260] No connection to the *Thompsonville banana peddler* of the same name. Both Squirsky and Katz would relocate to Thompsonville.

Seemingly unable to shake the saloon bug, Heinz purchased the saloon of E. F. Vogel at 58 North Main Street in Thompsonville in December of 1911, requesting that the liquor license be transferred to him from Vogel.

Four months later, Heinz sold the café to John Jakowicz, a Polish dry goods dealer from the North End. Jakowicz bottled his own liquors and sold them in glass containers marked with his registered name.

Pure Rye and Bourbon
Whiskey
8 YEARS OLD
95c---25 oz. bottle
Best on the Market
SOLD BY
JOHN JAKOWICZ
58 North Main Street   **Thompsonville, Conn.**

By the middle of 1916, Jakowicz seemed to have tired of the venture and sold his 58 North Main Street location and liquor license to John G. Cheneski, who would fall into ruin in just a few years. Jakowicz would return to focus on his core meats and grocery business, ultimately moving into a building then known as the *Old Macaroni Factory*[261] on Whitworth Street.

---

[261] Location unknown

The April 4, 1912, edition of the Thompsonville Press announced the sale of Cunningham & Hannon's saloon and bottling business[262] to Frank and Louis Boggio.

It's Pure---That's Sure.

Ask your dealer---He'll tell you that the discriminating public

Demand Superior Mineral Water Co.'s Soda.

From your dealer or direct from us.

Superior Mineral Water Co.

48 North Main St.   Phone 228.

On February 21, 1916, the Harry Squirsky and Albert Katz bottling plant, located at 48 North Main Street, near the north end of Freshwater Pond, was renamed the Superior Mineral Water Company after the works were purchased from Julius Heinz and subsequently burned to

---

[262] Also known as The Thompsonville Bottling Works and later as Bogey beverages

the ground.

The plant would be rebuilt but later removed to Enfield Street, leaving Thompsonville behind, as had most bottlers.

18: POSTMORTEM

Thompsonville was granted its first post office during President Andrew Jackson's second term. It was located in an office in Hiram Belcher's & Company's store on Main Street, which James Scrimgeour had erected in 1832. The stagecoach would deliver mail to the office between 3:00 and 4:00 a.m. and sort it for delivery later in the day.

Squire Henry Kingsberry was the first official postmaster, although he never performed the duties, deferring to the assistant postmaster, Hiram Belcher, and his postal clerk, Robert Morrison.

In 1842, the Aberdeen, Scotland, émigré George W. Martin, a former clerk at Andrews, Thompson & Company of New York, assumed the position of postmaster from Kingsberry. Martin was, at the same time, superintendent of the carpet mill while living in his home[263] on Pearl Street near today's Asnuntuck (then called Park Street). Martin's front lawn had served as the site where Dr. Joseph Harvey was installed as the pastor of the First Presbyterian Church in 1839.

---

[263] John L. Houston occupied the home after Martin, and Nathan Sisitzky occupied it next. Sisitzky will be discussed in a later chapter.

After a few years, the baton was passed to General George C. Owen, who had transplanted to Thompsonville from Tariffville in 1835. Owen had been a brigadier-general in the state militia from 1842 to 1844.

In 1849, Joseph S. Harvey took over the reins of the postal service, serving until 1852, when Judge Jabez T. Tayler assumed the role for only one year, passing the torch back to Owen, who continued to hold the position until 1861.

In 1861, Abraham Lincoln appointed John Houston to the role, who served until 1872, and his widow, Agnes, succeeded him. Houston had emigrated to Thompsonville from Scotland in 1832 and assumed the position of head dyer. He and his wife were among the primary movers who organized the First Presbyterian Church and remained active in it for years.

Although Mrs. Houston was the recognized postmistress, Miss Margaret Arnott did the real work while living at 37 Prospect Street[264] in the village. In truth, Arnott had been performing the postmistress duties since mid-1869, when Houston had become too ill to handle the responsibilities. In 1871, the village unanimously supported her in replacing Houston, but it was not to be, as Houston's wife was the United States Postmaster General's choice.

Margaret, her sister Elizabeth, and their younger brother James were born to James and Mary Arnott, who had emigrated to the village from Scotland in the early years of Thompsonville, then known as Lovejoy's Ferry (or as The City).

Soon after her rebuttal as postmistress, Arnott moved to

---

[264] William Tate built the house while employed by Shubael Parsons, a village painter. It became more famously known as The Demon House due to reports of unexplained ghostly phenomena within the residence.

Boston, where she took up residency and became a successful bookkeeper, a role she filled until the end of her years. Whether her disconsideration led to her relocation to the Massachusetts capital is unknown. Whether any of her anger at being passed over for the postmistress position was embedded in the Prospect Street home, if that was even a possibility, is also unknown.

Arnott's Uncle, Robbert Liddell, became the village's oldest surviving Civil War veteran, passing away in 1919. Liddell had fought as a member of Connecticut's Eighth Regiment, joining the battles of Newbern, Roanoke Island, and Antietam. He had actively participated in the Temperance and Prohibition efforts, having forsaken the demon liquor in 1873.

Liddell fell ill and spent most of his remaining days in the Prospect Street House while under the care of his nieces. After his passing, Elizabeth fell in the home, breaking her leg and hip, crawling to the living room couch, where she spent an entire day in agony until a neighbor discovered her the following morning. She passed soon afterward, and the house remained empty for years.

In 1886, James Arnott's name was submitted to become the new postmaster of the village, causing a massive uproar in Thompsonville, prompting Senator Eaton to state that he would not recommend 'a thief, a jail-bird, or a sneak like Arnott' to the position. This resulted in a lawsuit brought by Arnott against the Bridgeport Standard, the newspaper that had published the senator's accusation.

The plaintiff, Arnott, complained that the use of 'or' indicated that he was guilty of being all three things. He lost the case and the appeal. Perhaps his anger, combined with the disappointment left by his sister, was embedded in the walls of 39 Prospect Street, leading to future hauntings in that home.

When Margaret Arnott left the assistant postmistress post, she was succeeded by Miss Agnes Stewart, who was subsequently anointed Postmistress by President Andrew Garfield. This raises the question of whether this was done to address the perceived slight against Miss Arnott.

Stewart was the daughter of Charles Stewart, who had landed in Thompsonville from Kilmarnock, Scotland, in 1829. During her tenure at the Post Office, the office was relocated to the south side of the newly constructed bank building on Prospect Street.

Doctor Chester Johnson followed Stewart in 1886, serving until 1897, when Tudor Gowdy of the regionally famous Gowdy Gin Distillery took over. The anti-temperance postmaster served until 1913.

After Gowdy, James T. Murray was appointed by the infamous President Woodrow Wilson and served until 1922.

Perhaps there was something about being a postmaster.

Henry J. Lacey's name may not be as recognizable as others. Still, he was highly regarded in the village, and his namesake had an even greater impact at the national level.

Henry James Lacey Sr. was born in Syston, Leicestershire, England, in 1816, and his son, Henry Jr., was born in the same village in 1844. The family emigrated to the United States in 1849, landing in Boston, Massachusetts.

The Lacey family moved to Thompsonville, Connecticut, in 1858, Henry Sr. securing a job as a weaver at the carpet mill.

The elder Lacey was a member of the Masonic Lodge and a founder of Saint Andrews Church in the village. He served as the Sabbath school superintendent for a year before a full-time pastor was identified.

Often, a man's true measure is reflected not only by his actions but also in the quality and actions of his offspring. If this is true, Henry Lacey and his wife Catherine were idyllic parents.

Henry J. Lacey Jr., West Fitchburg, Massachusetts, merchant. Courtesy Mrs. James L. West.

On July 26th, 1862, Henry James Lacey, Jr. enlisted in Thompsonville, CT, and joined Company D of the 16th Regiment of the Connecticut Volunteer Infantry. The infantry moved quickly south and joined the Army of the Potomac as Robert E. Lee invaded Maryland. His first taste of battle was at Antietam, where he sustained a bullet wound to his leg. He was transferred to the United States General Hospital in Chester, Pennsylvania, for recovery.

Returning to war three months later, he took part in the Battle of Fredericksburg. Surviving the skirmish, he and his regiment were transferred to Plymouth, North Carolina, where Lacey Jr. was promoted to Corporal on April 16th. For 14 days, the Union troops were laid under siege by soldiers under the guidance of Confederate General Hoke. The garrison surrendered to the southern commander on April 30, 1864.

Lacey Jr. was sent to the Confederate prison at Andersonville in Georgia, an experience he wrote about in his manuscript, 'Personal Experiences of the War of the Rebellion.' He spent seven months in Andersonville, then was transferred to Charleston, South Carolina, and later to Florence, South Carolina, where he remained until February 28, 1865, when he was paroled.

> *I cannot find words in the human language to express my thoughts at the recollection of this horrible place, and the tears leave my eyes as look back upon the barbarous and inhuman treatment of the soldiers whose misfortune it was to be confined here.*

> *As we entered the enclosure, a spectacle met our eyes that almost froze our blood with horror, and made our hearts fail within us. Before us were frames that had once been erect, now nothing but walking skeletons, covered with filth and vermin.*[265]

Henry Lacey, Jr. had begun his imprisonment at 140 pounds and had left at 82 pounds.

---

[265] Personal Experiences of the War of the Rebellion. Henry James Lacey Jr. 1898. Self-Published. It was the same battle where Robert Liddle fought.

Discharged on July 9, 1865, he moved to Providence, Rhode Island, where he married Mary Pearce the following year. Henry Sr. passed away in 1871.

Henry Jr. worked in the grocery business until he relocated to Poquonoc Bridge, Connecticut, in 1880, where he continued to toil in the same line of goods. He served as postmaster for the small town during that same period, a position he held until he moved to Fitchburg, Massachusetts, in 1884, where he was also appointed postmaster. Once established there, he purchased a grocery store at 3 Westminster Street from resident William Baldwin. He operated it until July 1898, when he retired and published his war memoir, passing the business on to his son Charles.

Henry Lacey Jr. was chosen, among other survivors, to represent the State of Connecticut at the dedication of a monument erected at Andersonville, Georgia, on October 23, 1907, in memory of Connecticut men who suffered in southern military prisons between 1861 and 1865.

While Henry James Lacey Sr.'s works carried forward for many years, their echoes slowly vanished. However, Henry

James Lacey Jr.'s words still resonate today as he empathetically recalled the horrors he and his fellow soldiers endured at the Andersonville Prison in his military memoir.

An interesting way to measure the impact of one's life is to count the number of people who attend their funeral.

The West Fitchburg Methodist Church was filled with mourners at the passing of Henry J. Lacey, Jr., while more than 2500 people assembled at the Thompsonville Cemetery gravesite of his father, Henry James Lacey Sr.

These were honorable and valuable men, indeed.

Other notable men passed away during this period.

John Matthewson, the ale producer, died in 1879 at the age of 69, leaving the distillery in the hands of the probate court and, ultimately, his sons. His estate was valued at $100,000 [~$3 million in 2020].

Henry Thompson, discussed in earlier chapters, passed away in 1871. For the first time, the bell he had purchased for the Episcopal Church was rung for his passing.

Orrin Thompson's death on January 31, 1893, marked the end of his legacy. Although previous pages represent his life well, his death was best expressed in his obituary in the Hartford Courant on February 6, 1873.

He has lived a long and useful life; has survived most of his contemporaries and all of the partners with whom he first became associated in mercantile and manufacturing operations; has held fast to his integrity through many vicissitudes, and has leaned steadfastly for a lifetime upon the precepts and promises of the Gospel of Jesus Christ.

The old town cemetery of Enfield, where the dust of six generations now mingles and where the ashes of many of his kindred repose, will open its gates tomorrow to receive his remains. There his tombstone, with the place for the last date left blank, has waited his coming for nearly thirty years. Its brief record will soon be completed; but his more enduring memorials will be the prosperity which he has brought within our borders, and the universal esteem in which his memory will be cherished by his fellow townsmen.

Not only were the famous and relatively famous at risk, but so were average citizens, especially during the mid-1870s in Thompsonville, as reported in various local newspapers.

Thompsonville has seldom experienced so unhealthy a season as the present, and the mortuary record is rapidly growing larger. Five persons lay dead in the village Thursday of last week, and several are now dangerously sick. Pneumonia is the prevailing complaint, and its ravages are not confined to the aged, many of the deaths being of persons in the prime of life. The wife of Dr. Parsons, who died from this disease on Monday, was only sick three days, while the widow of Erastus Olmstead died on Tuesday, after a very short illness.[266]

Thompsonville physicians report much more than the usual amount of sickness for the past season, typhoid fever, pneumonia, and spinal meningitis have been the prevailing diseases. A considerable portion of the cases have proved fatal.[267]

The infectious challenges continued into the following year, as recounted in the Litchfield Enquirer, November 23,

---

[266] Connecticut Western News (Salisbury) Feb 26, 1875. Pg 2.
[267] Meriden Daily Republican April 9, 1875. Pg 2.

1876, edition.

> *Thompsonville's French-Canadian quarter[268], in the north part of the village, is infested with smallpox. The children in the public schools have been vaccinated, and every precaution taken to contain the disease within its present limits.*

Conventional methods of combating disease proved effective, but that didn't mean local physicians weren't immune to trying novel approaches as cures.

> *A novel treatment was practiced on a Thompsonville the other day. For his disease it was decided to try the efficacy of a 'ground sweat', for which purposes the man was stripped, and laid in a hole in the ground, and the covered with earth, a hole being left for him to breathe through.*

> *It is not announced whether a cure was effected. The man is between fifty and sixty years old.[269]*

If one did succumb, the town was strict about paying for the upkeep of cemetery plots, as a notice published in several regional papers proved.

> *If cemetery-lot owners do not settle within three months, their lots go by default, and the bodies will be removed.[270]*

There are no records of whether this threat was ever acted upon or of the location to which the dispossessed were removed.

---

[268] A section of Thompsonville commonly referred to as 'Frenchtown'. Many mills, carpet and other, had sections around them named similarly.

[269] Meriden Daily Republican July 31, 1877. Pg 2.

[270] Springfield Republican November 14, 1876. Pg 7.

For a small village during that period, there were numerous undertakers, including Edwin King, Arthur Leete, John Loring, R. A. Mitchell, J. Hughes, and William Mulligan. Some, like Mulligan, offered undertaking as an extension of their core business, Mulligan's being 'home furnishings'.

King was one of the undertakers who carried Stein's Patent Caskets.[271] Samuel Stein, who had incorporated his business in 1872, began selling his patented wooden caskets from his Rochester, New York, manufacturing facility. He achieved national notoriety after designing and building the coffin for Ulysses S. Grant in 1885.

Stein must have been the government's preferred casket provider, as coffins continued to be purchased from the company, as the clerk of the House of Representatives reported. In a 1891 report, a Stein casket was provided, along with the undertaking services from W. R. Spear, 19 pairs of silk gloves, a hearse, a barber's fee [presumably for the deceased], and attendees' costs. The coffin had a full plate-glass top, unusual for that time.

---

[271] Stein received Patent Number 132,605 on October 29, 1872, for an *Improvement in Burial Casket*.

Unusual but not unheard of.

In 1848, Almond Fisk of New York patented an airtight coffin consisting of two fitted metal shells joined together to complete the sealed environment. A glass plate, cemented in place over the face of the deceased, provided an unobstructed view of the departed.

A Fisk casket was used to inter John C. Calhoun, a South Carolinian Senator, in 1850 after the politician passed away from tuberculosis. The Senator was buried and disinterred multiple times over 25 years with no visible deterioration to Calhoun, prompting 12 U.S. Senators to sign and send a letter to Fisk extolling the virtues of his patented metal sarcophagus.

In 1877, Joseph Askins of Orrville, Ohio, was awarded a patent for a glass-metal burial casket, subsequently establishing a joint stock company called the *Askins Glass Casket Company* and setting up a manufacturing facility in the same city. Soon, a second facility was added in Elida, Ohio, and a third just over the border in Ontario, Canada. The company's directors included Joseph, his brother Jacob Askins, and seven others. Based on reportedly strong sales, the number of employees ramped up to fifty within a short period.

The company was so successful that a competitor, led by a former Askins employee, W. C. Lautner, established the Wooster [Glass] Burial Case Company in the nearby town of Wooster, Ohio, by February of 1880. Although the number of employees was not reported in an article published in the February 25 edition of the Wayne County Democrat, the paper noted that between 60 and 100 caskets were in various stages of completion at that time.

Given the market receptivity to the glass coffins and the rapidity with which competitors established themselves,

Askins began seeking willing partners in other parts of the country. One of those possible partners was revealed in the May 19, 1881, edition of the Thompsonville Press, where it was reported that Joseph Askins would meet with prospective interested parties in Mechanics Hall to propose his business plan and present samples of his product for consideration.

If this industry should be located here, the first building needed would be the foundry which could have considerable business from outside parties, including, probably, the Hartford Carper Company.

It is expected that when full capacity of production is reached, that two hundred and fifty persons would be employed.

The iron framework of two samples which he has for exhibition were completed and made ready for the paint with the patent emery wheels made by the Vitrified Wheel Company of Westfield, Mass.[272]

As reported in the following week's edition, the presentation and prospects for the business were so well received by those in attendance that half of the required capital of $50,000 had been raised through stock sales, with shares priced at $100 each.

Within a few days, shareholders met to formalize the paperwork. By that time, an additional $10,000 had been purchased, bringing the total subscription to $30,000.

In order that nothing should be done in haste and that every available means should be used to examine into the matter, Mr. W. Calderwood, as a representative of the stockholders, started yesterday morning for Ohio, where the first manufactory of the kind was established three

---

[272] Thompsonville Press May 19, 1881. Page 2.

years since. He will probably reach Ohio today and will make thorough examinations and inquiries, returning if possible by Saturday evening.

Should everything prove satisfactory, parties stand ready to take the remaining stock at once and work will be commenced as soon as possible. There are several places where the works could be located, but it is probable that the Brainard Warehouse will be bought, with land adjoining.[273]

By June 9th, everything seemed to be in order with the establishment of the new glass burial case company in Thompsonville, as the shareholders met at Dr. Loren Howard Pease's home to organize the company and formally elect officers. The early consensus was that William Calderwood, the same individual who had inspected the Ohio manufactories, was the front-runner to lead the concern. The still burning question was where the manufacturing facility would be located. The issue with the Brainard site was the inflexibility of the Dime Savings Bank of Norwich, owner of the property, as to the sales price, prompting the group to consider other sites, such as:

...the Wool lot, B[enjamin] Bright's lot, Philip Downey's lot[274], B. F. Lord's lot[275], and others.

Plans for a new building have been drafted and it is estimated that buildings such as would be wanted to begin business in and which are much larger than the Brainard warehouse, could be built for a figure not far from what is

---

[273] Thompsonville Press May 26, 1881. Page 2.

[274] Each along the CT River and RR Tracks towards Warehouse Point

[275] As above BUT northerly rather than southerly

asked for that property.[276]

By June 23rd, the building committee, comprising Loren Howard Pease, William Calderwood, and Niles Pease, had selected a location and, along with Joseph Askins, had begun soliciting proposals to erect the required buildings. The contract was eventually awarded to the Watters Brothers of Longmeadow, Massachusetts, who had submitted the winning bid of slightly less than $8,000.

Calderwood was born in Glasgow, Scotland, in 1838. He spent his youth along the banks of Loch Lomond and his early adulthood in Edinburgh.

International

YOU may safely depend on The "International" for that swing and dash, so essential to up-to-date Dress. The name spells Reliance. It not only assures correctness of style and fabric, but economic and perfect tailoring as well. And the most important thing of all is the knowledge and assurance that once you place your order with The International Tailoring Company, you may safely rely on getting what you ask for. This is why we take measures for those up-to-date Metropolitan Tailors.

Wm. Calderwood,
Pleasant street, Thompsonville, Conn.

He emigrated to the United States in 1870, along with other family members, all of whom were weavers, aboard the steamship Australia, and eventually settled in the village of Thompsonville.

Although his relatives pursued employment at the carpet company, William established a grocery and general store in the village.[277]

He and his wife, Ellen Alderman of Lockport, New York,

---

[276] Thompsonville Press June 9, 1881. Page 2.
[277] Calderwood worked the store until his 75th year, retiring and moving to Springfield, Massachusetts. He passed away in his 91st year.

had eight children during their residency, the last of whom was born when Calderwood turned 50.

The Articles of Association of the New England Glass Burial Case Company and the entirety of the subscribers were published in the July 7th edition of Thompsonville Press. This included 44 residents of Thompsonville: one from Scitico, three from Somers, two from Hartford, three from Suffield, two from Longmeadow, and one each from Boston, Springfield, and Pittsfield.

By August 15th, 1881, the Hartford Courant reported that the manufactory would be completed within six weeks and would begin producing caskets by the beginning of 1882. The Meriden Daily Republican followed up with a similar report on September 21, echoing the Courant article's sentiments but projecting that production would begin as early as October 1881.

January began with the rising hopes and dreams of those who had purchased stock in the fledgling company. The concern continued to add employees, reaching 50 by the 19th of the month. A casket 'trimmer' was lured away from Stein's Patent Caskets to work at the new Thompsonville manufactory and quickly demonstrated that the glass-metallic coffin could be covered in cloth as neatly as a wooden one.

The New England Glass Burial Case Company appears to be destined to become one of the largest manufactories in Hartford County. It was organized in July, 1881, and has erected in the south part of Thompsonville a foundry of 40 feet front and 100 feet deep, paint shops and finishing rooms 80 feet front, 100 feet deep and two stories high.[278]

One week later, on the 27th of January at 10 a.m., a terrific gale from the northwest swept through Thompsonville, blowing out the east and west walls of the newly erected Burial Company's Foundry. Within ten minutes, the Watters Brothers were on site, effecting short-term repairs, offering to repair the structure at no cost. The offer was refused, and the casket partners acknowledged the destruction was an Act of God rather than poor workmanship.

Perhaps it was an omen, but it nonetheless reflected the honor of both parties.

All during 1882, newspaper reports extolled both the virtues and the sales of the fledgling operation, the Hartford Courant quoting several undertakers as saying the glass-metallic constructs:

...would revolutionize the old and appalling forms of

---

[278] The Meriden Daily Republican January 20, 1882. Page 4.

caskets.

Undertakers fell over each other to advertise their participation in selling the Thompsonville product.

By August, those reading between the lines could see the first storm clouds on the horizon. The Thompsonville Press reported on the progress of the new wooden casket shop as the company expanded into more conventional burial containers.

> *October 1st is the time set by the Supt. of the casket works to get their new wood casket shops into working condition. The building is already up, and the machinery, which consists of saws, planes, moulders, shapers, lathes, etc., besides a new 50-horsepower engine are already ordered. The company has secured the services of Mr. Hall, of Grand Rapids, Mich., an experienced and competent manufacturer of wooden caskets.[279]*

In the September 10th edition of the Springfield Republican, the newspaper reported that with the recent additions, the company had the largest works of any kind in New England, if not the United States.

By December of 1882, the Thompsonville Iron Foundry had begun to advertise its own casting services.

---

[279] Thompsonville Press August 17, 1882. Page 2.

In October, the Thompsonville Press reported that the New England Glass Burial Case Company had received several thousand casket orders from Cuba, as if some impending disaster was on the horizon.

By March of the following year, the impending disaster became clear.

The New England Glass Burial Case Company, Thompsonville, has suspended but will pay all indebtedness.[280]

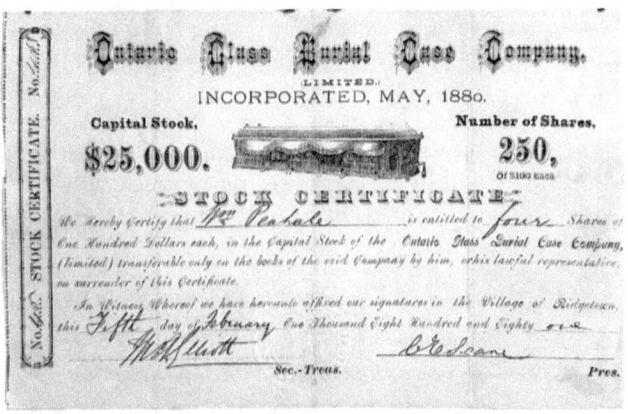

A similar scenario occurred to the north at the Ontario Glass Burial Case Company in Ridgetown, Ontario, Canada. The casket company was established in a timeframe comparable to that of Thompsonville, the Canadian firm formed in December of 1880, and its expectations echoed those of the small Connecticut village.

He [Askins] felt sure the company would be a fine success both for those who went into it and for the town. All the speakers had nothing but good words for Mr. Askins,

---

[280] The New London Day March 14, 1884. Page 4.

whose dealing here had been highly honorable, while benefitting himself he had done a good thing for Ridgetown, and for this, he must, in consequence, be considered a public benefactor.[281]

Eight months later, at the Provincial Fair in Hamilton, Ontario, the new firm exhibited one of its celebrated glass caskets to great fanfare.

The exhibit of the Ontario Glass Burial Case Company, manufacturers of the celebrated Askins' patent glass burial case, and for which W. M. Chapman's Sons are agents in this city, is already one of the attractions of the Fair. Of its kind, this exhibit is the most elegant exhibit to be seen anywhere.[282]

The jury is out on whether the actual casket displayed was manufactured by the new firm, as an article almost 12 months to the day noted the impending construction of a manufactory due to tax considerations.

At Ridgetown, a by-law granting a loan of $5,000 for ten years, free of interest, and to exempt Ontario Glass burial case company's building and plant for taxation for a like time, was voted on yesterday and carried.

The company guarantee to build immediately a brick factory and to employ at least thirty skilled workmen all the year round. The company will give a mortgage on the building, ground and plant as security to their fulfillment. The new company will have a capital of $50,000.[283]

By July 16, 1883, the company had ceased operations. Eerily similar to the Thompsonville iteration.

---

[281] The Lima Democratic Times December 18, 1880. Page 5.

[282] The Hamilton Spectator September 22, 1880. Page 4.

[283] The Hamilton Spectator September 6, 1881. Page 1.

Had Askins been a scam artist? It seemed unlikely, as neither the Ontario nor Thompsonville operations had paid him in anything but stock options, which were only promissory notes based on future success. But an article in the *Fort Wayne Weekly Sentinel* might indicate otherwise, as it reported Askins' visceral reaction to a response by postmaster Charles Rice to a request from, most likely, a potential investor from Chatham-Kent, Canada, a mere 30 miles from Ridgefield, the site of the proposed burial case partnership at the time, as to Askins' character.

SUE AND BE HANGED

Prospect of An Interesting Slander Suit at Elida, O.

Elida, O., Oct. 8, 1879 – Our little village is stirred from the center to circumference by the prospects of a large-sized slander suit. From the face of the returns, it seems our postmaster, Chas. B. Rice, received a letter a short time ago from a party in Chatham, Ont., asking about the reputation of Joseph Askins, a citizen of the village. Joseph was there trying to get up some kind of corporation or stock company to manufacture the Askins glass burial case. Charlie answered the letter and gave the general history of the Askins family, including Joseph. Last Friday Joseph arrived from Canada and stated that Charlie was going to the penitentiary whether or no, and proceeded to lay the matter before the grand jury, which was in session in Lima. They examined the papers, but said it came not under their jurisdiction. The matter now lies in this shape: Joseph claims that he can make a case and will sue for $10,000 damages, while Charlie says he may sue and be hanged to him, as he can prove all he wrote. Further developments will be promptly reported.

19: MOTHER NATURE &
ROBERT MCCRONE

The warmth of Spring in 1880 broke, and the last gasp of winter became a distant memory. But it was New England, and the weather was fickle.

On May 28, 1880, at one o'clock in the afternoon, a violent gale visited the villages of Suffield and Thompsonville, wreaking havoc and destruction. What some experienced as a simple thunder shower, others met the full force and fury of a genuine tornado as it tore across the two towns, sparing lives but not property.

Hundreds of trees were uprooted, roofs of barns and homes were scattered across the landscape, and businesses were destroyed.

The storm appeared to the west as a usual darkening sky before a summer thunderstorm. Soon, though, dust clouds swirled around the base of a forming funnel, and a driving hail preceded the tempest.

The maelstrom moved from Suffield to the Connecticut River. By then, the tornado was about one mile wide, kicking up waves like those on an open ocean during a squall. The steam ferry boat was anchored near the Thompsonville shore, and those onboard hung on for dear life, remaining inside the cabin for fear of being thrown into the roiling waves. Just south of the ferry, a barge lay in calm waters, defining how distinct the passing tornado was in cutting the impact line.

The storm moved in a northeast direction, tearing slate from the railroad freight house roof and driving it through the clapboards of the homes just across the road. On the eastern side of the tracks, a dozen or more houses just north of the train station lost their chimneys like dominoes toppling one after the other.

Nearly half a mile east of the river, and as far north as the village, the wind rolled up the slope over the open fields and smashed in Edmund B. Alden's 36 by 80 feet tobacco shed in which Mr. Alden was busy. Though the timbers and roof now lie flat, he escaped unhurt, and a horse in the shed was dug out of a hole in the pile of rubbish just large enough to contain him.

South of this building stood a well-built brick shed 160 feet long and 64 wide, surmounted by a cupola, under which a kiln of 30,000 bricks was burning, and another of nearly 100,000 was just being started. The roof was taken off and scattered over an adjoining yard in which a lot of green brick was drying, the damage being considerable.

A little further southeast stood a neat two-story brick horse barn, 36 by 42 feet, with 16-inch walls, in which seven horses were stalled. The upper story of this building was shaved off clean and scattered around, not a horse being hurt. A piece of the roof, however, struck Ernest Hortier, a French laborer, cutting him a good deal but not dangerously. Across the road to the north, in the cellar of a tenement whose 'L' was shattered, were two men, but neither was hurt.[284]

TERRIFIC GALE!

Buildings Destroyed!

Chimneys Down!

Trees Uprooted!

Roads Blocked!

Boats Smashed Ashore,

&c., &c.

Edmund Alden's fine brick barn was demolished, but, strange to say, the wooden barn beside it was uninjured. His old red barn, brick kiln, and some of his finest orchard trees were blown down. Mr. Alden was seriously injured by the falling debris.

---

[284] Springfield Republican May 29, 1880. Page 4.

Mr. Kenney's house in the hollow, just north of Mr. Alden's, was also torn into fragments.

Mr. Seth Alden's tobacco shed was destroyed. A large number of valuably shade trees were uprooted. A large willow tree on the Brookside was twisted from the ground and thrown into the brook.

A great poplar tree south of the Globe Hotel was blown across the road. Boats on the river were broken, driven up on shore, and overset. Three large trees were destroyed at the ferry, two were blown over in John Houston's yard, two at Charles Thorogood, two on the corner of North Main and Maple Sts., and two opposite, two in front of George Barber's place. Two trees behind Samuel Cook's house were torn up and thrown into the brook. A large tree in front of Francis Chapin's, fell, just grazing the house.

Travel is impeded by the blocking of Gray Brook bridge.

Three trains were stopped north of this place by trees thrown upon the tracks. About one hundred trees were uprooted on Robert McCrone's farm, and his barns, greenhouses, and tobacco sheds were laid flat. Mr. Gariside's tobacco shed was demolished.

Over twenty-five large shade trees were blown down between Seth Alden's and Robert McCrone's farms. The slamming of a door broke one of Thomas Mansley's show windows. Ten barns were blown down in Suffield, and probably more are to be heard from. [285]

The storm lasted only a few minutes but left years of recovery in its path. It was a reminder of the kind of interruption a seemingly calm Spring morning can present

---

[285] Thompsonville Press May 28, 1880. Page 2.

to unsuspecting people. It would be four years before Mother Nature displayed her unpredictability again.

New England farmers thought the freezing weather that arrived on May 28th, 1884, and held firm through the following day, was bad, but the Black Frost[286] that followed on May 30th was the killing frost they feared.

The air had been dry that Spring Friday, and the hoarfrost that would have protected the young plants as an insulating layer had failed to form. The water in plant tissues froze, fatally damaging the plant's structure.

To the north, in Massachusetts, throughout Vermont and New Hampshire, it was reported that apple, pear, plum, and cherry trees had dropped their early blossoms. Cherries and grapes were spoiled for the year. Currants, asparagus, peas, cabbage, and rhubarb, commonly hardy plants, were either wilting or turning pale in spots.

Garden plants grown on vines froze solid, and the new wood on grapevines was killed. In most farms, ground that had been turned over in expectation of planting had frozen hard enough to support a man's weight. The first plantings were a total loss.

Friday morning's temperature in the region ranged from 22 to 29 degrees, following the two previous days' lows of 32 degrees.

Some farmers set and maintained fires in their fields, which they tended throughout the evening until the morning sun provided a modicum of warmth, thereby saving some of their crops.

---

[286] Black frost is a severe frost that occurs when the air is dry and vegetation turns black. It's a killing frost that can damage and kill plants and trees.

The frost greatly damaged fruits and vegetables throughout Connecticut, freezing the young greens of potatoes, corn, and beans and forcing farmers to plow under their fields in hopes of a second planting.

In Thompsonville, a frost like the one on May 30th hadn't been seen since 1816, known as the 'Year Without a Summer'. Severe climate abnormalities dropped temperatures worldwide, resulting in crop failures and significant food shortages across the Northern Hemisphere. The freezing temperatures from May through August were record-setting.

Although the three frostbitten days of May 1884 may not have been as devastating globally, the effects were impactful regionally.

To state that the destruction by last Friday morning's frost, or rather freeze, the greatest known within the memory of the oldest inhabitant, is but repeating what almost everyone has said, but the old saying that 'what everyone says must be true,' helps to sustain the statement, and we will give it as a fact. For the mercury to drop to 24 degrees above zero, on the 30th of May, means destruction in the fullest sense of the word.

In Enfield alone, the loss can hardly fall short of twenty thousand dollars, and many put it nearer fifty thousand. To enumerate the varieties of vegetation that were damaged or destroyed would be a hard task and it would be but stretching it a trifle if we said that everything that has made a new growth since winter responded to the blast of that cold morning. Even the foliage upon the trees of the forest, the oaks, chestnuts, butternuts, ash, and others, was to a degree killed, and the undergrowth has the appearance of a fire having passed over the entire ground.

It is generally believed that the fruit crop, such as pears, plums, cherries and apples will be lessened at least three-fourths, while grapes, excepting where grown in sheltered localities, are entirely ruined for this season. The berry crop, including strawberries, raspberries, and cultivated blackberries, is said to be damaged more than a half, and one grower of the latter believes the crop entirely ruined for this season and badly damaged for next by the killing -of the new growth of canes. With the field crops, corn and potatoes, it made a clean sweep, not leaving a vestige of life above ground and in many cases freezing down to the seed.

While everyone loses more or less...Robert McCrone had one and a half acres set out with tomatoes and four acres planted to melons and summer squash, all of which were covered with rhubarb leaves but were entirely destroyed; seven acres of potatoes, part of which were covered with earth by horse hoes, but the covering amounted to nothing; two acres of early sweet corn, cut completely to the ground. His early peas, which were budded out, are badly damaged, and set back at least two weeks. Mr. McCrone states that after carefully examining at least fifty apple sets he was unable to find one that was not damaged or destroyed. He believes that at least one fourth of the entire production of New England is totally destroyed.[287]

But once again, Robert McCrone and local farmers proved resilient, salvaging what they could and replanting, hoping for a later harvest.

Four more years would pass, and once again, Mother Nature showed her unpleasant side, challenging the village residents, particularly Robert McCrone.

---

[287] Thompsonville Press June 5, 1884. Page 2.

Sunday, March 11, began as an unseasonably warm day.

But New England's weather is fickle, and the day began to turn decidedly colder. The rain that had been lightly falling during the day turned to snow at 10 p.m. as Thompsonville's residents and shopkeepers turned in for the night, most secure in believing that the falling flakes represented winter's last gasp.

Upon awakening the next day, the village was met with three inches of fresh powder. It wasn't enough to stop the beginning of the week's work or school activities, as the residents of Thompsonville were a hardy lot.

As the morning turned into early afternoon, the good people of the village began to look at the skies with concern. The flakes had not increased in size as they do in a late winter storm, but the number of flakes had risen dramatically, and visibility had been severely impacted.

Unknown to the layman at the time, an area of low pressure had formed along the East Coast with rotational winds from the Atlantic Ocean pulling moisture over the northeastern states. A classic nor'easter had formed, and Thompsonville was ground zero to the storm that would become known as the Great White Hurricane.

The wind then blew furiously and it was almost impossible for a person at that time to face the storm. At least 18 inches of snow had fallen on a level, but drifted it was much deeper. Many streets were in places filled to the level of the fence tops, while at other places, the banks turned up much higher.

As the fury of the storm continued to rage, people of mature years began to apprehend possible danger. Schools were closed early, and clerks were allowed to go to their homes with instructions not to return that day.

Superintendent Upson of the carpet works directed that

the whistles be blown at 4:30, an hour earlier than usual, and the operatives allowed to seek their homes by daylight.

At this hour it was absolutely dangerous for a person to attempt to go any great distance in the storm alone. Much of the way, the snow was waist deep, while banks that were from four to twelve feet had to be surmounted. In cases like the latter, it was only possible to crawl or roll.[288]

Suffield, Connecticut post-storm 1888 [unknown street].

No passenger trains passed this station going south after ten o'clock Monday forenoon, while no train arrived from New York after Sunday. The last regular train to go north was the 6.41 train Monday morning.

A special was made up at Hartford, composed of two engines, baggage, and a passenger car that passed this station about 12 o'clock and succeeded in reaching Springfield in the afternoon. The engines were heavily loaded with snow and resembled moving snowbanks.[289]

---

[288] Thompsonville Press March 15, 1888. Page 2.
[289] Thompsonville Press March 15, 1888. Page 2.

Connecticut received between 20 and 50 inches of snow across various parts of the state, with snow drifts reaching 12 feet or more. To the south, New Haven recorded drifts measuring 40 feet.

By Tuesday morning, the winter hurricane had lost most of its strength, although snow continued to fall throughout the day. The carpet mill remained closed, but Westfield Plate and G. H. Bushnell opened for manufacturing. Getting to work proved difficult, if not impossible, as waist-deep snow covered the roads. Schools were ordered closed for the remainder of the week.

Men were put at work with shovels as early Tuesday as possible and a passage dug through Main Street wide enough to allow a team to pass along.

B. W. Bright, with two horses and a bob sled, broke a passage through Prospect Street. B. F. Lord, with four horses, went through Main Street and Pearl to South Pearl, meeting Henry C. Woodward near Selectman Davis's, he having succeeded in reaching that point with men and a yoke of cattle.

Lord's team was followed by Bright's and the two teams went down South Pearl, returning the same way. James Logan and William Alcorn, with a double team and a number of men, broke a road from Maple Street through South Main to Pearl.

By night, passageways had been made through nearly every street in the village. H. S. Brainard succeeded in reaching Main Street with his milk sleigh, where he readily disposed of the lacteal fluid and returned. W. H. Lane succeeded in reaching the village with a load of yeast and reached some of his customers by taking the yeast in a water pail and making his way through the snow from house to house.

The. scene on Main Street was truly grand.

The snow was piled up on either side of the single driveway from six to ten feet in depth. Crossings were dug at intervals, and the buildings, with snow piled on the balconies and lower roofs, presented an unusual appearance. From the eaves of the lower carpet mills hang stupendous icicles from ten to fifteen feet in length, the wind evidently twisted and bent them as they congealed, leaving them a wonder to behold.[290]

As Wednesday unfolded, employees returned to work as if what winter had wrought had been a minor annoyance.

The work of breaking and clearing roads was continued all day Wednesday and will be continued for some days to come. The selectmen have over a hundred men employed shoveling and alt the teams that can be secured drawing the snow out of the* principal thoroughfares.

No serious accident or great loss of property is reported In the village.

A portion of the boiler house to the old Stockinet Works

---

[290] Thompsonville Press March 15, 1888. Page 2.

was crushed in by snow falling from the roof above. The roof to the old weave room, as it is termed, sunk from 12 to 15 inches under its heavy weight of snow, but being a truss roof, no damage resulted. The snow was removed yesterday, and the roof is all right again.

Robert McCrone, florist, undoubtedly sustained the heaviest loss of anyone in this vicinity. A large amount of glass was broken in his greenhouse and in places the roof was entirely crushed in. He was snowbound at Springfield. Fuel ran short and many plants were damaged or entirely ruined by being frozen. He stated this morning that he had $600 worth of flowers that he should have sold in two or three days, which were a total loss. He believes his entire stock of roses fit to use at Easter are ruined; The loss on the building and flowers he estimates at $3,000, about equally divided He appears not in the least discouraged, but hopes to have the glass replaced soon and a new start made.[291]

In the days following the storm, temperatures rose quickly, and the snow melted away within a few weeks, leaving only shared memories of the event.

Although no lives had been lost in Thompsonville, the rapid melt uncovered the bodies of missing unfortunates in other towns and left others with the cost of rebuilding their lives and livelihoods.

Robert McCrone suffered more than anyone else from both weather events, but he was a hardy New Englander built to withstand challenges.

Following the tornado of 1880, a brief article painted a

---

[291] Ibid

picture of the businessman.

> *There is probably not an intelligent man in town who does not feel a hearty sympathy with Robert McCrone. It is only a short time since he lost his greenhouses to fire. He was just getting so well going that the memory of the disaster was blunted, when the tornado comes to give another blow. He is no whiner or grumbler, but really, if a helping hand can be worthily extended to anyone, it is to him.*[292]

It is rare for someone to enter our lives and leave an indelible mark, as Robert McCrone did on the good people of Thompsonville. He was a farmer, gardener, vegetarian, constable, tax collector, state representative (twice), board member of relief, and a talented orator. He had taken another man's child, Randall Bostwick, into his home when the boy's father had left him with him, unable to care for the lad, and Robert had raised him as his own.

How many of us will have multiple newspaper columns regaling our lives and our impact upon our brethren after passing on? Personal stories speaking of us in glowing terms? Honoring and exalting that some were lucky enough to know us and call us their friend?

He was a Man amongst Men. Exceptional in every way.

His life is best captured in the eulogies penned by others.

IN MEMORIAM

He is gone and we shall see his familiar form no more. Let me place one sprig of green upon his grave.

His nature must have been fine in its beginning, but doubtless, it was refined again and again by sad experiences which would have hardened and corroded most

---

[292] Thompsonville Press June 4, 1880. Page 2.

souls.

If he died owing aught to any man, remember that the world owed him a thousand times more than he owed the world.

He was not careful about his attire. He cared for better things than fashion. He believed the religion of the future would be the religion of truth, but to him, Christianity was the leading star. He had no creed. He lived above all creeds. He had no thought of self. He who has the purest religion has self-most in abnegation.

We cannot say he was a perfect man; he had defects, but they were not of the heart. He was gentle as a lamb when contending with you about non-essentials, but as fierce as a lion when contending for a principle he believed in.

His love embraced all humanity. He was one of the first to vote the free-soil ticket in the town, because he believed that the colored man, as the rest of mankind, deserved his freedom; and it was very appropriate that a colored man should speak at his funeral.

He admired the beauty of the flowers he loved and wrought among so many years, but he admired much more the beauty of true manhood.

He could convince one of a belief he had just by asking a question, sooner than most men could by a long argument.

No intelligent lady ever got in familiar discourse with him without soon discovering beneath his rugged exterior the purity and simplicity of his nature. It was no task for him to convince any intelligent person of the purity of his motives and the generosity of his nature.

[indecipherable text]

Let us not [decry] his departure, for he was like a little child. 'Of such is the kingdom of heaven.' [293]

These weren't the only words to memorialize the life and legacy of the Thompsonville gardener. Film fans might recall the kindly Chauncey Gardiner from the movie Being There. Gardiner was a sheltered servant who spoke truthfully. His conversations were mistakenly considered simple, but the sincerity with which they were delivered reflected a profound, more honest knowledge.

Death of Robert McCrone

In the death of Robert McCrone, Enfield has lost probably her most remarkable man. We may indeed, we think, go farther and say that, in the judgment of those who have known him best and understood his real power and his actual influence as a thinker and debater, and as a strong man among strong men, it is true that he has been one of the most remarkable men of his day and generation, even thought that day and that generation are among the most remarkable thus far in modern history.

In Robert McCrone's case, no one who knows the history of Thompsonville from about the year 1840 till 1889, his most active years in some lines, can say that his town's people were ignorant of the fact that he was a man of unusual ability, and yet it is not probable that he has ever been appreciated at his real value by the majority of his acquaintances.

Born in Kilmarnock, Scotland, about the year 1819, he came to Thompsonville in 1831 and was at once set to work as a treading boy to a hand-loom weaver.

Circumstances beyond his control made all his life till his

---

[293] Thompsonville Press November 2, 1893. Page 2.

very recent years one of particular deprivation and self-denial. With an education, or rather a lack of education, that would have left an average man hopelessly ignorant, a passionate love of reading led him, by a singular purity of taste, to an acquaintance with the best literature, and educated him, in reality, far above the level of many a mere college graduate.

He was not a character easy to describe. It was a Scottish nature to the very core and, therefore, a complex one.

The strongest of all his strong traits was his intense love of right, his profound reverence for truth, and his loyalty to his own conception of god, which loyalty made faithfulness to all right and truth as he saw them inevitable. An uneducated man, deprived by the conditions of his daily life of all the refining influences of a happy home life, thrown almost entirely upon men, even for his intimate friendships, he was, as few men are, a man of his own kind; but it was a noble kind, and a kind that will start free and clear as few do in the life whose doors have just opened to receive them.

At eighteen, a seeming accident led him to study and adopt the theories of Dr. Graham, the vegetarian, and from thence to the end, no animal's blood ever in any degree ministered to his. It was a theory, perhaps, but not an ignoble one, and no man of our time has lived up to a higher ideal on all such lines as he.

From the first he was a whole-souled opponent of slavery. None who heard him in his passionate appeals against its monstrous wrongs can ever forget them. At such times, he spoke as one inspired, and some of the best critics have said that no national speaker excelled him on these subjects. He held his hearers spellbound, dominating them

*as only masters can dominate — one moment convulsing
them with laughter, another wringing tears from et=yes
unused to weep, and making every man see tot eh time
being — whether he would or not — right, pity, justice,
brotherhood as his intense soul saw them.*

*He might have been great as a statesman, as an orator,
as a reformer, as a great leader of thought. Vast
potentialities were his had his lot not been cast in different
lines.*[294]

For some unknown reason, the Thompsonville Press
skipped a week in publishing. The edition of November
16th was the next to go to press. It contained yet another
remembrance of Robert McCrone, a reprint from the
February 22, 1862, newspaper, as the country headed into
the dark days of the Civil War. The writer described an
unnamed gathering of locals held at Mechanics Hall to
commemorate Washington's birthday, and this was the first
time he was introduced to the Thompsonville gardener.

Several speakers had held forth, including John L.
Houston, Teacher Peck, Rector Gregory (new to Saint
Andrews), T. M. Sheridan (referred to as The Constable),
and Squire (Judge) Briscoe. After the crowd had sung the
Star-Spangled Banner, a call went up, inciting Robert
McCrone to take the stage to address the crowd.
Reluctantly, he did so to raucous applause.

*When silence at last reigned, again rung out that strong
voice, 'Mr. Chairman, ladies and fellow citizens,' and in
less than two minutes he was fairly launched in the speech
of the evening, and all was unheeded save the torrent of
philosophic, patriotic, and prophetic words that poured
from his lips with marvelous impetuosity.*

---

[294] Thompsonville Press November 2, 1893. Page 2.

He sketched in rapid review the past, its failures and its lessons; the present, its duties and its perils; the future, its hopes and its fruitions, when our beloved country should emerge from its destined baptism of blood, refined by fire, redeemed by suffering, disenthralled through costly sacrifices from the overshadowing curse of slavery

As he approached the close of his speech, with those confidant predictions uttered in the early and gloomy hour of the war, he seemed to assume the office and dignity of a prophet, as he stood upon that platform, with his tall figure erect, head thrown back, nostrils dilated, eyes flashing fire, and his right hand outstretched heavenward as though summoning the denizens of both worlds to witness his prophecy of the sure salvation of the imperiled union, the ultimate peace, prosperity, and glory of the greatest republic.

It was a grand speech. It has always seemed to me the best I have ever heard from him, but this may have been because, on this occasion, it was so new, so unexpected, so astonishing a revelation of power from so unexpected a source. My enthusiasm could scarcely be restrained from some unseemly demonstration of feeling.[295]

The writer had surreptitiously prepared a speech of his own, which paled in comparison to McCrone's, and was glad he had not been called upon. The relatively uneducated McCrone had educated the writer George S. Martin, inspiring him to become a better author and orator from that evening forward. His words in his memorial to the gardener of Thompsonville certainly spoke to his own eloquence.

Perhaps it was fitting that John W. Copley, the business

---

[295] Thompsonville press November 16, 1893. Page 2.

manager of the Church and North families of Shakers, purchased the auction sale of McCrone's property.

Years earlier, at the Annual Meeting of American Florists in Philadelphia, Pennsylvania, Robert McCrone had participated in answering questions submitted by the crowd assembled in the hall. It was reported that McCrone responded to queries with a good deal of wit, who 'had his way' with the crowd and 'vindicated the State of Connecticut by bringing down the house.'

As quoted by the Oshkosh Northwestern newspaper on May 17, 1882, when discussing how to get rich in farming, one can only think that his tongue-in-cheek response could have been applied to many life situations.

Keep down the weeds and use plenty of manure.

20: BRASS AND BROMIDE

Seventy-six trombones led the big parade,
With a hundred & ten cornets close at hand.
They were followed by rows and rows,
Of the finest virtuosos,
The cream of every famous band.
Seventy-six trombones caught the morning sun,
With a hundred & ten cornets right behind.[296]

Thompsonville, Connecticut, Cornet Band, circa 1900

Cornet bands were popular during the late 19th and early

---

[296] Seventy-Six Trombones lyrics (*The Music Man* movie)

20th centuries because the instrument's large mouthpiece and valve configuration made it suitable for community bands with diverse skill levels. The cornet also produced a warmer, softer tone than the trumpet and was considered more pleasing to the ear. It was also easier to hear outdoors, making it ideal for town gatherings and celebrations.

Thompsonville was blessed with four bands during this period.[297] The Carpet City Brass Band was active in 1904, performing in Thompsonville. The Thompsonville Cornet Band[298]Active in the 1880s and 1890s, the organization was initially led by John Wall Martin in its early years. The Thompsonville City Band, separate from Carpet City, was active in the same period. Brown's Cornet Band performed during the same years as Thompsonville Cornet.

Thompsonville City Band in costume circa 1908.

John Wall Martin was born on June 21, 1852, to George Wall Martin and his wife, Catherine Elizabeth Anderson.

---

[297] Detailed in *The Brass Bands of the World* compiled and published in 2019.

[298] At times referred to as Martin's Band of Thompsonville.

George had emigrated to the United States in 1844 on the Ship *Martha*, which had left Liverpool, England, destined for Ellis Island. He has sailed with at least three other weavers, John Fallows, Francis Fisher, and George Griffiths, each of whom had their sights set on employment at the Thompsonville carpet mills.

For whatever reason, young John never made it past the 6th grade, most likely taking on the duties of a tread boy in the carpet mill to help with his growing family's bills by 1864. The 1870 census confirms that John was employed in the carpet mill, but within two years, he had shifted his sights and, at 26, established himself as a cigar manufacturer in Thompsonville. He maintained that occupation until he closed his operation and moved to Springfield, Massachusetts, in 1922, passing away 22 years later at 91.

During his life in Thompsonville, he served as a vestryman at Saint Andrews Episcopal Church, was a member of the Doric Lodge of Masons, the Friendship Lodge, the Independent Order of Odd Fellows (IOOF), and the Enfield Encampment.[299]

One of his other positions was teacher and leader of the Thompsonville Cornet Band, a 'metal band' he led for 20 or more years from the 1880s through the early 1900s. He gave up the band leadership position to offer private lessons on the violin and cornet, and whether the former band retained another leader or ceased to exist is undetermined.

---

[299] The Grand Army of the Republic (GAR), the largest of all Union Army veterans' organizations, was the most powerful single-issue political lobby of the late nineteenth century, securing massive pensions for veterans and helping to elect five postwar presidents from its own membership. To its members, it was also a secret fraternal order, a source of local charity, a provider of entertainment in small municipalities, and a patriotic organization.

JOHN W. MARTIN,

Teacher of Violin and Cornet.

On and after Sept. 15th will be pleased to see former pupils and all others wishing THOROUGH INSTRUCTION on either or the above-named instruments.

J. W. MARTIN,

Formerly Teacher of Thompsonville Cornet Band.

RESIDENCE—

Lincoln street, - Thompsonville, Conn.

Post-office box, 227. . 16-tf

Whether the Thompsonville Cornet Band and William S. Brown's Cornet Band played at odds with each other is unclear. Still, they occupied the same entertainment space in the village and beyond, offering social engagements for village residents and their friends.

A rare opportunity for an excursion and basket picnic, at low figures, will be offered to our citizens on Friday, July 15th, by the Thompsonville Cornet Band.

The band has chartered the steamship River Belle and Gallup's Grove for the afternoon and evening of that day and will give all who avail themselves of the opportunity a pleasant boat ride and an afternoon in the grove.

The first boat will leave here about noon and return home from the grove at about 7 o'clock, in time to take a second party up the river for an excursion, stopping on their return for a dance.

The full band will accompany each oat and enliven the party with some nice music on the water.[300]

The Cornet Bands also acted as 'goodwill ambassadors' to other regional locales.

Windsor Military Band and St. Casimir's Lithuanian Society marchers walk on Broad Street during a 1916 parade. Windsor Historical Society.

Brown's Cornet Band went, by invitation, to Windsor last Saturday evening, to visit the Windsor Cornet Band.

On its arrival there, it was met at the depot by the Windsor Band, in full uniform, and the two bands paraded through the principal streets, halting on the green, where they played several airs to an enthusiastic crowd of spectators.

After which, they proceeded to the Town Hall, where

---

[300] Thompsonville Press July 7, 1881. Page 2.

tables loaded with refreshments awaited their coming.

After supper, speeches and Windsor cigars (which are sure to be good) were in order. On returning to the green the two bands gave a concert, and, as our informant says, made considerable noise.

The Thompsonville boys returned on the steamboat train, and all were loud in praise of the way they had been treated, and declare that all they want to do now is to get a chance to show the Windsor boys that Thompsonville can't be outdone on an occasion of that kind.[301]

Although William S. Brown was the spiritual leader of the Brown's Cornet Band, officers were elected to their positions annually. In 1885, R. C. Gaines was appointed president; Samuel McAuley was the sergeant and treasurer; Brown was the leader; Fred Clee was the secretary; and W. H. Loring was the assistant secretary. Whether the Thompsonville Cornet followed suit with elected officers is unknown.

What is known is that these brass bands entertained the good people of Thompsonville from the late 1800s through the early 1900s at social events, local and national celebrations, river regattas, and parades, all while dressed in full regalia.

Was there a purer form of entertainment to be had at that time? The reports conjure up thoughts of men in suits and women in their finery on crisp summer days, enjoying the company of family, friends, neighbors, and possibly even political rivals, sharing a moment of peace and glad tidings, encouraged by the melodies of local men in costume playing cornets.

They were good times indeed.

---

[301] Thompsonville Press June 8, 1882. Page 2.

Thompsonville was never a rich village in terms of monetary wealth. It was rich, though, in the type of brotherhood that came from a shared ancestry and experiences as emigres. Even though photography became relatively accessible with the release of George Eastman's Kodak camera in July 1888, the price point was still a financial stretch for residents of Thompsonville.

Who, then, would capture important moments, events, and people of the village?

Nathan Page Palmer was born in Peachem, Vermont, on May 3, 1843, to John Palmer and Hannah Page. When he was young, his family moved 12 miles northeast to Danville, where they settled for a while.

Palmer reportedly acquired the photography bug as a youth, but whether on his own or through mentorship in the art is unknown.

On September 8, 1862, Nathan, then 19, joined the war effort, enlisting as a private in Company B of the 15th Vermont Volunteers. About one year later, he received his honorable discharge and, within 30 days, re-enlisted as a private in Company D, 1st Vermont Cavalry.

He received his final discharge on June 21, 1865, about one year before the end of the national conflict, having fought in major conflicts in Gettysburg, Cedar Creek, New Town (Virginia), Mount Jackson (Virginia), Lacey Springs (Virginia), and Waynesboro (Virginia).

While at Gettysburg, he fought under General George Stannard. He also served under General George Custer, participated in Major General Philip Sheridan's raid, and was part of the last march that drove Major General Edward Johnson to surrender to the forces of General William Tecumseh Sherman.

At the close of the war, Nathan Page Palmer returned briefly to Danville, taking up photography again. He soon relocated to Boston, Massachusetts, and then to Springfield, Massachusetts, before finally settling in Thompsonville, Connecticut, in 1869, where he set up a photographic studio in the village.

N. P. PALMER,

PHOTOGRAPHER,

Thompsonville, - Conn.

PICTURE FRAMES OF ALL KINDS.

Views of Residences made to order.

Copying, Enlarging and Finishing in Ink, Water Colors and Crayons a specialty.

Lightning, and later processes used daily at my studio.

Sittings made in cloudy or rainy weather

On October 21, 1871, Palmer was secure enough in his occupation to marry Sarah Shackleton. The couple soon had two children: a son, W. Prescott, and a daughter, Olive.

The recorded personal legacies of many men and women are often disproportionate to the lives they actually lived. The lives of the kinder and gentler among us are left less committed to paper than those whose impact has been more eventful, positive, or negative.

Such was the life of Nathan Page Palmer, who, as his St.

Johnsbury Republican newspaper obituary stated, would be remembered by the town's older residents as a pleasant, genial man who made and held many friends.

His legacy, though, would be captured in the hundreds or thousands of photographs of people, places, and events he left behind. Each reflects the man behind the lens.

Photo of Mansley's Block, Main Street, Thompsonville, circa 1881. The image shows Thomas Mansley's store to the right and Charles Berberich's candy store to the left. An unknown dentist's office is on the second floor above Mansley's. The event the people are watching is unknown.

There is no one collection of Palmer's photos. When uncovered, they seem to have been put up for sale, scattering his legacy across a wide array of collectors. Perhaps this is for the best, as his photographs have captured the imagination of a host of individuals who have acquired a taste for the craftsman's skill and insight.

Through his single cabinet cards of people or stereographs of farms and buildings, he introduced the purity and innocence of the village during his time to others who might not otherwise have heard of Thompsonville,

Connecticut.

By 1903, Palmer had shelved his camera and assumed the mantle of Realtor and Insurer, selling his studio to F. L. Beauman.

A surprising amount of personal information about Palmer was revealed in his 1917 record, which was requested by Marcus Holcomb, the governor, and received by William Hughes, the Military Census Agent for the State.

Nathan Page Palmer photographed a simple cabinet card of an unnamed young boy, the date of which is unknown.

Nathan Page Palmer was a man of more diminutive stature at 5 feet 5 inches. He lived with his wife, Sarah, at 26 Main Street, Thompsonville. He had a physical disability, which remains unclear due to his handwriting. He couldn't drive a car, but he could ride a motorcycle and a horse. He seemed to have no other mechanical skills.

But he was one hell of a photographer, and, as each photograph is uncovered, we are all the richer.

21: CHARACTER

In September 1879, four residents of Connecticut Village founded The Vitrified Wheel Company. One of the investors was a familiar name in Thompsonville: Dr. Loren Howard Pease.

During his lifetime, Pease helped establish numerous businesses in the village, including the Glass Case Company, which failed miserably, and the Westfield Plate Company, which prospered for years. But that is the history of great thinkers. They are unafraid of failure or success.

Charles Alden, an industrialist, moved to Ashland, Massachusetts, in 1856 and purchased the Shepard Paper Mill on the Sudbury River east of the village. He modified the mill to manufacture emery, which was used to grind and polish metal. Alden had won the sole right to import stone from Smyrna, Turkey, thereby securing a virtual monopoly on emery production.

As the Civil War broke out, the need for Alden's emery erupted, production skyrocketed, and the businessman reaped the rewards.

In 1867, Alden sold out to a stock company, in which he was a large owner. The new entity was named The

Washington Mills Emery Company. It was the first abrasive producer in the United States, and its sole product at that time was imported Turkish emery ore. Washington Mills continued in business until about 1877, when the city of Boston purchased the company, its structure, and its water rights. Less than one year later, the building was destroyed by fire.

Charles Alden circa 1877 (Ashland Historical Society)

Alden had built another emery mill near the previous

one, leveraging his manufacturing patents. The Vitrified Emery Wheel Company, a company organized and certified on August 30, 1871, was established. This company manufactured emery wheels extensively used in grinding and polishing metals.

After operating for a few years, the company and its structure were sold to the City of Boston to support the Boston water supply system, just as Washington Mills had been. The building was demolished in 1877.[302] This closed the door to Alden's involvement with producing emery wheels in Ashland.

But it wasn't the end of the emery wheel.

The similarly named Vitrified Wheel and Emery Company was established in Westfield, Massachusetts, and organized and certified on September 23, 1873[303] , possibly shortly after the sale and closure of the Vitrified Emery Wheel Company of Ashland[304] sometime before 1874.

In contrast to that assumption stands the article from the October 10, 1876, edition of the Boston Evening Transcript:

By the action of the Boston Water Works in flowing in Ashland, all manufactories and mills dependent on water power there will be forced to leave the town. The city of

---

[302] History of Middlesex County – Ashland. Page 233.
[303] Report of the Tax Commissioner of the Commonwealth of Massachusetts for the Year ending December 31, 1888.
[304] Public Documents of Massachusetts: Being the Annual Reports of Various Public Officers and Institutions for the year 1874. Vitrified Emery Wheel Company of Ashland listed as having been sold by that time.

Boston has purchased the mill of the Cutler Brothers and of the Vitrified Wheel & Emery Company.

The following article from the Springfield Daily Republican provides some clarity in an attempt to reconcile the establishment of the Vitrified Wheel and Emery Company (in Westfield) in 1873, its valuation in 1874, and the forced sale and evacuation of the [original] Vitrified Emery Wheel Company (from Ashland) in 1876.

Westfield

NEW $100,000 BUSINESS ENTERPRISE

Westfield is congratulating itself that it is soon to number the Ashland emery wheel company among its manufactories, as that company has voted to remove to Westfield as soon as proper quarters can be secured.

The emery company has a capital of $100,000, of which $40,000 is owned at Westfield, and H. J. Bush is one of the directors.[305]

The Ashland Emery organization was initially established as a stock corporation with a manufacturing location (Ashland) and an ownership location (Westfield). When the city of Boston bought out the Ashland factory, ownership would naturally have looked to Westfield to relocate its facilities.

In any case, by late 1877, the company had located a site, retrofitted the building, and was prepared to move equipment from its previous site to its new building before the end of the year.

In May 1878, an article in the May edition of the American Machinist announced the development of the Vitrified Emery Wheel, featuring a breakthrough

---

[305] Springfield Daily Republican August 1, 1877. Page 6.

configuration for which they had been awarded a patent.

By September, the company reported rapid growth and a more prosperous condition than it had ever experienced.

This made the following announcement challenging to understand, as the company was prepared for exponential growth.

No organizational changes were announced, no management upset occurred, and no event would have prepared the casual observer for the newspaper report.

The Articles of Association for the *Vitrified Wheel Company*, which had four shareholders named, one of whom was Loren Howard Pease, were published in the September 23, 1879, edition of the Hartford Courant.

Most surprisingly, Article VI of the document stated:

The said corporation is established and located in the village of Thompsonville, in the Town of Enfield, and State of Connecticut.

Dated at Thompsonville, this 13th day of September 1879.

How could that be?

How could an established company, with stockholders, be formed as a new company without some sale or buyout, none of which was reported in any local or regional newspapers?

A clue comes from a report in the December 17, 1879, edition of the Green Mountain Freeman newspaper:

> *CORUNDUM WHEELS* – *Corundum is the next hardest substance in nature to the diamond. Rating the hardness of the diamond at twelve, corundum stands at eleven, while emery averages but eight and a half. The problem, attempted by so many, of finding a base strong enough to hold corundum without interfering with its cutting qualities, we are informed,* **has at last been solved by a Connecticut company***, by an ingenious process of 'vitrification'…it is predicted the discovery will revolutionize the wheel business of the world.*

The publication's association of the discovery with a Connecticut company supports the suspicion that the Thompsonville stockholders must have purchased and reorganized the Westfield organization, with manufacturing remaining in the state of Massachusetts.

A 1907 Connecticut Government publication listing stock corporations organized under general law noted the Vitrified Wheel Company as located in Thompsonville, supporting the transfer of ownership. The reorganized company was formally incorporated on December 27, 1879.

Two pieces of information providing clues to Vitrified Wheel's ownership were published the following year in the July editions of the Springfield Republican and the Thompsonville Press.

The Vitrified Wheel Company has declared a dividend of $3^{1/2}$ percent on their $60,000 capital, made in the six months **since they reorganized on the ruins of the Vitrified Wheel and Emery Company.**[306]

Last Monday, a semi-annual dividend of $3^{1/2}$ percent was declared. **Dr. L. H. Pease, of this place, is the secretary and also director of the company** *and was present at the meeting. He feels much pleased over the results of the past six months.*[307]

The Springfield article described an event in which the Vitrified Wheel and Emery Company ceased to exist as an entity, paving the way for new ownership and a rebranding as the Vitrified Wheel Company.

Westfield Snowstorm and Flood of December 1878

---

[306] Springfield Republican July 7, 1880. Page 4. (Author emphasis)
[307] Thompsonville Press July 14, 1880. Page 2. (Author emphasis)

Without transparent reporting associated with a specific event, one stands out and fits the timeframe.

On December 10, 1878, a heavy snowfall followed by a twelve-hour rainstorm swelled the Westfield River. The dike along the river collapsed in several places, sending floodwaters rushing through downtown Westfield.

Newspapers reported on the flood and its aftermath, citing that Westfield was the most affected area. Businesses and mills were washed away, leaving cleanup simple, as there was nothing to clean up – it had all been washed downstream. Some companies, like Steer and Turner's Organ Factory, posted rewards for anyone who found and returned their tools and equipment.

Although not specified in the reporting, one can only expect that the deluge impacted the Vitrified Wheel and Emery Company to the point of shutting it down, opening an opportunity for Thompsonville investors to step in and rescue the organization.

The flood's impact on the factory followed a fire that had burned through the building on April 5th of that same year. The $10,000 insurance policy barely covered the loss from the inferno. It was almost as if the building had been cursed, fated to be destroyed.

The company had recovered from the fire, but perhaps the flood proved too much, and the owners were happy to move on.

The true story of the purchase, reorganization, and renaming of the Emery Wheel Company may be unrecoverable. Still, the new owners did not plan to relocate the business to a new location. The good citizens of Thompsonville understood the impact that losing a business can have on a town, and they chose not to relocate the company to the small Connecticut village, even if it would have meant jobs for Thompsonville for years to come.

They chose kindness and compassion.

As the new iteration of the Emery Wheel Company rose from the ashes, the following appeared in the Hartford Courant, further clarifying the relationship between the Connecticut village and the Emery Company.

ENFIELD

The emery wheels made by the Vitrified Wheel company, **whose legal headquarters are in this town**, *have been adopted by the United States government as the standard, and the company is now supplying the United States arsenal at Rock Island. The works are located in Westfield, Mass.*[308]

The grinding, polishing, and cutting wheels were second to none, and Westfield, not Thompsonville, would reap the benefits.

But instead of thinking about what might have been had the company been relocated after a natural tragedy, it is better to reflect on the human choice to rebuild Vitrified Wheel on the ashes of its former site.

The choice was the right decision, and it reflected well on Thompsonville.

This would stand in stark contrast to Westfield's attempt to purloin a Thompsonville business just a few years later.

The United States Department of the Interior National Register of Historic Places Form notes that the Westfield Plate Company was initially founded in Westfield, Massachusetts, in the 1870s as a manufacturer of casket hardware but cites no references. The document even states that the company experienced exponential growth, which necessitated the need to seek new sites for expansion.

At first blush, the statement seems to have been fabricated out of whole cloth — or possibly not, as the following article, published in 1885, references the rudimentary works in Westfield.

---

[308] Hartford Courant December 6, 1887. Page 6.

A corporation formed in Enfield last September, but of which little has been known in this vicinity, has taken a new aspect and provides an enterprise for this place.

The corporation was organized under the name of The Westfield Plate Company, for the manufacture of coffin hardware, including textile trimmings, etc. The capital stock is $50,000, all of which has been taken and is largely owned by our village people.

*The works are to be located opposite the freight depot, on land now occupied by Matthewson Bros. & Co.'s coal and wood sheds. The building is to be 30 × 100 feet, and will be ready June 1ˢᵗ for the machinery (**which is now running in Westfield**).[309]*

The following week's local paper noted that in addition to rapid work moving forward on the construction of the company building:

*The works, **which are now at Westfield**, employ ten hands, but will probably be somewhat enlarged on coming here.[310]*

On September 12, 1884, as some of the redeemed bonds of the failed New England Glass Burial Case Company were being consigned to the boiler in the lower mill of the carpet manufactory, the Articles of Association of The Westfield Plate Company were published in the September 15, 1884, edition of the Hartford Courant. The shareholders were listed as A. M. Thomas, H. W. Morgan, Charles Stevens, H. W. Ely, and L. H. Pease. Thomas had been assigned 1996 shares, while each of the others had a single share apiece.

---

[309] Thompsonville Press April 30, 1885. Page 2. Author emphasis.

[310] Thompsonville Press May 7, 1885. Page 2. Author emphasis.

The company's principals were two familiar Thompsonville businessmen: George T. Mathewson, principal owner and director, and his brother Albert H. Mathewson, who served as treasurer and manager of the operation. As mentioned earlier, they were partners in the Mathewson Brothers & Co. Brewery, started by their father, John Mathewson. They also ran a coal, wood, and ice business along the village waterfront.

In 1885, the officers of the Westfield Plate Company raised $50,000 to construct a new industrial loft along the tracks of the New York, New Haven, and Hartford Railroad and across from the line's freight depot.[311]

The brick for the new building was furnished by no other than the Brickyards of H. D. Alden in Thompsonville, which had provided kiln-baked bricks for many of the large brick buildings in the village. On June 18th, it was projected that the structure, known as Mathewson's Building, would be completed and ready for occupancy in about 10 *days*. The Thompsonville Press operations would also take up space in the building.

By July 2nd, production equipment began arriving from Westfield and was rapidly installed in the waiting space on the first floor. Within a week, the new company was testing equipment and preparing to hire new employees.

Within no time, three new patents[312] had been applied for and assigned to the fledgling operation, and the items were being forged on-site and made ready for sale.

In October of the following year, 1886, the company's

---

[311] National Register of Historic Places Registration Form. Pg 15.
[312] H. M. Morgan for a textile handle, A. H. Thomas for a winding machine, and H. W. Morgan (again) for a rubber compound substitute (for insulating wires)

needs required the building to be expanded by another 15 feet. Construction was completed two months later, and the new boiler was installed in the space, increasing the plant's available power.

The finest silver, oxidized and gold-mounted funeral trappings, casket handles and plates, ever sent out by the Westfield Plate Co., are on the eve of being shipped as samples. There are above eighty different styles of handles, put up in handsome cases, the bulk of them the most elaborate and artistic designing.[313]

By December of 1887, the casket plate manufacturer was encroaching on the Thompsonville Press production space:

Extensive alterations in the interior arrangements of the Westfield Plate Co.'s works, are in progress. A large part of the upper floor at the rear of the Press office, largely used heretofore for storage purposes, is being done off and will be filled with machinery. The increased business and demands for better facilities to execute orders promptly has led to this move.[314]

In August 1889, the business was at it again, erecting an addition on the west side of the factory to serve as a storehouse. Business was booming.

However, nefarious activities were afoot over the border in Westfield, Massachusetts, where negotiations were underway to persuade Westfield Plate to return to the town where it had originated years before.

In an article in the Springfield Republican titled:

GULLIBLE DOWN-STREAM PEOPLE
Hoodlumism and Other Topics of the Carpet Town

---

[313] Thompsonville Press April 18, 1887. Page 2.
[314] Thompsonville Press December 15, 1887. Page 2.

the unnamed correspondent mocked the good people in the village to their south as if speaking to them directly:

Thompsonville people are not a little exercised over the prospective removal of the Westfield Plate Company from this place, but unfortunately, no means are proposed that might induce the concern to remain. The chances are that a final decision to go may be reached before any steps can be taken, for the matter has already been brought to a head.

If the concern goes to Westfield it will be entirely independent of the Textile company, as $40,000 in stock has been subscribed for, provisionally, should the report of the Westfield investigating committee prove favorable. The concern is far from being badly located at present, but more room is needed to relieve the night force.

W. O Collins of your city says if a change of location must be made he would much prefer that the enterprise should go to Springfield, so that in case Westfield intentions would not be brought about your board of trade is likely to consider the industry in a similar view. It is understood that the Westfield subscriptions range from $250 to $5000 which amounts ought to be within the means of a large number of folks here.

With the rather gloomy outlook for the carpet business, the town doubly needs small, diversified manufacturers that could easily be started with the money paid out for rum and lotteries every two or three years.[315]

The reference to the town as a village full of drunks and gamblers was appalling, especially in light of how honorable

---

[315] Springfield Republican June 22, 1890. Page 2. Author emphasis.

Thompsonville investors had conducted themselves years earlier in working to keep the Emery Works in Westfield after a natural disaster.

A few days later, a more innocuous follow-up report echoed the possible relocation of the factory, citing growth rather than the Thompsonville residents' inebriation and questionable moral character.

W. O Collins of this city, who is a large stockholder in the Westfield Plate company of Thompsonville, manufacturing coffin and casket trimmings, would be glad to have that concern transplanted to this locality. The company has outgrown its present quarters there and some influence has been brought to bear toward taking the plant to Westfield, but a hitch has been reached. The business is likely to be shifted from Thompsonville sooner or later and this city would be more likely to secure it than any neighboring place if, upon investigation, it should prove a desirable addition to local industries.[316]

By the 29th of the month, the hounds had been called off, and the business would seemingly remain in Enfield despite the vitriolic feelings of the neighbors to the north.

The town seems likely to retain the Westfield Plate company for the present, after all. The project of the Westfield men fell through because the concern declined to allow them to look into their books.

Some of the examiners interpreted the action to mean that the business was being done upon small margins. However, this may be, the company is not to be blamed for disliking to have its books ransacked, and yet some guarantee should be made before outsiders can be expected

---

[316] Springfield Republican June 25, 1890. Page 6.

to jump into a new business.[317]

The correspondent's position seemed *face-saving* at best, as, in their determination, how could any business not want to relocate away from Thompsonville? The poachers from Massachusetts retreated – their true character lay bare.

The Penny Press of October 6, 1891, reported a fire in the buffing room at the Westfield Plate building on Monday, the 4th, which resulted in approximately $500 in damage to company stock due to water and chemical extinguishers. It predicted trouble right around the corner.

By November 5th of that same year, expansion was on the minds of Westfield Plate yet again.

> *The Westfield Plate Company are compelled on account of the growth of the business to enlarge this building and has secured plans for an addition to be built on the west of their present building, 40 x 70 feet. The company now have something over 60 names on their pay roll and expect, with the addition of more room, to be able to employ twice that number.*[318]

On August 10, 1892, the unthinkable was reported in papers all over the Northeast, from the Boston Daily Globe to the New Haven Morning Journal and Courier to the Pittsburgh Dispatch.

> *Fire has again done its work in our village, laying in ruins the entire plant of the Westfield Plate Company and wrecking the office of the Thompsonville Press.*

---

[317] Springfield Republican June 29, 1890. Page 5.
[318] Thompsonville Press November 5, 1891. Page 2.

The flames were discovered at about 4 o'clock Tuesday morning. Constable Wilson and Night Watchman baker, who were on duty in the Carpet Company's yard, were the first to give the alarm, and, contrary to the rule of the carpet company, besides causing the fire bells to be rung, directed the gong sounded. Ebenezer Henry, an employee of Mathewson Bros. & Co., who lives in the near vicinity of the Plate company's building, bridled a horse and rode to the home of A. H. Matthewson, treasurer and manager of the company, and aroused him. During the meantime, the alarm had brought out the fire department.

The flames were then mainly confined to the north end of the building, though the thick smoke that penetrated

The Westfield Plate Co. Burned Out.

The Parsons Printing Co. Suffer Severely in the General Wreck.

A STUBBORN FIRE !

The Plate Co.'s loss almost complete — Will probably rebuild on same site—To occupy The T. Pease & Co.'s mill temporarily—The Press issued to-day---The Firemen fought the flames heroically —Incidents, insurance, etc.

the entire building was so dense that it was impossible to enter and part. The combustibles fed the fire into fury and rolls of flames leapt from windows and cast their glare over a wide area.[319]

The buildings and contents of both the Plate and the Press companies were total disasters. They contained metals and machinery, but were molten slag, worth no more than scrap.

Inventories, merchandise, and stock were unusable, with insurance coverage perhaps covering half the loss.

T. Pease and Sons Lumber offered space in their nearby building for the plate operations as it considered its next move.

To the north, once again, the poachers stirred.

Other places have offered liberal inducements to the Westfield Plate Co. to relocate elsewhere. Springfield offers the site of the recently burned shoe factory, on which a large chimney, boiler, and smokestack are estimated to be worth between three and four thousand dollars. Thompsonville must ensure that this industry does not leave town.[320]

The Westfield Plate Company has resumed work with a full complement of men in T. Pease & Sons' planning mill, where they will do business for the present.

It has not yet been decided whether the company will rebuild its burned factory.

It has received several tempting offers to locate elsewhere and may accept one of them.[321]

---

[319] Thompsonville Press August 11, 1892. Page 2.
[320] Thompsonville Press August 13, 1892. Page 2.
[321] The Journal (Meriden, CT) August 26, 1892. Page 1.

That other people and other places realize the advantages to be gained by enterprising manufacturing companies is easily understood when it is known that the Westfield Plate company has received overtures from at least a dozen places to locate elsewhere.

Springfield's offer was stated last week, but other invitations still continue to come from various direc-tions. One offer of a building site and buildings, valued at $5,000, or $5,000 in cash, comes from Pittsfield to have the company locate there. Another proposition equally good comes from Brockton [Massachusetts]. Windsor Locks Electric Light Company has a building and will do the right thing if the company will come there.

Probably the best offer comes from Owosso, Michigan. That city will provide advantageous buildings for the manufactory, and the Owosso Casket company of that city, one of the largest consumers in casket hardware in the country, offers to give them all their trade. We believe, however, that the company, which has wonderfully prospered since its establishment in business here, is not ready to leave the place yet, and certainly not if they can be given a fair show to rebuild on an enlarged scale on their old site. The unsettled condition of the grade crossing question prevents any extension at present. [322]

One occupant of a burned-out building was permanently relocated. The Thompsonville Press moved to new quarters in Spencer's block at Asnuntuck Street and Thompson Avenue.

But Westfield Plate rebuffed the offers to relocate.

Perhaps they had invested too much in the village in terms of manpower and skill development, or the thought

---

[322] Thompsonville Press August 25, 1892. Page 2.

of relocating was overwhelming. In the end, business continuity prevailed over all other possibilities, as orders remained unfulfilled, and the most expeditious route to getting up and running again lay in Thompsonville.

Just what kind of enterprising go-a-head material the Westfield Plate Company is composed of is well illustrated by the way they have surmounted the difficulties arising from the complete destruction of their manufactory two weeks ago last Tuesday morning.

Today, they are established in the T. Pease & Sons company's building, with nearly or quite their full force of operatives at work, and by Saturday night, will have every department in complete running order.

Not a moment was lost after the fire; new machinery was ordered, buffing wheels were made, vats for the plating solutions were built. The new machinery all had to be set up and provided with proper driving pulleys and driving belts attached.

A representative of The Press visited the company in their new quarters Wednesday afternoon and found the place really a hive of industry. The three stories of that large building have all been utilized, and the main departments each assigned a suitable place. Temporary partitions of cloth have been improvised for the present.

The engine, which has lain idle since the T. Pease & Sons company closed the mill, is again running, and the regular sounding of the whistle reminds one of the former busy days at that mill. The company's five traveling salesmen, who were called off the road after the fire, have been started out again, and by Monday of next week, the company will be filling orders again as usual.

The two weeks' delay has naturally accumulated a large

number of unfilled orders. To meet this demand, the company has had the mill wired for electric lamps, and next week will begin running extra hours.

A force of help larger than the company has ever had will be put to work. The company's office in the old building, which was only slightly damaged, has been repaired and will be the company's headquarters.[323]

Within two weeks, even the office was relocated onto the second floor of the Pease Building, thereby completing the process.

Then, on December 29th of that same year, a late Christmas miracle for the village. Albert Matthewson, the treasurer and manager of the Plate Company, announced the company would stay in the village, and he had purchased for himself a tract of land at the corner of South Pearl Street and Enfield Street. The property was locally known as the Captain Jabez King Estate and included a few buildings and four acres of land, which he planned to clear and erect a home second to none.

The statement was echoed in the January 10 edition of the Penny Press:

The Westfield Plate Company at Thompsonville, this state, has decided not to accept an offer to move to Springfield, Mass.

The village collectively exhaled.

By February of the New Year, a new building had begun to be erected for Westfield Plate on the site of the old footprint. The new structure would dwarf the earlier, being

---

[323] Thompsonville Press August 25, 1892. Page 2.

three stories high, 38 feet wide, and 172 feet long. The new structure would dwarf the earlier, being three stories high, 38 feet wide, and 172 feet long. The building would be constructed in three practically fireproof sections to prevent the recurrence of the 1892 inferno nightmare.

By 1906, the company was firmly ingrained in the village's fabric, as shown in a letter submitted by an unnamed correspondent to the July issue of the union workers' publication of *Our Journal.*

> *The boys under your jurisdiction must think that Thompsonville has long since been erased off the map, but if you will kindly publish this letter in your next issue, they will find that such is not the case.*
>
> *In case any of our western brothers come east in search of recreation, they will find Thompsonville located on the bank of the Connecticut River, almost mid-way between two great cities of Hartford and Springfield, and all members of the No. 52 employed by the Westfield Plate Co., manufacturers of fine casket hardware, linings, and*

garments.

It is conceded to the above company by all of its customers that its products are superior to any on the market, and little wonder, as the company employs none but first-class craftsmen; all of which are clean union men, except five or six who have sinned within the last year by allowing themselves to be suspended for nonpayment of dues, but all of whom are really good fellows, and will be back in the fold [soon]...

This time, Thompsonville came out on top despite Westfield's efforts to capitalize on disaster and wrest the company away from the village of immigrants.

In the end, then, who were indeed the immoral people?

There would remain one more *swing-and-miss business opportunity to disrupt the good people of Thompsonville.*

In 1895, bicycles were a national craze in the United States, with more than 300 manufacturers producing them. The *safety bicycle*, with two equal-sized wheels, was the most popular style. Bicycle sales increased from 30,000 in 1890 to over 400,000 in 1896 and upwards of 900,000 by 1898.

Cycling wasn't just a casual sport. For one gender in particular, it represented a sense of freedom. Susan B. Anthony, on reflecting on the importance of the bicycle, said:

Let me tell you what I think of bicycling. I think it has done more to emancipate women than anything else in the world. It gives women a feeling of freedom and self-reliance. I stand and rejoice every time I see a woman ride by on a wheel...the picture of free, untrammeled womanhood.[324]

Portrait of Violet Ward and Daisy Elliot, circa 1895 (courtesy of Museum of the City of New York)

With the rise in popularity, bicycle manufacturers fought local laws limiting when and where bicycles could be ridden on city streets. The makers also lobbied for better roads and more paving years before the automakers joined the fight.

In Thompsonville and surrounding towns, bicycle races began to gain in popularity.

Among the local bicycle riders who will enter the bicycle races to be held at Suffield next Saturday are Henry Ball, Edward Pease, William Kothe, and Stewart Young.[325]

By the mid-1990s, Thompsonville had a range of stores and services available to bicyclists.

---

[324] The New York World, February 2, 1896. Page 42.
[325] Thompsonville Press September 12, 1895. Page 2.

On November 28, 1895, the second-largest bicycle manufacturing plant in the country exploded in flames in Toledo, Ohio.

The factory, owned by the Lozier Company, whose headquarters were in Cleveland, burned to the ground in 30 minutes.

When it erupted into flames, 500 workers were manning the plant, none of whom were inside the building.

The explosion of a massive tank of enameling fluid sprayed the structure with flammable liquids, making the flames impossible to fight. Although eight firefighting companies responded, only two hydrants were available.

The loss was estimated at $500,000, with insurance covering only $350,000.

Within one week, Charles Moore, treasurer and general manager of Lozier, placed an order with the Pratt & Whitney Company of Connecticut for $40,000 worth of equipment to replace that lost in the Toledo inferno.

While the company got back on its feet, there were rumblings in the industry. Lozier was considering another production site in the northeast, realizing the futility of relying on a single location to produce bicycles.

Multiple towns began to consider the possibility of landing the production facility, with Manchester, Connecticut, being the first and most active. The vacant Union Mill property seemed best suited to accommodate the bicycle manufacturer.

On June 12, 1895, Lozier representatives headed east, including H. A. Lozier, president, and C. J. Moore, treasurer and general manager, to visit prospective sites. Although Manchester was a scheduled stop, the group also visited Thompsonville at the invitation of the local board of trade.

Representatives of the Lozier Manufacturing Company were here on Tuesday and looked over the vacant buildings of the Carpet Company in view of establishing an eastern branch of their industry. These gentlemen were met and entertained by representatives of the Board of Trade, William Calderwood and Tudor Gowdy. After buildings had been looked over, a drive was taken through the resident portion of the town. It was a brief and purely business visit, and little could be actually ascertained as to the probability of their selecting Thompsonville as the location of their eastern manufactory.[326]

The tour included three cities: New Haven, Bridgeport, and Rockville, Connecticut. It seemed there were vacant mills aplenty across the state.

The past week, officers of the company visited a number of proffered locations, including ones at Bridgeport and Thompsonville. The latter place, from all accounts, made

---

[326] Thompsonville Press June 13, 1895. Page 2.

the best offer through its wide-awake board of trade. Not only will Thompsonville give the bicycle company free rent for five years in a vacant carpet factory there and pay all taxes and insurance, but it will also pay the freight bills of all machinery that the company will bring to the place.[327]

By June 19th, Lozier and Thompsonville were in serious discussions about establishing the eastern factory in the village. The June 2nd edition of The Meriden Daily Journal reported that Thompsonville would be awarded the new plant but that a new building would need to be erected as available carpet buildings were found unsuitable.

This proposition has been accepted and already part of the 20,000 needed to put up the building has been subscribed. It may cost Thompsonville $50,000 or $75,000 all told to get this industry, yet the people there must think it is a good investment judging by the anxiety they manifested to secure it and the liberality of their offers.[328]

By the 20th, the Hartford Courant reported that more than half of the funds needed to erect the new building had been pledged, and that the balance would soon follow. Six days later, the same newspaper reported that less than $2,000 remained to be subscribed.

On the 27th, the plans for the required building were received from Lozier, measuring 400 feet in length, 40 feet in width, and three stories in height. Lozier confirmed in writing that they would visit the village shortly to complete negotiations. The initial site of the plant was to be located on the *Wool Lot* overlooking the Connecticut River near the

---

[327] The Meriden Daily Journal June 17, 1895. Page 4.
[328] The Meriden Daily Journal June 20, 1895. Page 4.

railroad tracks.

Lozier manufactured the popular Cleveland bicycle in Toledo, Ohio.

By July 1st, Lozier representatives, including its president, had arrived in Thompsonville and were finalizing plans for the new plant's exact location. On July 2nd, the articles of agreement between the Toledo company and the Thompsonville Board of Trade were signed, and the work of preparing the construction site began that same day.

The site required the demolition of three buildings to clear the property, and the residents were summarily evicted.

All over the state, towns reacted to Thompsonville's aggressiveness in pursuing and landing the company, collectively wondering why their towns lacked the foresight and initiative, while others spewed sour grapes.

> *That is the way progressive towns get business and the rule being made by progressive towns, slow behind-the-age places, no matter what their advantages, get left. There is the whole story in a nutshell: you pay your money and you*

take your choice. Business is business in this age more than any of its predecessors, there is but little sentiment in it, and businessmen go where they get the most for what they have to give.[329]

On August 8, 1895, an advertisement appeared in several local papers for 25 brick masons to work on the Lozier bicycle factory as construction was in full swing. At the same time, over the border in Toronto, Canada, Lozier was completing the erection of another production plant.

Meanwhile, in Ohio, the 800 workers employed by the bicycle company went on strike against their employer as wages had been reduced for two years to keep the manufacturer solvent. Within one month, the action was settled to the satisfaction of both sides, and production resumed.

In October, Lozier contracted to increase the Thompsonville plant footprint by erecting an additional two-story building for a machine room. The original building fund was still not fully funded, so the town established a committee to pursue the delinquents.

On November 30, 1895, an advertisement appeared in several local papers for 25 machine tool makers to work on the Lozier bicycle factory, as construction had been completed and the firm began to focus on production.

Nationally, the country was gripped by a financial crisis known as the Panic of 1895. It was characterized by a decline in gold reserves (from $190 million to $60 million in four years), bank runs, and a threat to the gold standard, which, for the layperson, meant fear and an unwillingness to take on debt. The downturn was so severe that, before

---

[329] The new London Day July 5, 1895. Page 2.

1930, the period was referred to as *The Great Depression.*

Unknown to most citizens, a financial group led by the despised J. P. Morgan exploited a loophole in a law passed by Congress during the Civil War, which allowed the government to issue bonds that could be exchanged for money, rather than relying on gold reserves. The country's finances were stabilized, and the United States avoided default, although a full recovery would take years.

It was no wonder that companies like Lozier turned to private citizens and public entities for the funds necessary to construct and expand their operations.

Thompsonville and its residents had stepped up to the plate, and the results were palpable.

THOMPSONVILLE NOW BUSY

LOZIER PEOPLE TO WORK NIGHTS

Thompsonville now and Thompsonville a year and a half ago are quite different places. The dullness is giving was to activity, the empty tenements are nearly filled up.

Indeed, a bright young businessman of the place did not hesitate to say today that next Spring would undoubtedly see a good sized building boom here in the village. It is hard to secure a desirable tenement, and the constantly increasing force at the Lozier company's factory will require more room.

This company, by the way, begins to run both night and day next Monday and expects to have by that time 173 employees. These will run in two 'shifts' and this number will be constantly added to . Superintendent Judson says that the demand for the positions are so great at present that he could run a factory double the size.[330]

March 1896 brought the good news of an order for 2,000 Cleveland (Lozier-branded) bicycles to be shipped to Russia. The company projected upwards of 25,000 orders for the year.

By this time, the Thompsonville factory employed 325 people and ran at maximum capacity. There was every expectation that the facility would expand.

In May, C. J. Moore of Lozier arrived again in the village, where he expected to remain for a few weeks. While in Thompsonville, Moore was given the deed to the building as the company had exceeded the investments in personnel and equipment required to transfer ownership of the structure to the company.

Rumors abounded that Lozier was considering moving their entire operation east, and Thompsonville wasn't alone in considering inducements to make that decision easier.

Lozier then presented their demand to the Thompsonville Board of Trade. In business for less than one year, the group required a $20,000[331] loan at 4% interest to enable the company to double the size of its manufacturing plant. A plant to which they then held the deed.

The request was further colored by the suggestion that the company might leave the village without the Board of Trade agreeing to their demand.

Lozier seemingly had a valid complaint, possibly influenced and encouraged by Thompsonville's northern neighbors.

To maintain a workforce of 300 employees in the village,

---

[330] Springfield Republican November 24, 1895. Page 3.
[331] Some sources mention a $100,000 loan at 4%

the company had run through between 1,500 and 2,000 workers in six months, many of whom came and went continuously, with most registering complaints about someone or something.

Was it the quality of the workers or the quality of the town? To the north, in Massachusetts, a recent adversary lay in wait, considering the opportunity.

On May 28th, the Thompsonville Board of Trade met and agreed to extend a $25,000, 4% loan to Lozier, believing the action was sufficient.

Behind the scenes, Westfield, the business antagonist in Massachusetts, reached out to Lozier, proposing a $75,000 subscription for the company to build and relocate its operations to the town. Thompsonville was caught off guard.

Middletown, Connecticut, also appeared to have been involved in backdoor negotiations, as reported in a newspaper.

MIDDLETOWN LOSES IT

LOZIER BICYCLE COMPANY WILL GO TO WESTFIELD

It is feared that the Lozier Bicycle Company, which was expected to locate here, will move to Westfield, Mass. The businessmen of that place feel confident that they will secure the industry and have made all arrangements to have the company locate there.[332]

On June 15th, Lozier laid off 200 workers in their Thompsonville plant, presumably until the beginning of September. The 50 workers remaining would work every

---

[332] Meriden Daily Republican June 12, 1896. Page 6.

other two weeks.

In Westfield, the $75,000 in promised subscriptions fell short by $14,000 on the due date. Still, the bicycle magnate was satisfied with the Massachusetts businessmen's promise that the goal would be reached, and a contract was signed to move forward. In return for the pledged $75,00, Lozier would employ no less than 500 hands per day for a period of five years.

Surprisingly, on August 1, most of the Thompsonville Lozier workforce, previously laid off, was called back to work, and by early November, the full force was back at work.

In the same month, on August 6, Lozier put the Westfield factory construction out to bid. Thompsonville felt the familiar burn of the shiv in its back.

By August 20, George R. Blodgett, a local contractor in Westfield, won the construction bid and began advertising for 50 hands to start erecting the factory. The structure was targeted for occupancy on January 1 of the following year.

Unlike Thompsonville, where employees had secured whatever vacant tenement spaces they could find when hired at the Lozier plant, Westfield entrepreneurs formed a stock company called Cycle Heights. They purchased as much available property around the new Lozier plant as possible to construct new housing, which they expected to have ready by mid-winter of 1896.

The last payment of the $75,000 subscription was made to the Lozier Manufacturing Company in the spring of 1897.

At the end of December 1897, there were rumblings of discontent in Westfield as the Lozier Company, which had begun work in the Spring of that year, had yet to comply with the scale of employment it had promised. The townspeople held a meeting about the situation, but no action was taken, even though the company employed 200 fewer than the promised 500.

Lozier suggested shutting down the Thompsonville plant and transferring the equipment and jobs to Westfield to address the shortfall. To do so, though, the company would require the town to cancel the remaining balance of the five-year contract (three were left), enter into a new agreement, and transfer ownership of the building to Lozier.

To the delight of Thompsonville, the Westfield Board of Trade refused the Lozier overture.

Initially.

But Westfield reconsidered, and a new agreement was signed, signaling the eventual closure of the Thompsonville operation and its transfer to Westfield by the spring of 1899. The new deal was for a term of 4 ½ years, with a guarantee of 400 factory employees, only a slight increase from the number employed under the previous contract.

As part of the new arrangement, Lozier offered a few scraps to Thompsonville, who had paid for and transferred ownership of the factory in their own village to the bicycle company. They would install six machines in the old Pease Lumber Company building to produce piecework for the cycles manufactured in Westfield.

But by June 1899, the Thompsonville operation had neither been closed nor transferred to Westfield. In fact, Lozier was asking for the building to be expanded and for the company to be given more time to conclude the operations in Connecticut.

Westfield was over a barrel.

Between 1895 and 1904, over 1,800 separate businesses merged into approximately 150 'trusts', where shared interests bonded them in an attempt to 'rationalize' the industries. Less than a third succeeded. One of the more spectacular failures was the American Bicycle Company, which included about 50 companies that produced at least 60% of the bicycles and bicycle parts in America. The Trust, established on August 31, 1899, was too small and narrowly focused, poorly organized, and lacked a clear objective.

The American Bicycle Company Trust acquired bicycle companies through cash, stocks, and bonds, with Albert G. Spalding serving as president, Colonel George Pope as vice president, and Harry Lozier as one of the ten directors. The previously independent bicycle manufacturers now bowed to the trust's will, and decisions were based on the cartel's needs rather than the brand's needs.

In many ways, the creation of the bicycle trust reflected the diminishing interest in pedal-powered transportation and the downward spiral of sales as department stores sold serviceable bicycles for less than $50 each.[333]

---

[333] By the time the trust itself collapsed in 1902, national production had fallen from 1.2 million bicycles a year to

In April 1900, the American Bicycle Company Trust announced the pending transfer of the parts assembly equipment and jobs to the ABC Westfield plant.

Westfield was gleeful.

By May, there had been no word of how the vacant Thompsonville factory would be disposed.

In July, word reached the village that the Goodson Graphotype Company of Jersey City, New Jersey, with a capitalization of $5 million, was interested in purchasing the Thompsonville plant and relocating its operations there, with no assistance or inducements required from the village Board of Trade. That same month, the ABC Trust proposed that Westfield sign over the deed to the Massachusetts factory to the bicycle conglomerate. The town rejected the proposal.

> *Not since the Lozier factory was opened in Westfield has business been so slow in starting this fall. Some say it is the election, but the general opinion is that the bicycle business is not destined to be the great success in the future as it has been in the past. The facilities for traveling about the country in the rapid and convenient trolley cars at a cost within reach of even the poor man, must have its effect on the bicycle industry, and then, too, the motor wagons are coming into more general use.*
>
> *Locally the assessors find a big falling off in the number of bicycles owned by the citizens, and it is a common remark that less bicycles have been seen on the streets this year than for several seasons.*
>
> *Many of the businessmen and other citizens who owned wheels and formerly took long rides are now seen walking or patronizing the electrics. If the conditions are such here,*

---

about a quarter of that figure.

are they not so elsewhere?

This is not to infer that we are to lose our big bicycle industry, for there is still a demand for bicycles, and there will, of course, continue to be. The question is, will that demand ever become as great as it has been in the past?[334]

Meanwhile, in Thompsonville, the first carload of equipment belonging to the Goodson Graphotype company arrived on October 24th, 1900.

The familiar whistle used by the Lozier bicycle company was blown yesterday for the first time, calling the men who are getting things ready for the company to their work.[335]

The ears of Thompsonville people have listened joyfully for the last three mornings to the whistle from the old Lozier factory, which shall henceforth be known under another name.

It is a sound that makes people happy since it means business, prosperity to businessmen, and a bank account to the working man. This whistle has been off duty for a long summer vacation and is jubilant because of its return to action. Its glee is evident from the fact that of its own accord, it has awakened the people at the hour of 3 in the morning and continued its joy until curbed by the janitor.

Manage Goodson was in town today looking after the setting up of the machinery, of which a carload has already arrived and two more are expected next week. The machinery from the Providence branch is that which is now arriving, and it will require several weeks to get it all set up. A dozen or more men are engaged in giving the factory a renovation, and carpenters are at work making

---

[334] Springfield Republican October 21, 1900. Page 6.
[335] Springfield Republican October 26, 1900. Page 2.

other repairs.[336]

In Westfield, there was a quiet concern. The wresting away of the bicycle company from Thompsonville, once considered a commercial victory, was proving to be worrisome as the bicycle market began to dry up.

In September 1900, American Bicycle announced it would use the former Lozier factory in Toledo, Ohio, to make steam cars. The automobile was now the talk of the town among Massachusetts hopefuls, and if it found a market, it was a strong possibility that it would be made at the Westfield factory.

The bicycle business is much quieter than usual, and the demand for wheels seems to have fallen off to quite an extent. The motor wagon would fill in the gap nicely and be the means of keeping the factory booming, as the demand for these vehicles is constantly increasing.[337]

There has been some talk of manufacturing automobiles at the factory, but nothing definite has been decided in that direction.[338]

In Thompsonville, the Goodson Graphotype Manufacturing Company promised to more than make up for the loss of the Lozier bicycle parts-making business, as it had employed more than 40 men by the end of December.

In 1901, the American Bicycle Trust Company failed.

In 1902, the American Bicycle Trust Company was reorganized into the American Cycle Company.

---

[336] Springfield Republican October 28, 1900. Page 2.

[337] Springfield Republican November 20, 1900. Page 8.

[338] Springfield Republican December 11, 1900. Page 8.

In 1903, the American Cycle Company failed.

In 1904, Goodson Graphotype moved its manufacturing facilities to New York.

In the decades-long back-and-forth struggle for commerce supremacy between Thompsonville, Connecticut, and Westfield, Massachusetts, who can say who was the winner and who was the loser?

Perhaps neither.

At the very least, Thompsonville had conducted itself honorably. It did not try to exploit another town's misfortunes by luring away an established business.

It did not denigrate a rival town's character by criticizing its inhabitants' moral fiber.

The actions of a town and its people speak a lot about both, and Thompsonville could sleep at night.

22: INCENDIARY

Sometimes, it is just more straightforward to let another author's words describe an event. The following is taken directly from the Thompsonville Press newspaper of December 05, 1889[339].

Work of the Flames

The Stockinet Mill in Ruins

The Firemen do a Grand Work

The most destructive fire to have ever visited this village occurred last Thursday night, when the entire building owned and occupied by the Hartford Carpet Co., known as the Stockinet mill, was destroyed, along with its contents.

The fire originated very near to, or in the base of, the tower on the south side of the building. It was discovered by Thomas Ash, a young man living in a house on 'the Green.' He, being sick at the time, his brother John, of baseball notoriety, was first to give the alarm. This was

---

[339] Most grammatical errors are from the original author, although punctuation has been added at specific points to clarify without impacting intent or content.

within a few minutes of 11.30 p.m.

The night watchman of this mill, Lemuel Loughlin, had completed his eleven o'clock rounds and turned in at his headquarters on the opposite side of the street. Ash, after notifying him, ran to the engine house. Constables Wilson and Beehlor, with Watchman Sloan, had just eaten their lunch, and, as Wilson stepped to the door to look out, he saw the tower windows of the Stockinet building red with flames and at the same moment heard the shout of 'Fire.'

Loughlin attempted to ring an alarm with the large bell in the tower, but on opening a door in the tower, he found the flames and smoke so dense that he was obliged to give it up. Sloan rang the alarm with the White Mill bell, while Wilson hastened to notify the officers of the Carpet Company, as well as Foreman James Morrison of the fire department and several firemen. The gong was also sounded.

It was apparent from the very start that it was a most serious fire. No means could prevent the entire destruction of the large building itself, while every building in the vicinity was in imminent peril. The fire, which, when first seen, was entirely confined to the tower, rapidly spread to each floor of the building, and for a brief time volumes of black smoke poured from every opening, crack, and crevice.

As the windows gave way, the flames burst forth, furnishing a fearful yet grand spectacle. Not only the dry timbers and oily floors, but the wools and worsteds stored there furnished the very best of material for feeding the flames.

The fire department responded promptly, and while it was useless to attempt to check the flames in the doomed building, a most admirably planned and executed fight was made to prevent their spread to surrounding property.

The steamer was stationed at the hydrant at the rear of

the bank block and furnished two excellent streams. Four other streams were supplied by the Carpet company's force pumps and two by the hydrants of the Water company. Foreman James Morrison of Fire Engine Co. No. 1, along with his men, fought the flames from the north side. The flat tin roofs of the stores and blocks along Main Street provided excellent positions for the firemen, from which points the roofs and sides of the buildings were kept drenched.

Despite these efforts, however, several of the buildings caught fire at various times. The newly organized volunteer hose company from the south end, under the direction of Foreman Henry Bennett, did good work. The streams from the hydrant near Judge Briscoe's, also front of the dye house, proved more effectual than at any previous occasion.

In less than half an hour from the first alarm, the roof of the main building had been literally eaten away by the flames, and for the next hour, the building was a roaring furnace, sending sparks and burning embers high in mid-air. Fortunately, the wind was light, but what there was scattered the sparks and burning embers over nearly the entire northern part of the village.

As the devastation of the flames progressed, large sections of the walls fell, sending up volumes of sparks, and no one, except an eyewitness of this spectacle, can fully comprehend the terror it sent to the hearts of our citizens as they saw the showers of burning embers falling upon the roofs of the buildings. Thanks to an overruling Providence a drenching rainstorm had preceded the fire on the morning before, and everything was wet. Had it been the opposite — everything dry — no human power could have prevented our village from today being in ashes. The firemen worked faithfully, they did their part heroically, and today the industries of the village move on as though nothing unusual had taken place.

How the fire originated will probably remain a secret, but according to the best information, **it is believed to have been incendiary**.

It has been well demonstrated that the fire originated in the lower story, very close to, or in, the tower. The watchman had sounded the hour at eleven and made his circuit of the entire building, as the record in his watch shows, leaving the basement of the mill at about 11:10 p.m.

Night-watchman Loughlin states that at eleven o'clock, he entered the mill through the tower. He went up the stairway to the top floor of the tower and struck the hour of 11 o'clock with the large bell. From there, he passed to the attic, turned a key in his watchman's watch, and then to the next floor and so on down, turning a key at opposite ends of the building, requiring him to walk the entire length of the building on each floor.

He also made a circuit of the basement and out, leaving the mill yard through the gate exactly in front of the tower. He then proceeded to the barn and turned a key, returning to his headquarters in the old Stockinet office. After reading a paper for a few minutes, he proceeded to eat his lunch. He was just in the act of taking his pail of tea from the stove when Ash called him out. The flames were then confined to the tower. He ran to the gate he had so recently passed out of, finding it closed and fastened as usual. He threw it open and attempted to enter the tower, but found it impossible due to the fire and smoke. He noticed that the fire was most fierce in the elevator part of the tower, which was divided off from the stairway by a solid brick wall. On finding that it was impossible to ring an alarm, he proceeded to aid the fire department. He states that he made his 11 o'clock round entirely alone and that he was particularly on the alert for fire, as many other places had suffered recently.

That a fire could have been smoldering at 11, he believes entirely impossible, as he would have detected it by the smell. His only theory is that **some fiendish person set the fire through one of the windows at the base of the tower**. A strange coincidence is that the fire occurred just three years from the day he began watching this mill. He is a young man well known in this community and son of Felix Loughlin, engineer at the wash house.

The president of the company, Hon. John L. Houston, the superintendent, Lyman A. Upson, and Paymaster James B. Houston, were among the very first to respond to the alarm. Each from the earliest moment fully comprehended the seriousness of the situation and did their utmost to avert a most terrible conflagration.

President Houston immediately hastened to the telegraph office and, as soon as the night operator arrived, sent dispatches to Hartford and Springfield, informing the city officials and chiefs of the fire departments of each place of the impending danger to our village and requesting assistance. He also communicated with Supt. Davidson, who ordered special trains from each city for use of the fire departments. Mr. Houston remained at the telegraph office from the time the fire broke out at 11:30 until it was deemed safe to let the outside engines go home.

Superintendent L. A. Upson acted as chief, and no one could have done more masterly service; he was acquainted with every part and condition of the burning structure and its surroundings, also the means available to cope with fire. He acted quickly and apparently made no false moves, as the results show. His orders were carried out with readiness and dispatch, and Paymaster J. B. Houston proved an excellent lieutenant to Mr. Upson, filling an important position.

At 12:56 a dispatch came from Hartford saying that a special train, with steamer, had just left that city. Following this came another that Springfield had sent two steamers. Before the arrival of the Hartford steamer at 1:26 the fire had reached its worst and the two special trains were sidetracked, with orders not to unload the steamers unless other fires broke out. The firemen from both cities bad come to help, and when they found that the fire was under control kindly relieved our firemen at various points.

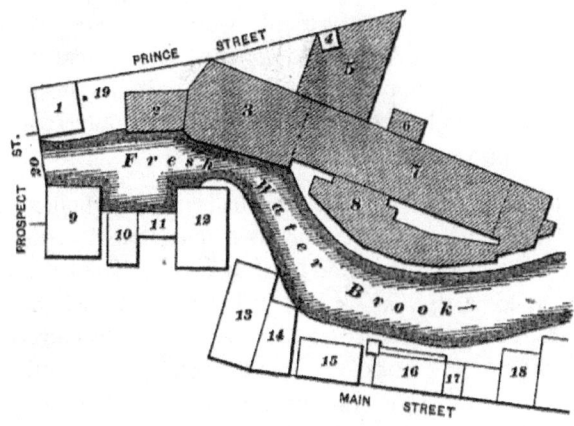

THE SHADED SPACE SHOWS GROUND PLAN OF THE BURNED STRUCTURE.

Key to Diagram.

1. Bank block, including Post-office.
2. Two-story building built in 1870.
3. Five-story building built in 1870.
4. Chimney.
5. Boiler-house.
6. Tower where fire was first discovered.
7. Main building built in 1844-5.
8. One-story Stockinet dye-house.
9. John Hunter's block.
10. Union market.
11. Grist-mill shed.
12. Grist-mill.
13. Mrs. J. C. Simpson's block.
14. G. L. Noble's block.
15. Geo. Leete's block.
16. Thos. Feeley's block and Sullivan's bakery.
17. Old Post-office.
18. Hartford Carpet company's office.
19. Hydrant, location of steamer.
20. Prospect street bridge.

The building, or more appropriately, buildings, were erected at different periods. The main section, No. 7 in the sketch, was the first building erected by the Enfield Manufacturing Co., and was built In 1844 and '45 for the manufacture of stockinet underwear. Nos. 2 and 8 were built in 1870, at which time the large chimney was moved to its present location, No. 4, and the boiler-house, No. 5, was also erected. A few years later, at the winding up of the Enfield Manufacturing Company, the entire property was purchased by the Hartford Carpet Company. The structure was over 300 feet long, averaging 50 feet wide; sections 3 and 7 were three stories high, adjacent to the basement and attic. The building was used for sorting, blending, and storing stock. Edwin Whitley, foreman of the sorting department, has occupied the fourth floor of the main building for the past 12 years. He had between 40 and 50 persons in his employ, primarily women. There was no machinery in use in the building; the large boilers in the boiler house adjoining were used solely to provide steam for the dye house and to operate a powerful force pump for fire and other purposes.

The stock at this time was unusually light, brought so on account of the inventory, which is taken at this season and would have been completed in a day or two. The total loss upon building and stock will fall little, if at all, below $200,000. With insurance of $15,000 on the structure and $160,000 on the stock, the insurance is placed with 16 different manufacturers' mutual insurance companies.

PARTIAL VIEW OF THE RUINS FROM THE SOUTH-WEST.   (FROM A PHOTOGRAPH.)

Crowds of people assembled along the streets to witness the burning, and all with expectation and dread, fearing that adjoining property would become ignited, and not only adjoining property, but that at a distance, for burning embers fell upon the roofs of houses as far north as the extreme limits of the village, while along Main and Pleasant streets sparks fell in perfect showers. So bright was the glare of the flames that it was seen for miles around, reflecting upon buildings as far distant as Hartford.

The building had always been considered by the Carpet company as well protected against fire. Shortly after its purchase by the company, during Mr. Houston's superintendency, the windows on the north side were removed, and the openings bricked up. Undoubtedly this precaution did much towards preventing the flames from reaching the buildings at the north. As it was the heat was so intense that the window casings to George Leete's building and Mrs. J. C. Simpson's building caught on fire several times. Leete's building suffered the most of any, over 150 lights of glass being cracked by the intense heat. One or two articles inside of A. R. Leete's store became ignited but with the aid of pails of water the fire was kept from doing any great injury, though many articles of furniture were scorched or blistered by the heat. Thomas Feeley's block, occupied by himself and Morris Sullivan, was injured but little. Clothing on a line on the rear porch caught fire, also a barrel of wood was found on fire. These were each thrown into the brook. By closing the blinds at the rear the heat was kept from the glass and not a pane was cracked. G. L. Noble's block, occupied by Patrick J. Sullivan as dwelling and saloon, was damaged to the amount of $25 to $30, Mrs. J. C. Simpson's block about $50, and George Leete's $60. D Robertson & Co.'s stock of dry goods was slightly damaged by smoke, as was also Arthur R. Leete's stock. Insurance on all this property has been adjusted through F. E. Ely and David Brainard, insurance agents. The old grist-mill, a landmark, was where possibly the fiercest battle with the flames occurred, but this point was carefully guarded by Foreman James Morrison, who centered one of the powerful streams from the «teamer here. The old wooden structure, the nearest building to the fire and as dry as tinder, once in flames, would have proved a serious combatant. Foreman Morrison realized this and made sure that it was well protected. The other stream from the steamer was carried to the new dye-house, now in process of construction.

People living in close proximity had just reason for feeling terribly alarmed, and many gathered up their valuables preparatory to a hasty leave, while others actually moved their household effects to safer quarters. It was an hour of the most intense excitement, yet the very best of order was preserved, and wonderful to say not a person was seriously injured, though Foreman Bennett of the volunteer hose company was hit upon the head by a falling brick.

Supt. Upson's wife very happily conceived providing hot coffee for the firemen and others, and, aided by Reverend William Hart Dexter did an act that was heartily appreciated by all. In place of nothing better, crackers and cheese were dispensed at the engine house free to all, and hot coffee was also furnished by the Allen House.

Matthew McAuley, now residing on King Street, was for 28 years watchman of this mill property, but retired three years ago, being succeeded by Lemuel Loughlin.

William L. Wilson, foreman of the old weave shop and for 54 years in the employ of the company, was at his home in Suffield when the fire broke out. He had his team hitched up at once, and with three others drove to the ferry and came over the river and hastened to his department in the 'long' mill. He was naturally much concerned to find the long weave room filled with smoke and feared lest the building was already on fire. He made a careful search, remaining in his department until nearly daybreak. The firemen and others who took positions upon the top of this building kept it well wet down, though at times the showers of sparks were almost blinding.

Possibly this large fire and its results may give us a little better idea of the vastness and importance of the Hartford Carpet company located in our midst, when we stop to think that, though $200,000 worth of their property was destroyed in a single night, not a spindle was stopped or a person of the 1800 employees thrown out of work for a single day, but on the contrary new forces set to work clearing away the debris. What will be done towards rebuilding is not yet decided, and quite likely may not be for some time. Supt. Upson stated that they needed the room badly, but could get along all right for the present. Edwin Whitley and his employees were given quarters in the wash-house and all were at work again in the afternoon following the fire.

The Enfield Manufacturing Co., which was the original owner of the burned buildings, was organized about 1840, with Henry G. Thompson as president. Mr. Schoonmaker was also one of the organizers of the company. The first superintendent was a Mr. Steiger, and manufacturing of stockinet underwear was first begun by this company in a brick building owned and now occupied as a worsted shop by the Carpet company and located in the yard at the rear of the machine shop. The main building just destroyed was built in 1844-5. Mr. Medlicott succeeded Mr. Steiger as superintendent, and following him came Theodore W. Pease, lately deceased, and still later Mr. Weston, father-in-law of Benjamin W. Bright. For many years, and particularly in 1851-2, this company did a very flourishing business and formed an important industry for this village. Business was finally suspended about 1870, and the building was shortly after purchased by the Hartford Carpet Company.

This completed the newspaper report on the inferno. A townsperson, signing only his initials, submitted observations on the fire in the same edition.

Mr. Editor:

We have recently passed through a very trying event in this village. We were already in a state of anxiety over the sufferings of our brethren at Lynn and Boston, both those cities swept with devouring flames and still smoldering in ashes, when our own village was aroused with the alarm of fire.

The festivities of Thanksgiving Day were hardly over, people had scarcely retired to their beds, when they were summoned to the rescue. And no one who witnessed that conflagration but seriously questioned the safety of the village.

Far and near stores and dwelling-houses were threatened; within a radius of ten rods houses were heated almost to a state of combustion, and the elevation of the heat, accompanied with flaming sparks sweeping the entire northern part of the village, with all the factory buildings, made the heart tremble for the safety and comfort of our people. The old grist-mill was the key to the situation, and that saved, and the neighboring buildings protected, all was mastered. It was a creditable piece of work and all done by our local fire company.

While Hartford and Springfield both readily responded to the alarm of distress, and while such notification was very expedient, yet the work was done by the men here. Unless it was the work of an incendiary, which heaven forbid, no cause of the fire has as yet been discovered, and perhaps never will be. A theory, however, occurs to the writer which it may be useful to mention.

It was observed that the fire broke out in the tower and in an upper story. It was discovered, too, at about 11.45 o'clock. The watchman had previously gone his usual round, and all was reported well. Now may it not have been that a flame was generated by the friction of the bell rope? Or from the bell swinging in the tower? The time that elapsed afterward was just sufficient for such a spark to take effect, and the light woolen fabrics might easily have spread the flames through the entire upper part of the building.

So much for the theory, a theory which we venture to suggest in the hopes that it may attract attention to such causes of fire in future.

The losses also were great. The president of the Hartford Carpet company has already stated the losses in a general way as quite above $200,000. And we yet await any trouble that may come from the consumption of such a quantity of valuable material.

So much for the practical aspect of the fire. But, Mr. Editor, no manly observer of that fire but must be impressed with another aspect of it, viz., the heroic aspect.

No one who approached that building, or ventured to lend a helping hand, or who occupied a position near it, could but realize the danger of trying to master the fire. That great building was an enormous oven, and near approach to it meant endangering the life.

But what did we see?

Men, members of the fire company and others, exposing themselves heroically to the burning heat. The devouring flames swept almost into their faces, and had they not been clad in rubber suits and kept wet with water, not only would every rag been burned off their backs, but they must have perished in the heat. In looking at the work from a certain standpoint the men appeared to be standing in the very midst of the flames. One could not but recall Nebuchadnezzar's fiery furnace, in which were thrown the three Hebrew children, nor could we but discern with the eye of faith one like unto the Son of Man walking in the midst of the flames.

Sir, such heroism deserves more than a passing notice. Men can not be paid for such work. These noble firemen whom we hear of day by day risking their lives for the safety of people's homes and property, too often themselves with neither home nor property, and never to be known personally for any thing good that they ever did, do they not deserve to be called the heroes of humanity?

Sir, such noble men will stand the fires of the judgment, and their names, forgotten here, if they but believe on Him, will be found enrolled in the Lamb's Book of Life.

J. F. G

The letter to the editor was simple, but it reflected the community's sense of brotherhood and caring for one another. Each person looking out for the welfare of his neighbor, no matter what the personal cost.

A neighborhood of immigrants whose shared histories bound them together more than blood.

Scotch, Irish, English, French, German, and Canadian. They were willing to sacrifice more than most to maintain that sense of community.

23: BUBBLE WATER

Henry Daniel Cogswell began his first dentistry practice at age 26 in Providence, Rhode Island. When gold was discovered in California, he traveled west aboard a clipper ship for five months before landing in San Francisco on October 12, 1849. There, he set up an office and became the first practicing dentist in San Francisco.

Long before *Teeth Grillz* became popular among the hip-hop generation, Cogswell made a small fortune by pulling the rotted teeth of gold miners and decorating what was left with gold fillings made from their own ore.

Investing his dental earnings in stocks and real estate, Cogswell became one of the first millionaires in San Francisco. After retiring from his practice, he founded both the Cogswell Polytechnic Institute and Cogswell Dental College in that state.

His life passion, though, was addressing the drinking problems of the working classes. He planned to provide free drinking fountains in American cities, one for every 100 saloons. In this committed teetotaler's opinion, what the inebriated needed to quench their thirst was not alcohol but cool, clean water.

As a strident supporter of Prohibition, Cogswell built his

first drinking fountains in San Francisco, California, then set his sights on the sinful in the rest of the country.

Cogswell's temperance fountains, which he designed, often featured a giant statue of himself in a frock coat holding a cup and dispensing water to the parched masses.

Former dentist and temperance promoter Henry Cogsworth (public domain)

However, the intoxicated did not appreciate his gifts as much as he would have liked. The fountains proved irresistible targets for vandals, as drunken revelers, rowdy art lovers, and ordinary folks who deemed the statues in poor taste all desecrated or destroyed them.

Lavator Brainerd Lewis was born in Westfield, Massachusetts, on March 16, 1844. Within seven years, his Mother (Sophia Clapp), Brother (Harrison), and Father (Lavator Merrick Lewis) had passed away, leaving him on his own at the age of seven.

After his father's death, the 1855 census shows that the youth lived with his uncle Samuel Brainard and Martha Lewis, a farming family in the same town. Sadly, Lavator's aunt Martha died one year later in 1856.

Historical records show that Samuel relocated to Missouri soon after Martha's passing, leaving Lavator, then 16, behind in Westfield with his aunt Mary. It is unclear whether Samuel took his daughter, Augusta, with him when he moved out west or left her in the care of a local relative.

By all accounts, Lavator was an excellent student, as captured in the Westfield Newsletter of 1860.

As promised in our last issue, we give below the names of all scholars belonging to the high school who were perfect in deportment and recitations during the week ending Friday, Oct 12th.

Among the names of the 30 girls and 11 boys was Lavator Lewis, the star pupil.

In 1864, Uncle Samuel passed away, leaving Cousin Augusta orphaned. At 18, in 1866, she petitioned for guardianship[340] with Alexander McKenzie, a local farmer and Scottish immigrant. Whether there was a standing relationship between the Lewises and the McKenzies is unknown. However, five years later, in 1871, Alexander

---

[340] Guardianship was a legal arrangement where the court appointed a person to take care of a minor's well-being and to manage their estate, mainly if they were orphaned. The guardian was responsible for the child's property and finances rather than necessarily their day-to-day custody.

McKenzie was similarly appointed guardian of Lavator B. Lewis, Augusta's cousin. Lavator was 27 years old at the time.

It is not difficult to understand how Lavator would have benefited from guardianship. He was about to establish his own whip manufacturing business in Westfield, and a guardian would have provided necessary business insight, as Lavator had no parents or partners to consult.

By 1872, Lavator was an established and successful businessman with a whip factory on Elm Street and a home on West School Street. A vocal member of the Temperance movement, he often publicly stated that if society could prohibit the sale of gunpowder to ensure public safety, then the sale of liquor should be regulated for the same reason.

At a Good Samaritan meeting in front of City Hall on July 21, 1873, local residents, including Lavator B. Lewis, spoke out against prohibition.

The work is but half done when the grog shops are closed. There must be something to fill up the void made by taking away a man's liquor, billiards, and cigars. Let us open places where music, free lectures, eatables, and temperance drinks are to be found, and so keep the man saved from his cups and away from temptation.[341]

In a nod to his beliefs, Lavator set up a watering trough in front of his whip factory on Elm Street to provide clean water to the thirsty.

Lavator was painstaking in his approach to whip manufacturing. His attention to detail brought his products' national attention. It attracted quality craftsmen to his business and quickly made him wealthy, enabling him to expand his real estate empire.

---

[341] Springfield Daily Union June 14, 1873. Page 4.

In 1877, he purchased a much-coveted building, Stowe Place, at 10 Broad Street, and followed that by buying two lots of land on Holland Street from the trustees of the Methodist Church.

That same year, on July 14, 1877, Lavator, then 33, petitioned the court to release him from guardianship, stating that the arrangement was no longer needed. Clearly, with his business expertise on display, it was not.

Eleven days later, the court agreed with the petitioner and granted Lavator's request. Surprisingly, the published account in the Springfield Republican reported:

Lavator B. Lewis of Westfield, **formerly insane,**[342] *was discharged from guardianship.*

What?

By most accounts, Lavator was of sound mind and had only sought the guardianship of a trusted person who had performed the same service for his cousin Augusta. The description of Lavator as *formerly insane* could have reflected his eccentricity in business dealings and not his emotional state.

In any case, it was an interesting choice of words.

In 1881, Lavator continued to expand his holdings by purchasing a three-story block at the corner of Franklin and Elm Streets at a real estate auction. It was previously owned by Alonzo Whitney, a well-respected and successful farmer and real estate owner.

Three years later, Lavator had flipped the Broad Street

---

[342] In 1900, insanity generally referred to a severe mental illness, encompassing a wide range of symptoms, including irrational behavior, inability to reason, and violent tendencies, and was considered a legal term used to determine if someone was mentally unfit

mansion to J. B. Colton, whose company manufactured what was then claimed to be the best flavoring extracts in the world. When reporting on the sale of the property, a local paper noted:

> *More longing and envious eyes have been cast towards this place than almost any other in town, on account of its desirableness of location.*[343]

In 1886, Lavator purchased another building at the corner of Elm and Chapel and moved the entire structure to an empty lot at the rear of his whip factory.

By this time, Lavator was making more money than he could have imagined. His Elm Street property was occupied by his own whip company, Loomis & Becker's whip button manufactory, and, on the ground floor, H. W. Hammersley's grocery establishment.

In February 1888, L. B. Lewis decided to exit the whip manufacturing business and put his factory up for sale. The equipment was soon sold, and the lithographic company of George Sauter and Philip Pfeiffer took its place.

Freed from the challenges of manufacturing and promotion, Lavator turned to his other passions: investment banking and philanthropy.

One event in 1897 provided some insight into the eccentricity of Lavator, his desire for perfection, and his beliefs in *what was right*. As the country moved from horse-drawn carriages to mass transportation, the town of Westfield had proposed laying trolley tracks on the same roadway as its Franklin Street building. Lavator was adamant that the tracks should not be laid on his side of the

---

[343] Westfield Times and Newsletter November 12, 1884. Page 2.

street, as it would interfere with teams driving up or standing in front of his building.

He lost the argument and boarded up the front of his building rather than rent out the first floor, which had been occupied as a grocery store for years.

With time on his hands, he reflected on the earlier work Henry Cogsworth did with his Temperance Fountains. Although the fountains were a wonderful concept, they posed a challenge to those desiring an easy way to drink cool, fresh water when a cup wasn't available. Committed to prohibition, Lewis considered the problem and engineered a solution, a system that could be retrofitted to any fountain and deliver clean water to thirsty passersby through bubblers.

He sought no patent for his invention; instead, he began installing these devices in fountains all over the region at no cost to any municipality. In June of that year, an article in the Hartford Courant reported on his hope that the towns and cities where he had installed his invention would assume maintenance responsibility.

LAVATOR LEWIS'S IDEA

He has maintained Pipe Attachments to Drinking Fountains Long Enough

Lavator B. Lewis of this city has addressed a communication to the mayor and city government, in which he says: 'Lavator B. Lewis, who has made, connected, and maintained for a considerable period pipe attachments for water drinking purposes in seven of the city water tanks, located in front of City Hall, at South Green, on New Britain Avenue, at Parkville, foot of State Street, at the Tunnel and on Windsor Avenue, now asks that the city maintain these attachments perpetually, they having been extensively used. Said Lewis wants the goodwill of the drinking public and asks for no further consideration.

By July, requests for his bubbler plans were coming in from all over the country so they could be attached to existing fountains in other states, cities, and towns.

By August, even Thompsonville had a bubbler installed on the fountain near the White Mill, a gift from Lavator Brainerd Lewis of Westfield, Massachusetts.

THE NEW DRINKING FOUNTAIN

The new drinking cups, or bubble fountains, as they are properly called, which have recently been placed in three of the water tanks in town, have attracted no little attention, and favorable comment as well. It may not be generally known that these fountains are provided through the generosity of a man who, until a few days ago, was practically unknown in our town.

He is a Massachusetts man and his name is Lavator B. Lewis. He has acquired property in active business operations as a whip manufacturer. Desiring to use some of it, or some of the income from it for the benefit of his fellow men, he conceived the idea of providing free public drinking fountains.

The contrivance is simple, yet it meets the object admirably and thousands of thirsty wheelmen and others will have reason to be truly thankful for the generous provision made by this man. It is a pipe connection attached to the inlet of the tank, the top of the pipe extending a few inches above the surface of the tank, to which is connected a small cup. By a valve or cock the flow of water is adjusted so that it flow gently over the edges of the cup, very much like a bubbling spring.

Mr. Lewis has placed thirty-two of these fountains in Connecticut and eighteen in Massachusetts, he himself providing the cups and all attachments and superintending the connecting of them, the only expense to the town being the providing of a man to make the attachment.

The three bubble fountains are located at the watering tank near the White Mill, one near the Freshwater Bridge, and one on Enfield Street near the head of Bridge Lane. Prominent features that commend these drinking cups are cleanliness – the edges of the cups being constantly washed – and the fact that the cups cannot be lost or stolen.[344]

The bubbler near the Freshwater (Thompsonville to Suffield) bridge was connected to a water tank fed by a spring north of the village. Thompsonville was the proud owner of two Lewis Bubblers.

In the Fall of 1901, the water tank/fountain near the White Mill was briefly removed as trolley tracks were laid into the road. The following Spring, the tank and fountain were reinstalled, and a new bubbler was added. By that year, 64 Lewis Bubblers had been erected in regional Connecticut and Massachusetts fountains.

Two years later, Lavator Brainerd Lewis passed away. In a nod to a remaining icon that had reflected his eccentricity, the boards that covered the front of his Franklin Street building were removed.

In one of several obituaries, the following succinctly summed up his legacy:

---

[344] Thompsonville Press August 9, 1900. Page 2.

Mr. Lewis was of a quiet and unpretentious disposition and was not entirely understood by his neighbors.

During the latter part of his life, he traveled about looking after his banking interests and doing benevolent work where he found opportunity.

He was well known by officials of many towns of this state and Connecticut because of his work in the interests of a thirsty public by putting drinking attachments on many watering tanks. He was especially fond of children and delighted to please them, while he found many occasions to help the infirm and needy.

He will be missed by all, especially those in town who have been cheered and helped by his kind words and deeds.[345]

And certainly, by the thirsty residents of Thompsonville.

Delivering cool spring water to residents' homes had been considered as early as 1880, when Charles H. Briscoe, Loren Howard Pease, Frederick E. Ely, Shubael Parsons, George H. Barber, Albert A. Allen, Benjamin F. Lord, and John Hunter petitioned the Connecticut State Assembly to incorporate The Thompsonville Water Company. The petitioners asked that the company be

...authorized and empowered to construct, maintain, and repair such reservoirs as it may deem expedient or necessary; to construct, repair, and maintain dams across such streams as it may deem necessary, and to take, hire, or rent any lands, water-springs, dams, or works, and to construct, repair and maintain such pipes, canals, or

---

[345] Westfield Times and News-Letter October 20, 1904. Page 4

aqueducts as may become necessary or convenient for the conveyance of water to such points as it may desire in or near said village.

And said corporation is hereby authorized and empowered to open the ground in any streets, highways, and public grounds, with the consent of the selectmen, for the purpose of building, laying down, sinking, or repairing such pipes or conduits as may be required for conducting and distributing water within said village, provided it shall put such streets, highways, and public grounds in as good condition as before said laying, constructing, or repair.[346]

The petition was granted on March 24, 1880, with an initial ten-thousand-dollar subscription, which could be increased to thirty thousand dollars when required.

The first meeting of the corporators was held at Lord's Hotel on December 9, 1884. Frederick Ely[347] was elected Chairman, and Charles H. Briscoe as clerk. The organization's charter was accepted, and subscriptions were opened to sell stock.

The original concept was to tap the Pierce Brook[348], which was about one mile north of the village, and

...convey it to a stand pipe to be located on the top of the hill near the brick schoolhouse, to be high enough to give

---

[346] Connecticut Special Acts and Resolutions January Session 1880 Page 82.

[347] Ely was born in Hawaii, where his father was stationed as a missionary. Before moving to Thompsonville, Ely spent a few years as a merchant in Cleveland, Ohio. For 20 years before his death, Ely served as clerk and treasurer for the town of Enfield and Judge of Probate.

[348] Present-day Waterworks Brook

a pressure of one hundred feet, sufficient for the hydrants for fire purposes. It will be brought in the highways and will require seven miles of pipe to go over the different streets of the village.[349]

The Morning Journal-Courier of New Haven, Connecticut, reported that the Thompsonville Water Company was fully organized on January 5, 1885, with a stock capitalization of thirty-thousand dollars.[350]

The Thompsonville Press of January 8, 1885, echoed that report, adding that directors for the organization were chosen at that same January 5 meeting:

…William Birnie, C. L. Goodhue, Geo. H. Barber, C. H. Briscoe, and L. H. Pease. C. H. Briscoe was elected president, William Birnie treasurer, and L. H. Pease secretary.[351]

James Watson was born in England in 1815, but the town and his parents' names are unrecoverable, as is his year of emigration.

He married Caroline Hale Sparks in 1837 in a ceremony held in Glastonbury, Connecticut.

The specific route he took to land in Thompsonville, Connecticut, is unclear; however, it is clear that Watson had owned and operated a grist mill on Main Street in Thompsonville, along the Freshwater Brook, since approximately 1850, as indicated on a 1869 map of the village.

---

[349] Hartford Courant December 12, 1884. Page 4.

[350] The organization's charter was amended in January 1885 by a Special Act to adjust its capitalization to thirty thousand dollars from the original ten thousand.

[351] Thompsonville Press January 8, 1885. Page 2.

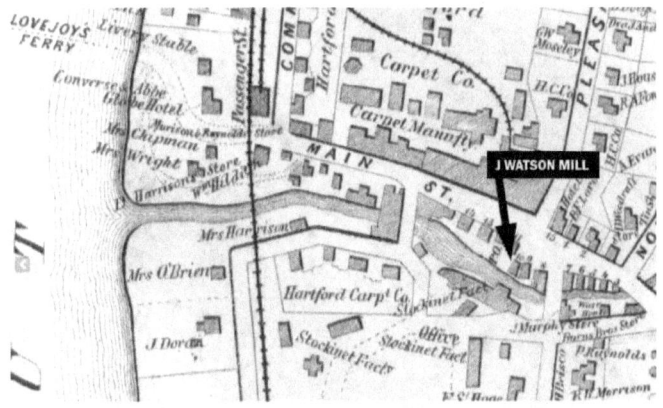

Baker Tilden 1869 map of Thompsonville, Connecticut showing the Grist Mill of James Watson on Main Street of the village.

William P. Robbins was born in Siam, Bangkok, to Samuel Robbins of Marietta, Ohio, and Martha Pierce Robbins of Enfield, Connecticut. William's parents were missionaries who returned to the United States soon after William's birth, settling in Enfield. Martha died when Robbins turned two years old, and Samuel passed quickly after his wife, leaving William and his older brother, Samuel Jr., to be raised by their Aunt, Mrs. Polina Lee, also of Enfield.

In 1873, Robbins married Adella Hills of Windham, New Hampshire, and the two took up residence in the northern section of Thompsonville on his grandfather's homestead. Robbins was the grandson of Deacon Luther Pierce and his wife, Amelia, both of Enfield. He began a milling business from the building known as the Pierce Shop, along the Pierce Brook[352] where Springfield Road intersected State Street. William and his bride built their

---

[352] Renamed as the Waterworks Brook after being sourced for village drinking water years later.

own house near his grandfather's home.

Early example of a mid-1800s Grist Mill located on a stream to power the grinding machinery (photo public domain)

In 1879, on March 14, Robbins, tired of the *daily grind*, sold the grist mill to James Watson, giving Watson two mills in Thompsonville. After the purchase, Watson rebranded the mill as the North Mill. Robbins relocated to Warren, Massachusetts to live near his brother.

Watson began advertising his milling operations when the Thompsonville Press began publication in 1880.

JAMES WATSON,

GRAIN, MEAL AND FEED for sale at reasonable prices. Custom grinding done at the usual rates. Corn shelled, or ground on the ear, at Watson's North mill, on the Springfield road. A full supply always on hand at Thompsonville mills.

By 1881, Watson also began grinding plaster and grains at his North Mill. A grist mill could also operate as a plaster mill by employing a separate set of grinding stones or by adjusting the separation of the burrs (mill stones). Ground gypsum wasn't used for construction as much as it was for fertilizer.

At some point in late March 1882, Watson sold the North Mill and the former William P. Robbins home to Christopher Wiseman.[353]

Christopher Wiseman has this week removed to the W. P. Robbins house, in the north part of the town, and next week will commence running the grist mill known as the North Mill. Our dealings with Mr. Wiseman and his experience as a miller assures us that the farmers that patronize him will be well served.[354]

Christopher Wiseman was born to James and Ann Wiseman in Grassington, Yorkshire, England, on September 16, 1838. Father James was a successful blacksmith while Ann tended to the home.

In 1861, the English census identified Christopher's occupation as a carter, which meant he transported goods by cart or wagon from the countryside into towns on market days. Seeking a better fortune, he emigrated to the United States in 1867. Upon his arrival in Thompsonville, he was hired as an apprentice miller at the Watson Mill.

Two years later, secure in his position, Wiseman married Janet Gemmell in a ceremony conducted by Reverend John

---

[353] By 1886, Watson acquired a grist mill in nearby Spoonville (another name for East Granby, Connecticut) where he ground corn, rye, oats, and other grains for the general market.

[354] Thompsonville Press March 30, 1882. Page 2.

Howson, the village Methodist minister.

The 1870 census identified Wiseman as a miller, or, as actually recorded in the document, someone who *worked in a grist mill.* Four years later, in 1874, Wiseman became a naturalized citizen, assuming all the benefits his new allegiance afforded.

As the new owner of the North Mill, Wiseman enthusiastically assumed his work, accepting and filling orders while advertising alongside the former mill owner, and congenial competitor, in the local newspaper.

Miscellaneous.

JAMES WATSON. GRAIN, MEAL and Feed for sale at reasonable prices. Custom grinding done at the usual rates. A full supply always on hand. Main street, Thompsonville, Conn.

CHRISTOPHER WISEMAN, DEALER in Flour, Meal, Grain, Feed, Etc. Custom grinding done at the usual rates Corn shelled, or ground on the ear, at the North Mill, on Springfield road. A full supply always on hand. Orders filled promptly and delivered free of charge.

Like the real estate tenet, it is all about location, location, location. Wiseman's Mill was situated on Pierce Brook, and the property included water rights that were used to power the mill's grinding machinery. The plans of the newly minted Thompsonville Water Company to tap the Pierce Brook to supply drinking water to the residents of Thompsonville created a cloud of concern about the viability of Wiseman's Grist Mill business, prompting the miller to take out a preemptory advertisement in the local paper announcing an abrupt change in payment terms.

NOTICE!

IF THE PLAN PROPOSED BY THE Thompsonville Water Company is adopted, my grist-mill at this place will soon be closed, and I shall be obliged to do a STRICTLY CASH BUSINESS during the short time I remain here.

All persons indebted to me are respectfully requested to call and settle without further notice.

CHRISTOPHER WISEMAN.

Thompsonville, Jan. 7, 1885.

In June 1885, two carloads of iron piping, four carloads of cement, various tools, horses, and workmen arrived in the village to install the infrastructure for delivering spring water to Thompsonville.

North of the village, Christopher Wiseman breathed a sigh of relief as the source water had been changed from the Pierce Brook to eight springs located on Samuel C. Smith's lot about one and one-quarter miles to the north of the village. The water concern purchased two and one-quarter acres from Smith, where a 40-horsepower engine would be installed to draw and pump water into a reservoir constructed on one acre of land purchased from Henry C. Woodward. Woodward's property had been surveyed as 40 feet higher than the original site for the reservoir on Robert McCrone's hill, which was located in the same general area.

Secure in believing that his location was safe from development, Wiseman addressed some concerning issues at his own site.

> *The dam at the North Mill – Wiseman's Mill – is undergoing repairs and is in fact being put into shape in a business-like way by a wheelwright from Springfield and Thomas Watters and his carpenters. Much time and patience has been expended in endeavoring to get along with a leaky dam,* **and now that the Water company is not going to interfere with the present water privilege**, *the necessary repairs are to be made at once.*[355]

At the same time, progress was being made on building the pumping station and reservoir, as well as on burying the water-delivery infrastructure in the village.

> *Pipe has already been laid through Alen Avenue and East Whitworth Street, as well as quite a distance on Pleasant Street. The location of the standpipe, which is to be located on H. C. Woodward's land, has been marked out and the stand pipe, or metallic reservoir, is being built at Hawkins's boiler works in Springfield, and is to be 40 feet in diameter and 25 feet high, with a capacity of about 250,000 gallons.*

> *The engine and pump, which will be located on the land purchased from S. C. Smith, is to be what is termed a duplex pumping engine and will pump 40,000 gallons of water an hour. The engine is being buit by Deane of Holyoke. With a mammoth pump of this kind and a reservoir located at a point above any building in the village, and with proper hydrants, which must be provided, the chances for success in fighting fires will be*

---

[355] Thompsonville Press June 6, 1885. Page 2. (Author emphasis)

greatly increased.[356]

BE VERY CAREFUL OF THE WATER YOU DRINK.

The above illustration shows plainer than the power of words the connection between wells and cesspools, and should startle every thinking person. The Thompsonville Water Company furnish pure wholesome spring water to a family for $8.00 per year.

Apply to GEORGE F. COOPER, and have pure water in your house.

Thompsonville Water Company.

Goodhue and Birnie of Springfield, Massachusetts, were the general contractors and designers for the effort, having previously completed a similar system in Revere, Massachusetts. It wasn't quiet work, as the Thompsonville

---

[356] Thompsonville Press June 6, 1885. Page 2

Press noted in its October 1, 1885, edition:

> *It is hardly necessary to note the fact, except for the information of the deaf or those living outside of a radius of five miles from H. C. Woodward's hill, that boiler makers are there at work putting up the standpipe for the water company.*

Three years before Lavator Lewis installed his first bubblers in water tanks in Thompsonville, it was:

> *...suggested that a public drinking fountain, supplied from the pure cool springs of the Thompsonville Water Company, would be an excellent move in the temperance direction.*[357]

As reported in the newspaper, it seemed that the locals sorely needed an alternative to alcohol.

> *People who are in positions to know state positively that the number of drunken people about the streets last Saturday evening was never equaled before in this place. No less than three drunken brawls are reported in the vicinity of as many different saloons, the latter bordering close on to Sunday morning. No arrests were made and if reports are correct, it would have been very difficult to tell where to begin.*[358]

To the north of the village, Christopher Wiseman had grown tired of the Grist Mill business by 1887 and withdrew, returning to his earlier roots as a carter. He purchased a Landau hackney to transport people to and from the train depot in Thompsonville. He also ferried

---

[357] Thompsonville Press May 19, 1887. Page 2.
[358] Thompsonville Press August 30, 1888. Page 2.

people to local family and social events.

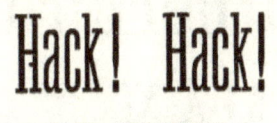

Hack! Hack!

FOR SERVICE.

I WISH to thank the public for the very liberal patronage given me in the past. With my new Landau Hack I am better equipped than ever for all kinds of carriage service. 'Bus for picnics, etc. Prices reasonable.

C. WISEMAN.
Pleasant street, Thompsonville.

While a buggy usually denotes a simple horse-drawn vehicle for transporting one or two passengers, carriages, including hacks, Gladstones, Landaus, Phaetons, and Victorias, were designed to convey multiple passengers in varying degrees of comfort. The Landau wagon's low body allowed everyone to see who was riding in the carriage, providing fodder for wagging tongues.

An example of a Landau Wagon—named after the German city of Landau, where it was first produced (public domain).

Wiseman's hack venture lasted 14 years until he died in 1901. George C. Rutherford of Thompsonville purchased and continued the business.

Geo. C. Rutherford.

HACKMAN,

Successor to C. Wiseman.

Having purchased from the estate of the late C. Wiseman the hack and livery business, I desire to announce to the public that my carriage will meet all trains from 8.02 a. m. to 7 p. m.; also other trains by request.

The traveling public is assured of prompt and courteous treatment.

Orders may be left at Geo. R. Steele's corner drug store, or at my residence on Maple street near the electric car barns.

GEO. C. RUTHERFORD,

Thompsonville, Conn.

In 1889, the charter of the Thompsonville Water Company was amended to allow the organization to extend its water-delivery infrastructure south to Warehouse Point and east across the Connecticut River to the neighboring town of Suffield. To supplement the increased water requirements, the company built an aqueduct to Pierce's Brook, which was the original source identified for fresh water.

James Watson retired from the Thompsonville Grist Mill in 1891. Philip Lovejoy, a descendant of the ferry operator for whom the village had originally been named, continued working at the Main Street facility until he retired in 1894.

That same year, a drought gripped the village, and residents who had opted to tap into the Water Company's pipes counted their blessings. Work finally began to lay pipes along the Connecticut Riverbed to deliver water to Suffield.

The pipes were made of lead, an unknown health hazard.

The Water Company took steps to secure its reservoir by installing a fence to keep animals from accessing the drinking water. Years earlier, the Enfield Board of Health had legislated a similar action to ensure the purity of the water at Watson's Main Street Mill.

All persons shall be and hereby are absolutely forbidden to deposit any urine or fecal matter, or any other filthy substance or thing in the mill-pond of the grist-mill used by James Watson, in the village of Thompsonville, in said Enfield, or in or on the bed or banks of said pond or where it can fall or wash into or upon said pond or bed.[359]

Given the possibility of contamination, one wonders why the Water Company took so long to protect the source.

Hmmm...that water's got a tang to it...

---

[359] Extraction from the Town of Enfield Board of Health notice issued by the Town Clerk on October 26, 1886.

24: FOX IN THE HENHOUSE

ENFIELD, CT., Jan. 8, 1900

To: Henry D. Alden, George H. Payne, and John F. O'Hear, selectmen of the town of Enfield, in the state of Connecticut.

Gentlemen: I hereby tender my resignation from the offices of clerk and treasurer of said town. Personal business matters require more and more of my attention and necessitate the taking of this action. Assuring you of my regret in leaving said offices and your association therewith, and requesting that you will kindly take immediate action, I am, very respectfully yours.

(Signed) Robert E. Spencer[360]

Spencer's request was reluctantly accepted. This action was not entirely unexpected, as he had expressed his intention to resign on multiple occasions.

Robert Emmett Spencer had served as town clerk and treasurer for the Town of Enfield since his election in

---

[360] Thompsonville Press January 11, 1900. Page 2.

January 1893, becoming the first Democrat to hold these positions since 1786. Spencer became so popular that he ran on Republican and Democratic tickets, giving both parties equal bragging rights. Spencer also filled the position of Judge of Probate in the town.

The margin of Spencer's victory in the election prompted the newspaper to provide additional background on the contest winner.

TOWN CLERK, TREASURER AND REGISTRAR.			
—Districts—			
1st	2d	3d	Total
Robert E. Spencer, d,	50	439	76	565
Frederick A. King, r,	60	233	79	372
JUDGE OF PROBATE.			
Robert E. Spencer, d,	50	419	71	540
Frederick A. King, r,	61	248	73	387

Robert E. Spencer, now in his twenty-ninth year, was born at Colchester, this state, though his early life was spent at East Haddam, where his father conducted a country store for a number of years.

In August, 1881, Roswell D. Spencer, with his family, located in this village, and, in company with M. W. Babcock, entered the mercantile business in the North Store.

Robert, after completing his education at the Hartford High School, entered the store as a bookkeeper and cashier, and a year later, on the retirement of Mr. Babcock, succeeded to his position in the store.

At East Haddam, while a boy, he sold papers and carried the mail daily, by which means he accumulated the *sum of $800. In 1885, with this sum added to his earnings at the North Store, he purchased of Levi P. Abbe the property on South Main Street known as the Woods Homestead, where a year later he erected a building in which was opened the North Store branch.*

He afterwards conceived the idea of establishing a bank and to practically prepare himself for such duties occupied a position for a few months in the Naugatuck National Bank, and in September, 1887, through his efforts was organized the R. D. & Robt. E. Spencer Banking Co., which institution has grown to a position of importance and trust.

In 1891 he spent several months in the South and West and while at St. Joseph, Mo., with J. W. Brockett of that city he established the firm of Brockett & Spencer, dealers in mortgage loans, and leased the safe deposit vaults at St. Joseph.

In September of the same year, on returning from Denver, he entered the meat business, buying the market outfit and goodwill of L. B. Allen. At the organization of the Enfield Mercantile corporation, July, 1892, this department and the grocery business established by J. W. Graham were united and have since been conducted as a corporation, of which Robert E. Spencer is the president.

The building, the second floor of which is occupied by THE PRESS, was erected for and is owned by this corporation. Mr. Spencer sold his property on South Main Street to Maurice Sullivan, taking a lease of the banking rooms for a term of years. Among other investments he purchased of A. H. Mathewson a charming residence on Pearl Street, where he is happily located with a wife and one child.[361]

The Spencer Bank's original location was inside the North Store, in the center of the facility, enclosed with wire screening. A three-ton burglar-proof safe purchased from the Hall Safe and Lock Company of Chicago, Illinois, rested within the secured space.

VAULTS, VAULT FRONTS AND **VICTOR COMBINATION BANK LOCKS.** 93 Dearborn St, CHICAGO, ILL. and Cincinnati Ohio.

In addition to traditional banking, the company opened a savings division for locals who desired to 'put a little money away each week'. It was a welcome addition to the village, attracting numerous smaller depositors.

Seven years later, on April 26, 1894, the R. D. & R. E. Spencer Bank became the first bank in the village to be robbed.

At about 11 a.m., three professionals began to work out a carefully prepared plan.

One man drove a team to the bank's door and called out to Roswell Duane Spencer, Robert's father, who was working inside the building, on the pretense of negotiating a loan. The elder Spencer stepped out and engaged the stranger, the two men moving slightly south toward the next-door clothing store.

---

[361] Thompsonville Press January 26, 1893. Page 2.

While Roswell's back was turned, a second man moved to Kennedy's saloon, signaling a third man who entered the bank. Maggie Handley, who lived across the street, witnessed the affair and called out to Mr. Spencer, her warning words inciting the lookout man to run.

The third man, already inside the bank, coolly asked Mr. Spencer to change a five-dollar bill for gold, which he did. The man then exited the bank, scurrying quickly away toward Central Street, disappearing around the corner.

The first man with the team drove toward Freshwater Bridge, where men numbers two and three leaped onto the carriage. The three quickly drove away.

It took R. D. Spencer a full twenty minutes to realize the game that had been played when he looked to the safe to withdraw some cash and found it 'lighter' by some twelve hundred dollars. With the constable out of town, the bank owner telephoned Hartford and Springfield to report the theft. The notification was to no avail as the bank robbers had changed their horse-drawn vehicles and were suspected of heading toward the Berkshires.

They were never apprehended.

Despite the minor setback, the Robert Emmett Spencer opened a new bank branch in Hazardville in 1898, on the corner of Main and Maple Streets, to serve that small populace. One year later, on October 27, 1899, Spencer's Hazardville bank was the first savings institution in that village to be robbed, giving the Spencers the unenviable position of being the first bank in both Thompsonville and Hazardville to be burglarized.

The Hazardville job differed from the earlier Thompsonville affair in that the eastern bank was broken into in the early hours of the morning, while people were sleeping.

The burglars had first broken into nearby stores to steal four heavy blankets. They soaked these in an open water tank on the street. Entering the bank through a rear window, the pair wrapped the safe in the wet blankets to deaden the noise of the explosives attached to the steel vault. The plan worked flawlessly. The front of the safe was blown from its body with a muffled blast, loud enough to alert residents to the robbers' activity.

The burglars were unaware that the firm had transferred hundreds of dollars to regional banks the previous day, leaving only a few random dollars, some documents, and a chest inside the safe. While the documents and $10 in notes were reachable, the chest was not, and the criminals left with little to show for their efforts.

The people's money seemed safe.

From burglars, anyway.

Twelve days after resigning as town clerk and treasurer for the Town of Enfield, Robert Emmett Spencer posted a notice on both the Thompsonville and Hazardville branches of the R. D. & Robt. E. Spencer Banking Company announced that it would suspend business pending bankruptcy proceedings in federal court.

Local businesses and farmers used the general banking business, while the savings department was patronized by working people.

The townspeople were stunned.

An additional note on the Hazardville Branch stated that customers would be paid one hundred cents on the dollar, thus ensuring their deposits.

No such words accompanied the Thompsonville note.

This action clarified the younger Spencer's decision to remove himself from the town offices.

Much excitement has been occasioned by the suspension. The firm has enjoyed the confidence of the townspeople.[362]

When the Thompsonville bank opened, it was capitalized at $25,000 [~ $780,000 in 2020 dollars]. By 1900, the elder Spencer guessed there were approximately $50,000 on the books [~ 1.5 million in 2020 dollars]. During the month preceding the suspension announcement, it was admitted that about $10,000 had been withdrawn by unnamed businesses or individuals [~ $300K in 2020 dollars].[363]

The following day, the monies withdrawn during the month preceding the suspension had climbed to $15K [~500K], which should have raised additional suspicions.

Roswell Duane Spencer, the senior partner, announced that all of the family's personal property would be liquidated, if necessary, to cover any depositor losses. The Spencers had enlisted Judge Charles H. Briscoe of

---

[362] Meriden Daily Journal January 23, 1900. Page 2.

[363] One has to question the timing of the withdrawals and if those businesses or people were notified of the pending suspension action. Their names are unrecoverable.

Thompsonville to handle their bankruptcy.

Small depositors remained anxious, most claiming to have on average $2,000 in the bank [~75,000 in 2020 dollars].

By January 25, the elder and younger Spencer's general statements about how debts would be repaid seemed to calm the villagers' nerves. However, an actual balance sheet report would not be available until attorney Briscoe filed it with the courts.

By February 2, the estimated value of the deposits with the private Spencer Bank had risen to $75,000 [approximately $2.3 million in 2020 dollars].

By February 5, the company's liabilities and assets were reported as far worse than expected. Their liabilities were slightly above $131,000, while their assets totaled approximately $37,000 — a shortfall of almost $100,000.

The hope for a dollar-for-dollar recovery by depositors vanished into thin air.

The great majority of the stockholders are working people who have laid away their hard earned savings in the two banks only to have them swept away by the failure.[364]

Few bank failures in Connecticut have been accompanied by such a poor showing of assets.[365]

On February 10, 1900, Robert Emmett Spencer was arrested and charged with misappropriating bank funds. The issue arose from a claim by William Hilditch, Sr., regarding a $600 bank loan note that was sold to Hilditch. The note taker repaid the note, but the funds were never

---

[364] The Meriden Journal February 5, 1900. Page 9.
[365] The Meriden Record-Journal February 6, 1900. Page 1.

passed on to Hilditch.

Slowly, other issues began to emerge.

As the courtroom drama unfolded, Robert E. Spencer admitted that the Thompsonville branch had been insolvent since 1892 and that every dollar deposited had been used to cover old debts since 1895. Spencer also added that no balance sheet had ever been created to determine the viability of the concern or condition of the business.

It is essential to remember that Robert Emmett Spencer had served as Enfield's town clerk and treasurer for seven years. He was revered, respected, and trusted with individual investors' money and the town's finances.

The people's confidence seemed to have been as misplaced as had the $100,000 shortfall [~ $3.8 million in 2020].

What had become of the money?

Spencer had speculated in land in Denver, Nebraska, and other Western and Southern states, which had all proved failures. Now looking old beyond his years, the young man denied he had speculated on Wall Street.

'Did you ever make annual balances to determine the condition of the bank?' asked Mr. Maltbie [prosecutor]

'No, we never did' said Mr. Spencer, 'but we were short since 1892.''So from 1892 down to the time the bank closed its doors you could never tell as to what its condition was?'

'No, we had no idea.'

'So, the money of every man who has given money into the bank since 1895 has been used to pay old debts and carry on these other investments?'

'That's practically true.' Said Mr. Spencer.

'How did it happen that you had no money in the bank on the day it closed?'

'Because it took all the cash we had on hand to pay the demands of Saturday.'[366]

The bank had been a Ponzi Scheme for five years.

The townspeople began to become bitter.

And it began to show.

TO SPENCER CREDITORS.

A Package Containing a Rope and Advice.

(Special to The Courant.)

Thompsonville, Feb. 23.

A package addressed to the creditors of the R. D. & R. E. Spencer Company was received from the mails to-day. On examination it was found to contain a rope with a noose on the end and a note stating, "A piece of this hemp properly used would serve the ends of justice better than the courts, and prevent many swindles." No name was signed to the note and there was nothing to indicate the place from which it was mailed.

Hartford Courant, February 24, 1900, article. Page 3.

And it began to worsen a little.

---

[366] Hartford Courant February 20, 1900. Page 4.

On February 28, 1900, Robert E. Spencer was charged with forging Ann Lawton's[367] signature to withdraw funds from her account at the Institute for Savings in nearby Springfield, Massachusetts. Unable to secure his $5,000 bond, he was taken to the Hartford County Jail.

The following day, Ellen Smyth, who had secured Spencer's $2,000 bond for the Hilditch embezzlement charge, asked to be relieved of that bond, and Spencer was transferred the responsibility for meeting both.

He remained in jail.

On March 8, 1900, the other shoe dropped.

The Meriden Journal reported that Robert Emmett Spencer had speculated and lost in the Stock Market, and that the failure of the Thompsonville and Hazardville banks could be traced back to massive losses in Sugar and Federal Steel in 1899.

> *From what has now been learned, it is supposed that he [Spencer] spent such time in New York. A well known Hartford man said that about two years ago he saw Spencer in a dilapidated condition in New York. He looked badly worn and excited, and was entering a saloon. It has also been learned that Spencer was a speculator on Wall Street and the name of the firm was given where he had placed his orders.*
>
> *It is said that he bought quite heavily of Sugar and Federal Steel.[368]*

On March 17, 1900, Robert Emmett Spencer finally resigned his position as Judge of Probate in Enfield.

---

[367] Enfield resident
[368] Meriden Journal March 8, 1900. Page 8.

On June 7, 1900, Robert E. Spencer pleaded guilty to the charge of forgery in the Lawton case, the Hilditch charge being nolled. State's Attorney Arthur F. Eggleston recommended a three-year state prison sentence, with release after two and a half years on good behavior.

While true sympathy is felt and expressed for his family, there are few outside of the family who think the sentence too severe.[369]

Surprisingly, there are no accounts of the residual damage to the ordinary citizens of Thompsonville and Hazardville caused by the mismanagement of their unsecured savings. Consider their average savings of $2,000 [~$75K in 2020] disappeared overnight, without the possibility of even partial recovery.

Even more surprising was that neither the obituary of Roswell Duane nor that of Robert Emmett Spencer mentioned the bank failure or its fallout. It was as if that part of their personal history had been excised, not worthy of the final published recollection of their lives.

But maybe there was just something about that name.

Herbert O. Spencer arrived in Thompsonville in 1903, shortly after the final meeting of the creditors of R. D. Spencer, R. E. Spencer, and R. D. & R. E. Spencer Company concluded. He gained employment with S. Willis Rockwell, who ran a successful dairy business in Enfield. Soon, he secured a position in the insurance business in Springfield, Massachusetts.

---

[369] Thompsonville press June 7, 1900. Page 2.

During the course of business, H. O. Spencer made the acquaintance of Zella Colburn, daughter of John A. and Maria E. Colburn, who owned a working farm in Enfield. Herbert and Zella were married on November 21, 1907, and the couple made their home with Zella's parents. Herbert offered to work at the marketing end of the farm for the following year, and by May of 1908, H. O. Spencer's peddling business began.

H. O. Spencer seemed to meet with immediate success, to the extent that by July, he had purchased the William T. Watson home on Russell Street for $4,800, with a cash down payment of $2,800.

He quickly established credit with his suppliers, and although his payments were not always prompt, his checks followed in due course.

That is to say, the checks followed, but the money didn't.

It wasn't until some banks began returning checks for insufficient funds that questions arose.

Unbeknownst to most people, H. O. Spencer had become the administrator for Mary J. Goodell's estate in Agawam, Massachusetts, while he was engaged in the insurance business in Springfield. Mary was the daughter of Paris and Martha Goodell. Her father was a laborer, and her mother was a dressmaker. Despite their stations in life, upon their deaths — Martha in 1878 and Paris in 1883 — Mary was left with an estate valued at around $8,000 (~$300,000 in 2020), a sizable amount.

As a single woman without children, Mary required assistance managing her estate as she aged, and Herbert O. Spencer was lucky enough to be appointed to the position.

Lucky for Herbert, not so fortunate for Mary.

Spencer had begun drawing down on Mary's money before his marriage to Zella. He had borrowed money from Zella and her father, John, to fund the wedding ceremony. John had been repaid, seemingly from Mary Goodell's funds, but his bride was not made whole.

The breaking point in Spencer's scheme came when the train station agent, Daniel J. Mullane, a former lieutenant in the United States Cavalry, decided Spencer had floated too many checks with him for services rendered and demanded a cash payment. With no arrangements offered, Mullane placed a lien on Spencer's property.

A panicked Spencer, only 25 years old and sensing his house of cards about to fall, hightailed it out of town. As word of his exit spread, other creditors came forward and attached liens to the young man's home.

The indemnity company that had furnished bonds to protect the Goodell estate when Spencer was assigned as administrator tracked Spencer's movements as he swept through Boston, Massachusetts; Albany, New York; Troy, New York; and New York, New York. The securities company reached out to Spencer's brother, and the sibling arranged to meet Herbert in Worcester, Massachusetts, where the two conversed and agreed to return to the Colburn home in Enfield.

Exhausted, H. O. Spencer confessed to Attorney William H. Leete. The pair traveled to Leete's home, where Police Chief Edward Bromage met them, arrested Spencer, and transferred the young man to the Enfield lockup. The following morning, Spencer appeared before Judge J. P. Davis, where he pleaded guilty to 'misappropriating funds for his own use.'

> *These developments put a peculiar phase upon the situation, and such acts as he has performed are considered by many as being those of a person slightly unbalanced mentally rather than one of one intentionally doing wrong, and certainly they are not those of a bright or clever rogue. While the public feels that, in justice to all, he letter of the law must be carried out, at the same time deep sympathy is felt for his young wife and the members of his family, who feel keenly the affliction brought by his acts, so lacking in brilliancy or intelligence.[370]*

At the young man's trial, the point was made that Spencer's father had indeed been removed to the McLean Hospital in Somerville, Massachusetts, shortly after his son's birth, as the elder Spencer presented with signs of insanity. Perhaps Herbert had inherited his father's penchant for magical thinking.

Still, the fact remained that H. O. Spencer had recklessly spent $5,800 of Spinster Goodell's funds [~ $220,000 in 2020 dollars], so punitive action had to be taken.

And it was. Superior Court Judge William S. Case

---

[370] Thompsonville Press November 26, 1908. Page 2.

sentenced Herbert O. Spencer to two years in jail for embezzling the estate's funds.

> *Every hour brings to light some new shady transaction in the young man's career. To straighten out matters it is believed Spencer will be forced into insolvency, with very little chance of the creditors getting any dividend on their claims.*[371]

In the 1910 federal census, Herbert O. Spencer was listed as an inmate.

His wife, Zella, filed for divorce soon after, eager to be free from the association with the name Spencer, as it had acquired an unwanted connotation in Thompsonville.

---

[371] Hartford Courant November 26, 1908. Page 18.

25: A RIDE DOWN THE RIVER

Frederick Harvey Prior was born on September 6, 1847, in East Windsor, Connecticut. His father, Harvey Skinner Prior, passed away when Frederick was 22 months old, leaving the family without a head of the house, a position his mother, Harriet Sabrina Kibbe, assumed.

Frederick was the youngest of five children and the third son of the marriage. The three brickmakers who lived in the family home were likely boarders whose rent provided income for the host family.

A complicating issue in tracing Frederick's history is that his grandfather, father, and uncle were all named Harvey Prior. Add to this that Frederick preferred to be called Harvey, and the challenge becomes clear.

What is clear, though, is that by 1868, Frederick Harvey Prior had been named Ferry Commissioner for the Warehouse Point ferry, a position he maintained until he was appointed station agent and toll-gatherer at the Enfield Bridge in 1879.

Frederick married Martha Barker in 1872, and the two set about making a family. Harriet Sabrina arrived in 1876, and Clifford Harvey in 1881. Prior was a member of the Masonic Morning Star Lodge in Warehouse Point and, by all accounts, was a valued community member with a large circle of friends.

This made his final action on February 3, 1889, even more challenging to understand.

There, at the toll booth in Thompsonville, Frederick Harvey Prior placed a gun against his temple and blew his brains out, creating an immediate employment opening. The official coroner's report cited the:

Effects of a bullet, shot through the head, from a pistol fired by the deceased himself.

The immediate cause of death was compression of the brain.

The deceased was only 41 years, four months, and 27 days old, and speculation centered around what was referred to as domestic troubles. Surprisingly, it took Prior a day to draw his final breath.

Andrew W. Scott, an acquaintance of Priors, attended the toll taker's funeral services. Scott had been a first lieutenant in the Civil War, serving in the 1st and 8th Connecticut Infantries. After the war, he settled in Thompsonville and found work as a carpenter. Years before, in 1840, he had married Eliza T. Ripley of Enfield, and the two were blessed with three children.

In 1870, Eliza passed away, and Scott moved to Windsor Locks. Once there, he rented the Old Stone Tavern in the southern part of the town, and his daughter and son-in-law lived with him.

After his wife's passing, Scott seemed to acquire a taste for gin, and the beverage often influenced the frequency of his work.

While at Prior's funeral, an attendee overheard Scott

remark that there would be another death soon, finding the comment most disconcerting.

Four days after Frederick Harvey Prior's death, on February 7th, Andrew W. Scott left his home, reportedly to travel to Enfield Bridge. One week later, the Thompsonville Press printed a few lines stating that the carpenter hadn't been heard from since, and that search parties had been organized to locate him.

On February 28th, the badly decomposed body of Scott was found frozen in the woods, his hands clenched on his chest, and an empty bottle of gin at his side. It was later learned he had purportedly been traveling to a small job in Suffield, and the liquor had caused him to lose his way, and he had succumbed to the elements.

Or, perhaps, he had simply fulfilled his own prophecy.

Sometimes, history calls upon the most ordinary among us to participate in a historic event. Our involvement need not be earned or based on a specific quality, competency, or morality. When events converge, someone concludes the action or records the activity for posterity.

Hosea Keach was plucked from anonymity.

Hosea Keach, formerly baggage master at Warehouse Point, has been appointed Consolidated road station agent at Enfield Bridge in place of Harvey Prior, deceased.[372]

Hosea Ballou Keach was born to George Hudson Keach

---

[372] Morning Journal and Courier February 13, 1889. Page 4. The death of Frederick Harvey Prior opened the door for the hiring of Keach as station agent.

and Mary Ann Sturdy on July 15, 1853, in Enfield, Connecticut. Hosea seemed to grow up nondescript, neither drawing attention to himself nor distancing himself from neighborhood children.

He married Hattie Maria Boleyn of Enfield in 1876, and the couple welcomed their first child, of seven, that same year. Records indicate that Hosea had become the baggage master for the Warehouse Point station by the time he was married.

The Warehouse Point railroad station. Archives & Special Collections, University of Connecticut Library. Photograph taken by Lewis Herbert Benton ~ 1929.

We can assume Hosea was attentive to detail. As baggage master, he oversaw all aspects of baggage handling, ensuring that luggage was tagged correctly, loaded onto the correct trains, and unloaded at the intended destinations. Other staff at a railroad station in the late 1800s included station masters, who were responsible for the overall operation of the station; booking clerks, who handled ticket sales and financial auditing; and porters, who handled luggage and assisted passengers.

When Prior took his own life in 1889, the railroad tapped

Hosea Keach to take over as station master for the Enfield Station. In addition to managing the station, the young man managed toll traffic at the Enfield Street Bridge while it remained open.

Enfield Bridge and Toll House after traffic was closed across the span circa 1903. Richard E. Roy Collection.

By the mid-1890s, the bridge's revenue and usage had declined, and it was very lightly patronized, as the spans in Thompsonville and Windsor Locks handled the majority of the traffic.

By 1897, the entrances to the Enfield Bridge were boarded up, ending horse-and-buggy traffic, but pedestrians and bicyclists loosened enough boards to allow free passage over the Connecticut River.

A freshet is a sudden rise in the level of a stream or river caused by heavy rains or the rapid melting of snow. It is most common in the springtime, but can occur at any time when weather events combine to create the appropriate conditions.

The appropriate conditions arrived in the Northeast on February 13, 1900, and continued for 24 hours.

A rainfall of about 3¹ᐟ² inches in the 24 hours ending at 5 o'clock yesterday afternoon brought on a sudden freshet which did damage throughout Western Massachusetts, and whose force was not spent last night. The Westfield and Miller rivers were particularly threatening yesterday, and the Connecticut River took the almost unprecedented jump of eight feet in 16 hours. At 1 o'clock this morning the water had reached 15 feet at the old toll bridge and was still rising rapidly.[373]

The February 14th headlines told the tale of mounting concerns in Massachusetts.

WILLIAMANSETT CAUGHT IT HARD

TWO DAMS WERE SWEPT AWAY

**Washout Flood in All Directions –
At Chicopee and the Falls**

ICE BLOCKADE AT CHESTER

**A $3000 Bridge Swept Away –
Electric Plant in Danger – Streets Flooded**

THE FLOODS CAME AT HOLYOKE

GRAND SIGHT AT THE BIG DAM

**Damage in Several Localities –
Washouts on Railroads**

---

[373] Springfield Republican February 14, 1900. Page 7.

The February 15th headlines reported more hardships.

THE HOUSATONIC RAGING

A Sick woman Nearly Caught in Bed by the Flood – Roads and Railroad Tracks Under Water

---

Blackington Mill Dam Goes at North Adams

The Hartford Daily Courant reported issues from Vermont through Connecticut as rain and melting snow raised river levels and caused havoc, with the water rushing toward the open sea.

The debris of the freshet which came floating down stream on Tuesday included a cow, a pig, poultry, wrecks of poultry houses, pens, and other small out buildings.[374]

The Connecticut River crested at 23 feet above its low water mark, and stayed there for a while as water from tributaries and the north fed its expansion.

Hosea Keach, station manager at Enfield Bridge Station, had been instructed to keep a close eye on the covered span, as concerns arose about whether the structure would withstand the increased volume of the freshet.

Having inspected the bridge multiple times during the morning hours, Keach stepped onto the bridge once again shortly after two o'clock in the afternoon. Sauntering down the wooden structure, serenaded by the rushing waters below and the sounds of ice and debris bouncing off of the piers, he headed cautiously westward toward Suffield on the opposite shore.

He had covered no more than two-thirds of the distance

---

[374] The New Hartford Tribune February 16, 1900. Page 3.

to the first pier when, with a crash, the central section of the bridge dropped into the cascading waters. Turning on his heel, he made a mad dash toward the Enfield shore.

Ten feet from land, the section containing him folded in half, the timbers in front of him rising, threatening to fall back upon the panicked station agent.

What happened next is a matter of conjecture.

Keach wasn't struck by anything that would have caused him to lose consciousness. Still, there was a gap in his memory that could have resulted from vasovagal syncope, or fainting. This occurs when the body experiences a sudden drop in blood pressure and heart rate due to extreme fear. Certainly, dropping into a raging river while trapped inside an oversized wooden coffin could meet the requirements for such a response.

When he regained consciousness, he found himself sitting atop a wooden crossbeam near the peak of the structure's roof with no idea how he had arrived there. Below his feet, the roiling black waters of the swollen Connecticut River had replaced the bridge floor as it carried the historic bridge and its lone occupant south, toward Warehouse Point.

There was only one building at the Enfield Bridge station, and that was the house where Keach and his wife lived. The building also served as the tollhouse for collecting fares when the bridge was in operation. This day, though, Kech's wife, children, and hired help were absent, and no one was there to witness the station master's plight.

The first moment of concern occurred when the 3:08 train, known as the *Afternoon Extra 53*, arrived at the station, and no one was there to greet it. The second moment came when the engineer realized the bridge was gone as well, and a connection was quickly made between the two.

As the train passed the Warehouse Point station, the rear brakeman tossed a note about the engineer's observations onto the depot platform, which read:

The old Enfield Bridge has gone, it is on the way down. [375]

E. Walter Bailey, station agent, shared the note with four men assembled there: Robert Abbe, Albert Lord, Arthur A. Blodgett, and his son Fred Harrison Blodgett.

Joseph Warren Johnson, an Enfield lawyer, was sitting in his office that afternoon, corresponding with William D. Marsh of Chicago, Senator William Dixon's nephew and one of the bridge's owners, in an attempt to draw attention to its growing instability. A visitor in Johnson's office, looking out the westward-facing window, remarked, 'What is that coming down the river?'.

Communicating the event to Suffield was out of the question, as the telephone cabling had been strung along the south side of the missing bridge and had been severed when the bridge collapsed.

The Southern New England Telephone Company had seven wires crossing the river on the structure, and by the breaking of the wires communication [had] been cut off between Somers, Somersville, Hazardville, and Enfield. [376]

Reports and inquiries were passed along the shoreline by telegraph or, where possible, by telephone, and the water's edge was soon teeming with interested onlookers.

"When I got my thinker to running. I didn't know how long it was, I said to myself, 'It will never do to stay in here, for nobody will know I am on the bridge.' You see,

---

[375] Springfield Republican February 16, 1900. Page 3.
[376] Ibid

my family were all away at the time, and there wasn't a soul about to see the bridge go down.

I couldn't realize that the old thing was floating because of the water inside and I couldn't see out. I began to wonder how I was to get a hole so as to let folks know.

Finally, I got hold of a heavy timber, half underwater, and sitting there cramped butted a hole through the end of the bridge, where the gate had been boarded up to keep people from going through. When I got my head through, I saw I was passing the island[377] and about a mile below [from where the bridge originally sat]. Then I knew something had to be done and done quick, for I thought the old bridge would bang up against the piers of the railroad bridge, and then goodbye to Hosea Keach. I thought of my family most, I guess, for I certainly gave myself up as a dead duck. I thought I was surely doomed.

Then I climbed out, putting one foot on the timbers nailed across the gate and the other on the top of the sign about horses not going faster than a walk, and getting hold of the shingles, pulled myself on to the top of the bridge, which was floating right side up. I found myself within 40 rods of the railroad bridge and could see the men standing there watching."[378]

One of the observers was Station Master E. Walter Bailey, who had grabbed a pair of field glasses as he stepped onto the Warehouse Point railroad span to scan the onrushing waters to the north for signs of the oncoming collapsed bridge. There, as two sections of the covered structure passed the island, he saw a man waving feverishly at the far end of the floating framework that rode closer to

---

[377] Terry's Island (now known as King's Island)
[378] Springfield Republican February 16, 1900. Page 3.

the shore.

As if steered by providence, the structure began to drift and turn, and the end Keach stood upon began to angle toward the railroad bridge.

Arthur Blodgett sent his son Fred to the baggage room to retrieve a coil of ½ inch hand line he had stored there after completing some recent banjo signal[379] work for the railroad. When he returned, Robert Abbe, the freight agent, took the rope and tied a bowline knot into the cordage, leaving about 30 or 40 feet free.

The bridge was coming in at about 10 miles per hour, as the normal current was strong near the base of the railroad bridge, and, with the increased water volume, it sped up significantly. The end of the floating bridge opposite Keach struck the railroad pier with a solid blow, and the end where the Enfield Station Master stood swung rapidly around in a half circle.

As the old ark of ruin came floating down to the railroad bridge, the two [Abbe and Blodgett] dropped it over the head of Hosea. He had strength and sense enough to loop it under one shoulder, and he was pulled up some twelve or fourteen feet to the railroad bridge safe and sound, not a scratch upon him, and only wet to the waist, but much exhausted.[380]

Keach lay there momentarily, catching his breath, and within a short while, rose to his feet and accompanied young Fred Blodgett on a trolley car north to Bridge Lane, where Keach departed. As luck would have it, a local farmer was passing by, and Hosea hitched a ride with him to his home at the Enfield Bridge Station, where he was met by his wife,

---

[379] A train signal that resembles the bottom of an inverted banjo.
[380] Hartford Courant February 16, 1900. Page 1.

Hattie.

It was reported that a good tongue-lashing followed.

Although there was great consternation over whether the remaining sections of the floating bridge might cause damage downstream, the concerns were unfounded, and they either broke apart or grounded themselves along the riverbank.

The two remaining sections of the bridge, still connected to the Suffield shore, were blown up on August 20, 1901, as a charge of fifty pounds of dynamite was secured to the last supporting pier and set off in a massive explosion.

Clouds of dust, mortar, stone, and pieces of timber burst from the sides of the bridge [and] a few seconds later, the remaining spans parted directly over the pier and fell with a crash. The span near the shore parted in the center one-half swinging in towards the shore and the other remaining near the pier. The second span was practically intact and remained where it fell.[381]

On December 6, 1920, Hosea [Ballou] Keach passed on to the other world, leaving this one darker for those who knew him, by his passing. His was not one of those lives that was constantly in the limelight, but rather a life whose constant objective was the quiet performance of duty.

He was a kind and loving husband and father, giving unstintingly of his strength and all that he possessed for the good of those who were dear to him. Many were the friends he made, all of whom he met once greeted him ever after with a glad smile of welcome and passed very happy

---

[381] Hartford Courant August 21, 1901.

hours in his company. He loved little children, and even animals knew him as their friend.

He was faithful to the task which his hand found to do, faithful beyond the usual faithfulness of men. He held on with determination when strength was fast ebbing, just to do his duty and play the man.

'Be thou faithful unto death, and I will give thee a crown of life.'

D. T. K. [382]

Years later, Edwin B. Fish of East Windsor, Connecticut, captured the tale in a poem, reprinted from time to time in regional newspapers on the anniversary of the event.

The old bridge stood a century or more,
Connecting Suffield with Enfield shore,
But in the course of time it began to decay,
The gate was closed and no toll to pay.
A few years after when the river was high,
It floated off to another nearby,
And on it, a shouting like all creation,
Was Hosea Keach of the Enfield Station.
A dangerous place for him to be,
No chance of escape that he could see;
With water roaring on every side,
He could not swim if he had tried.
The railroad bridge was drawing near;
He thought of home and friends so dear;
With strength most gone he still was brave,
Not knowing that he would be saved.

---

[382] Hartford Courant December 14, 1920. Page 8. Tribute written by Dewitt Talmage Keach.

'Bob" Abbe and others hearing his cry,
Ran out to the bridge where he'd pass by;
They lowered a rope, which he carefully caught
And pulled him up fifty feet to the top.
As he left the wreck it struck the pier;
From the men above went up a cheer.
It broke in pieces under his feet;
His life was saved by the daring feat.
He was about all in when he reached the top,
So they gave him a drink and something hot,
He walked home with his clothes all wet,
The experience he will never forget.
The wreck floated down the river so wide
Till it struck the shore on the Windsor Locks side,
Where a party of men, we'll mention no name,
Went to work and demolished the same.
They towed it over to Warehouse Point side,
And carried it home away from the tide;
A part of that bridge stands today on a farm
Where a launch is kept in a very small barn.
The old bridge is gone; They don't miss it I know,
As they have one above and another below.
We hope by next year these will be free,
For we're heartily sick of paying the fee.
Messrs. Abbe, Bailey, Blodgett, and Lord
Will vouch for this story, with one accord.
No doubt Hosea Keach, if so inclined
Would tell it to you at any time.
When these few lines some people see,
They may wonder who the author can be.
If to know his name is your wish
I will tell you — it is Edwin B. Fish.

PETER FLOYD SORENSON

www.ingramcontent.com/pod-product-compliance
Lightning Source LLC
Chambersburg PA
CBHW021209130626
46554CB00004B/1149